Ethics for Behavior Analysts

This fully-updated 3rd Edition of Jon Bailey and Mary Burch's bestselling *Ethics for Behavior Analysts* is an invaluable guide to understanding and implementing the newly revised Behavior Analyst Certification Board (BACB) Professional and Ethical Compliance Code. Featured in this new edition are case studies drawn from the author's real-world practice with hints to guide readers toward the ethical 'solution' and revised chapters, including how this new edition evolved alongside the revised Code and tips for succeeding in your first job as a certified behavior analyst. The complete, revised BACB Professional and Ethical Compliance Code is included as an appendix. This 3rd Edition improves upon what has become a go-to resource for behavior analysts in training and in practice.

Jon S. Bailey, PhD, Emeritus Professor of Psychology at Florida State University, teaches graduate courses for behavior analysts. Dr. Bailey is a founding Director of the Behavior Analyst Certification Board®, and he is past President of the Association of Professional Behavior Analysts (APBA).

Mary R. Burch, PhD, is a Board Certified Behavior Analyst®. Dr. Burch has more than twenty-five years' experience in developmental disabilities. She has been a Behavior Specialist, QMRP, unit Director, and Consulting Behavior Analyst in developmental disabilities, mental health, and preschool settings.

"*Ethics for Behavior Analysts, 3rd Edition* by Bailey and Burch is another winner. It covers all the essential elements of ethics in an accessible and comprehensive manner. With valuable new chapters, the most up-to-date information, and numerous case examples that facilitate a problem-solving approach to ethical issues, this book is an invaluable resource. Students and professionals in behavior analysis should keep it close at hand."

— **Raymond G. Miltenberger, PhD, BCBA-D**, Professor, University of South Florida.

"The 3rd Edition of *Ethics for Behavior Analysts* is a 'must read' for students of behavior analysis and seasoned professionals alike. It builds upon the huge success of the previous editions with the inclusion of Dr. Bailey's 'Seven Step Model' for solving complex cases and new case examples aligned to the BACB Professional and Ethical Compliance Code. It will continue to be a staple in my graduate ethics classes."

— **Rosemary A. Condillac, PhD, C.Psych., BCBA-D.**, Associate Professor, Centre for Applied Disability Studies, Brock University, St. Catharines, Ontario.

"This book is the 'go-to' ethics book for our field of applied behavior analysis. Bailey and Burch handle the universe of ethics with a perfect touch. Ranging from formal presentation of ethical requirements, to real-life examples that all readers will relate to, this book will raise the awareness of ethics and ethical conduct, which in turn will increase the chances that the clients who we serve will be treated humanely and safely."

— **Thomas Zane, PhD, BCBA-D**, Institute for Behavioral Studies, Endicott College.

"Bailey and Burch bring clarity to the BACB Professional and Ethical Compliance Code through cogent discussion of each element and thoughtful consideration of the myriad issues facing practicing behavior analysts. Practitioners of all levels will find valuable insight from numerous examples of real-life ethical dilemmas."

— **Dorothea C. Lerman, PhD, BCBA-D**, University of Houston, Clear Lake.

Ethics for Behavior Analysts

3rd Edition

Jon S. Bailey and Mary R. Burch

Routledge
Taylor & Francis Group

NEW YORK AND LONDON

Third edition published 2016
by Routledge
711 Third Avenue, New York, NY 10017

and by Routledge
2 Park Square, Milton Park, Abingdon, Oxon, OX14 4RN

Routledge is an imprint of the Taylor & Francis Group, an informa business
© 2016 Taylor & Francis

First edition published by Routledge 2005
Second edition published by Routledge 2011

Library of Congress Cataloging-in-Publication Data
Names: Bailey, Jon S., author. | Burch, Mary R., author.
Title: Ethics for behavior analysts / Jon S. Bailey and Mary R. Burch.
Description: 3rd edition. | New York, NY : Routledge, 2016. Includes bibliographical
   references and index.
Identifiers: LCCN 2015038979 | ISBN 9781138949195 (hbk : alk. paper) | ISBN 9781138949201
   (pbk : alk. paper) | ISBN 9781315669212 (ebk)
Subjects: LCSH: Behavioral assessment—Moral and ethical aspects—United States—Handbooks,
   manuals, etc. | Behavior analysts—Professional ethics—United States—Handbooks,
   manuals, etc. | Behavior analysts—Certification—United States—Handbooks, manuals, etc.
Classification: LCC RC437.B43 B355 2016 DDC 174.20973—dc23
LC record available at http://lccn.loc.gov/2015038979

ISBN: 978-1-138-94919-5 (hbk)
ISBN: 978-1-138-94920-1 (pbk)
ISBN: 978-1-315-66921-2 (ebk)

Typeset in Minion Pro
by Apex CoVantage, LLC

This book is dedicated to the memory of my dear friend and colleague Gerald L. "Jerry" Shook (1948–2011). You had a vision of a profession of behavior analysis and created the Behavior Analyst Certification Board as an instrument to bring it to life. You advocated for a code of ethics from the very beginning and encouraged me to promote it; you changed my life.

Jon Bailey, BCBA-D

Contents

**SECTION III   Professional Skills for Ethical
                 Behavior Analysts**

**SECTION IV   The BACB Code, Glossary, Scenarios,
                and Further Reading**

Preface

EVOLUTION OF THIS BOOK AND HOW TO USE IT

My first experience in ethics came when I was a graduate student in psychology in the late 1960s. I was working with a profoundly developmentally disabled young man who was confined to a heavy metal crib in the small ward of a private institution in Phoenix, Arizona. Blind, deaf, nonambulatory, and not toilet trained, my "subject" engaged in self-injurious behavior virtually all day long. His head-banging behavior against the metal bars could be heard 25 yards away and greeted me each time I entered his depressing, malodorous living unit. Day after day, I sat by his crib taking notes on a possible thesis concerning how one might try to reduce his chronic self-injurious behavior or SIB (we called it self-destructive behavior in those days). After a few informal observation sessions, and reading through his medical chart, I had some ideas. I set up a meeting with one of my committee members, Dr. Lee Meyerson, who was supervising the research at the facility. "I'm observing a subject who engages in self-destructive behavior," I began. "He hits his head 10 to 15 times per minute throughout the day. I've taken informal data at different times of the day, and I don't see any consistent pattern," I offered. Dr. Meyerson let me go on for about 10 minutes, nodding and occasionally taking a puff on his pipe (smoking was allowed everywhere in those days). Then he stopped me abruptly and, gesturing with his pipe, began to ask me questions that I had never thought about. Did I know my "subject's" name? Did I have permission to observe and report on this individual? Who gave me permission to look at this medical record? Had I discussed this case with any of my graduate student colleagues or shown the data in class? I had no good answers to any of Dr. Meyerson's questions. I wasn't thinking of my "subject" as a person, only as a source of data for my thesis. It never dawned on me that "Billy" had rights to privacy and confidentiality and that he needed to be treated with dignity and respect, not as just another "subject" to help me complete a degree requirement. As it turns out, Dr. Meyerson was ahead of his time in grilling me with ethical questions that would not actually come up in legal circles for another ten years (see Chapter 1). Dr. Meyerson's questions helped sensitize me to looking at what I was doing from an extra-experimental perspective. How would I like to be treated if I was a subject in someone's experiment? Or, how would I want my mother or sister to be treated? "With kindness, compassion and respect" is no doubt the quick response that most of us would offer. And so it is that ethics in psychology, and particularly in behavior analysis, can be easily personalized and made tangible if we will just stop and think about what we are doing.

Students today have a great advantage over my generation. We had no code of ethics to guide us; we had one foot in the animal lab and one in the world of academia, and we were trying to figure out how to transform powerful operant conditioning principles into effective treatments. It didn't dawn on us at the time that ethics was involved at all, until, of course, we encountered Dr. Meyerson. Today, graduate students in behavior analysis have nearly fifty years of applied research and practice to fall back on (and to learn from and be held accountable for knowing). In addition, they have a wealth of resources on ethics, including case law and precedent-setting legal findings. Finally, students today have a perfectly legitimate, thoroughly researched, and well-vetted ethics code specifically designed for our field. The current version of this document is the BACB Professional and Ethical Compliance Code for Behavior Analysts. In teaching the graduate course "Professional and Ethical Issues in Behavior Analysis" for the past 15 years, I have learned a great deal about the ethical issues that appear to be unique to our field and have been developing lectures and trying to discover ways of making ethics interesting, informative, and engaging for students who do not quite see the relevance or appreciate our cautious approach. One thing I've discovered is that although we now have an excellent ethics code, it is somewhat dry and, by itself, does not convey the urgency and relevance that it should. Reading the Code is something like reading instructions for computer software: it's clearly important, but you would rather just start using it.

Years ago, I was scheduled to give a half-day workshop at Penn State on ethics at the urging of Dr. Jerry Shook. In the process of preparing my materials, I wondered what kind of ethical questions the participants might have. Dr. Shook arranged in advance to have each participant write and submit to us two questions or "scenarios" that he or she had confronted in the work setting. When I got the questions, I realized that reading the scenarios suddenly made the ethical issues jump right off the page. I began trying to look up the correct responses (according to what was then called the BACB Guidelines), and this turned out to be quite difficult. Something was missing. An index of some sort would help, but none was available that I could find. Several all-nighters later, I had developed one. By the time Dr. Shook and I traveled to the conference, I had a new approach to teaching ethics. It involved presenting scenarios, having the students look up the relevant sections in the then-Guidelines for Responsible Conduct, and then having them present their proposed ethical actions. This approach teaches students that sometimes broad, ethical considerations always come down to some specific code items. My experience in using this method over the past several years is that it brings the topic to life and generates excellent discussions of very relevant issues.

One troubling problem I encountered in teaching the "Ethics for Behavior Analysis" course was that specific code items were often very much out of context or written in such stilted legal-ese that students did not understand why they were necessary or how they were relevant. I found myself often "translating" specific items into plain English. This process, along with providing some historic context and background about how and why certain items were important in our field, seemed to increase the level of under-standing for the students.

This book, then, is the culmination of this attempt to present a practical, student-centered approach to teaching ethics in behav-ior analysis. All of the cases are based on real examples but edited so as to avoid embarrassment or legal hassles, and the authors of the cases gave permission for their use (those in quotation marks are direct quotes from submitted cases). In addition, for each case, there is a commentary at the end of each chapter. In Appendix C, you will find practice scenarios that can be used in class or as homework, and we have now added "Hints" at the end of each one. You can, of course, develop your own scenarios based on the specific areas of application that you encounter in your practice of behavior analysis.

A final word about using this volume: this text is intended to be a practical handbook, and we specifically attempted to avoid making this an academic or theoretical work. Many people teach-ing ethics courses will routinely have students read the U.S. Con-stitution, view *One Flew Over the Cuckoo's Nest*, and research their state laws on limits of treatment, requirements for keeping docu-ments, maintaining confidentiality, and other relevant issues. My experience is that it takes some creative digging to find relevant readings. Exposing students to a variety of sources from Skinner and Sidman to Association for Behavior Analysis International (ABAI) position statements is useful in preparing them to tackle the world of ethical issues they will confront. We have tried to summarize what we consider the most important and pressing issues for new Board Certified Behavior Analysts (BCBAs) in Chapter 19: "A Dozen Practical Tips for Ethical Conduct on Your First Job." I hope you enjoy using this book and welcome input and dialogue on effective ways of teaching this most important topic.

—Jon S. Bailey
January 1, 2016

Evolution of the 3rd Edition

Not long after the publication of the 1st edition of *Ethics for Behavior Analysts*, we began receiving requests to give workshops on ethics at state association meetings and for other groups around the country. It was enlightening and educational to learn firsthand from practitioners about the ethics situations they were confronting on a daily basis. To facilitate our ability to refer to the participants' practical scenarios throughout the day, we began asking them to complete "Scenario Forms" before the workshop began. These scenarios generated lively discussions that gave practitioners a sounding board for the ethical challenges they were confronting in their jobs.

In role-playing exercises in the workshops, participants referred to the Guidelines for Responsible Conduct (now the Professional and Ethical Compliance Code for Behavior Analysts). We noticed that while workshop attendees might know what a particular Guidelines item said, they had a hard time coming up with the words and actions needed to handle a situation. This led to another new chapter, "Delivering the Ethics Message Effectively" (Chapter 17). A key addition to the second edition came from a development at the Texas Association for Behavior Analysis in 2005. It was there that Kathy Chovanec asked us why behavior analysts did not use a Declaration of Professional Services to help ward off problems presented by parents, teachers, and others. In collaboration with Kathy, we developed just such a document for behavior analysts (see Chapter 18 for this valuable document).

In the course of teaching ethics graduate classes, I've continued to learn about challenges that my students faced as they participated in practica and began to understand that their approach to ethics was homegrown. Some students had a difficult time giving up "personal ethics" and adopting our field's professional ethical guidelines. I soon began each class with this dramatic introduction, "Today is the last day of your civilian life. From this point forward, you are expected to join the ranks of professional behavior analysts and to learn and use our ethics Code for Responsible Conduct." From this came the idea for Chapter 5, "Everyday Ethical Challenges for Average Citizens and Behavior Analysts."

In the spring of 2010, the BACB undertook a review of the Guidelines. An expert panel consisting of certificants Jon Bailey (chair), Jose Martinez-Diaz, Wayne Fuqua, Ellie Kazemi, Sharon Reeve, and Jerry Shook (CEO of the Board) was created. The panel recommended rather minor changes to the Guidelines overall but did include some new procedures, including risk-benefit analysis. This topic is included in Chapter 16 "Conducting a Risk Benefit Analysis."

In August, 2014, the BACB's Board of Directors approved an initial version of the Professional and Ethical Compliance Code for Behavior Analysts. As of January 1, 2016, all BACB applicants, certificants, and registrants were required to adhere to the Code.

HOW TO USE THIS 3RD EDITION

Each year, I teach a semester-long graduate course called Ethics and Professional Issues for Behavior Analysts. I use *Ethics for*

Behavior Analysts for the first half of the semester and *25 Essential Skills and Strategies for Professional Behavior Analysts* (Bailey & Burch 2010) for the second half. By covering ethics first, I find the students become sensitized to the new way of thinking about how they should conduct themselves; then I introduce them to all the other professional skills they will need to be successful.

We hope that this 3rd Edition of *Ethics for Behavior Analysts* will be useful as you learn about and teach others about ethics.

—**Jon S. Bailey**
January 1, 2016

Acknowledgments

We learned a great deal from the hundreds of people who have attended our Ethics Workshops and thank you for the wide variety of scenarios you submitted, some of which appear in Appendix C. In addition, we would like to thank all the individuals who have submitted ethics questions via the ABAI Hotline; these have stimulated a great deal of thought and have contributed to the cases that you will find in this book. Devon Sundberg, Yulema Cruz, Brian Iwata, and Thomas Zane provided valuable assistance in the preparation of this book. We would like to acknowledge Dr. Dorothea Lerman for providing several new research scenarios for this edition. Finally, we would like to thank the Ethics Workgroup that produced the revisions to the Code, and special thanks go to Margaret (Misty) Bloom, the BACB's very capable attorney, for her efforts in assisting the Ethics Workgroup.

Disclaimer

This book does not represent an official statement by the Behavior Analyst Certification Board®, the Association for Behavior Analysis International, or any other behavior analysis organization. This text cannot be relied on as the only interpretation of the meaning of the Professional and Ethical Compliance Code for Behavior Analysts or the application of the Code to particular situations. Each BCBA®, supervisor, or relevant agency must interpret and apply the Code as they believe proper, given all of the circumstances.

The cases used in this book are based on the authors' combined 60 years of experience in behavior analysis. In all cases, we have disguised the situations and used pseudonyms to protect the privacy of the parties and organizations involved. At the end of some of the chapters, we offer "Responses to Case Questions" as examples of real, or, in some cases, hypothetical solutions to the ethical problems posed by the case. We do not hold these to be the only ethical solutions, but rather, each response is an example of one ethical solution. We encourage instructors who use the text to create alternate solutions based on their own experiences. Finally, we hope that the responses offered here will stimulate discussion, debate, and thoughtful consideration about ways of handling what are by definition very delicate matters.

One

Background for Ethics in Behavior Analysis

1

How We Got Here

There is nothing more shocking and horrific than the abuse and maltreatment of innocent people who are unable to protect and defend themselves. Atrocious incidents of physical and emotional abuse toward animals, children, women, and people who are elderly occur every single day in our culture, and they are often reduced to a few lines in the local news of the daily paper.

Individuals who are developmentally disabled can also be the victims of abuse. The reprehensible mistreatment of children and adults with disabilities is especially disturbing when the abuses come at the hands of your chosen profession. But this is exactly what happened in Florida in the early 1970s. These abuses changed the course of history for behavior analysis and the treatment of people with disabilities.

> **Aversive consequences were used with abandon in informal reactions to self-injurious, destructive, and inappropriate behaviors.**

The story of the evolution of our ethics Code for behavior analysts began in the late 1960s, when "behavior modification" was all the rage. Having started only in the mid-1960s (Krasner & Ullmann, 1965; Neuringer & Michael, 1970; Ullmann & Krasner, 1965), some of behavior modification's early promoters promised dramatic changes in behavior that were quick and easy to produce and could be carried out by almost anyone with an attendance certificate from a daylong "behavior mod" workshop. People calling themselves "behavior modifiers" offered rented-hotel-ballroom training sessions in abundance. There were no prerequisites for registering, and no questions were asked about the speaker's qualifications. The basic pitch was this: "You don't have to know why a behavior occurs (it was assumed to be learned—an 'operant behavior'); you need to know only how to manipulate consequences. Food is a primary reinforcer for almost everybody; just make it contingent on the behavior you want. For inappropriate or dangerous behavior, use consequences (punishers) to 'decelerate' the behavior." There was no consideration given to the notion of "causes" of behavior or that there might be a connection between a likely cause and an effective treatment. Further, no thought was given to possible side effects of using food (e.g., food allergies, weight gain) or how the food, often candy, might be handled. Indeed, Cheerios®, M&Ms®, pretzels, and other bite-sized snacks and treats were loaded in the pockets of the "behavior specialist" in the morning and used throughout the day as needed (a hungry behavior specialist might even have a few from time to time). Likewise, aversive consequences were used with abandon in informal, impromptu, and spontaneous reactions to self-injurious, destructive, and inappropriate behaviors. Some staff members were urged to "be creative" in coming up with consequences. As a result, hot pepper sauces such as Tabasco and undiluted lemon juice might be seen in the jacket pockets of staff members who were on their way to work on "the behavior unit."

In the early 1970s, "the unit" was frequently a residential facility for developmentally disabled individuals who had moderate to severe mental retardation, some physical disabilities, and troublesome behaviors. It was most likely a former veterans' or tuberculosis (TB) hospital, which might house 300 to 1,500 "patients." Custodial care was the norm until "behavior mod" came along and offered dramatic treatment for severe behavior problems.

With no code of ethics and essentially no restrictions, this "treatment" quickly drifted into flat-out abuse.

THE SUNLAND MIAMI SCANDAL

The Sunland Training Center in Miami became "ground zero" for an abuse investigation that rocked the state of Florida in 1972. The center had been plagued by high turnover rates since it opened in 1965, resulting in frequent understaffing and low-quality training. Surprisingly, the majority of staff serving as "cottage parents" were college students. In 1969, the superintendent resigned under pressure from an investigation into "allegations of resident abuse." It seems that he confined two residents in a "cell improvised from a large trailer" (McAllister, 1972, p. 2). Then, in April 1971, the Florida Division of Mental Retardation and the Dade County Attorney's office began an intensive investigation of resident abuse that concluded after a six-month inquiry regarding allegations of "infrequent and isolated cases of abuse" (p. 2) that the superintendent had dealt with the employees involved and taken appropriate disciplinary action. One of those professional employees, Dr. E., challenged his reassignment, and a grievance committee then uncovered what it considered to be a "highly explosive situation" involving resident abuse with the apparent knowledge and approval of top administrators. As a result, seven individuals were immediately suspended, including the superintendent, the director of cottage life, the staff psychologist, three cottage supervisors, and a cottage parent. Each was charged with "misfeasance, malfeasance, negligence, and contributing to the abuse of residents" (p. 4). Subsequent to this, Jack McAllister, the director of the State Health and Rehabilitative Services (HRS) Division of Retardation, formed a nine-member Blue Ribbon Panel "Resident Abuse Investigating Committee" composed of experts in retardation as well as an attorney, a social worker, a client advocate, and two behavior analysts (Dr. Jack May, Jr., and Dr. Todd Risley).

Interviews were set up with more than 70 individuals, including current staff members, former employees, residents, and relatives of residents (including one whose son died at Sunland Miami), with some interviews lasting as long as 10 hours. The committee also examined original logs, internal memoranda, a personal diary, and personnel records.

It seems that Dr. E., a psychologist who presented himself as an expert in behavior modification and joined the staff in 1971, had set up a truly ironically named program called the "Achievement Division" in three cottages, allegedly to study "some rather esoteric questions of statistical models for economic analysis" (McAllister, 1972, p. 15). Dr. E., over a period of the next year, established a "treatment" program that consisted of, or evolved into, abusive incidents, including the following: forced public masturbation (for residents caught masturbating), forced public homosexual acts (again for those caught in the act), forced washing of the mouth with soap (as punishment for lying, abusive language, or simply speaking at all), beatings with a wooden paddle (10 "licks" for running away); and excessive use of restraints, including one resident who was restrained for more than 24 hours and another who was forced to sit in a bathtub for two days. Restraints were routinely used as punishment rather than an emergency method of preventing self-injury. As if this were not enough, the list of horrific, systematic abuses goes on: a male client required to wear women's underpants; excessive use of lengthy (e.g., four-hour) seclusions in barren and unpadded rooms with no permission to leave to use the bathroom; public shaming by forcing a resident to wear a sign that said "The Thief"; food or sleep withheld as a form of punishment; another resident forced to hold feces-stained underwear under his nose for 10 minutes as punishment for incontinence; and another

> Dr. E. established a "treatment" program that consisted of forced public masturbation, forced public homosexual acts, forced washing of the mouth with soap, beatings with a wooden paddle, and excessive use of restraints.

resident forced to lay on urine-soaked sheets for repeated incontinence (pp. 10–11).

The "milieu" of the Achievement Division consisted of an utter
lack of programmed activities, which resulted in "profound bore-
dom and deterioration, unattractive surroundings, complete lack
of privacy, public humiliation, nakedness . . . , and lack of any
means of residents to express
their grievances" (McAllister,
1972, p. 13). One resident died
from dehydration, and another
drowned in a nearby canal in
his futile attempt to escape his
cottage at Sunland Miami.

> These revolting acts of
> abuse were the result
> of an attempt by Dr. E.
> to create a "superb
> behavior modification
> program."

At first glance it might appear
that such abuses would certainly
have to be the work of a few frus-
trated, angry, poorly trained employees bent on sadistic acts. However, the investigation revealed the contrary: these revolting acts of
abuse were the result of an attempt by Dr. E. to create a "superb behavior modification program" (McAllister, 1972, p. 14) using routine
"behavior shaping devices" (p. 15). The committee's explanation was
that this program "degenerated . . . into a bizarre, abusive, and ineffective system of punishment" (p. 17). In the Achievement Division,
these procedures were systematically applied, condoned by supervisors and professional staff, and recorded in daily living unit logs. The
procedures not only were used openly but also were, at least initially,
well researched. Dr. James Lent, a well-respected expert in behavioral
treatment, for example, had modeled a token program after one first
developed in Parsons, Kansas. One key ingredient was left out of this
and other aspects of the Achievement Division: monitoring of individual resident behavior. Rather, the emphasis was on guidelines for
treatment that gave the otherwise poorly trained employees a great
deal of latitude in their reactions. The three guidelines were as follows:
(1) emphasize "natural consequences of behavior"; (2) devise your own

immediate response to problem behaviors that might crop up where no other instructions apply; and (3) do not threaten—if you verbalize a consequence to a resident, "follow through on every contingency."

The investigating committee was adamant in its observation that none of the cruel and abusive procedures employed in the Achievement Division had any basis in the behavior modification literature or "any other modern therapeutic or educational methodology." They went on to suggest that because the cottage where the abuses took place was totally isolated from outside monitoring, it was entirely possible for "well meaning but poorly trained personnel" to try some mild form of these procedures and then gradually escalate to the bizarre applications that were ultimately achieved. Each instance was, as noted previously, in a daily log book, and, given no corrective action or response, a cottage parent would naturally assume tacit approval and then perhaps employ a "slightly more extreme form" of the procedure. "In this way, quite extreme procedures evolved in gradual steps from spontaneous initiation of less extreme procedures by the cottage staff, until . . . a pattern had been established of dealing with recurrent problems by escalating the intensity of whatever procedures happened to be in use for a particular resident" (pp. 17–18). This natural tendency toward "behavior drift" on the part of the staff is certainly not uncommon in residential treatment facilities. In the case of Sunland Miami, it was facilitated by a nearly total lack of monitoring by upper-level management. The written policies at Sunland Miami clearly prohibited abusive practices, but there was no evidence that these were "forcefully communicated" to employees, and, as was previously mentioned, the facility suffered from chronic turnover of staff, so ongoing staff training was superficial at best.

Another concern of the investigating committee had to do with the training and credentials of Dr. E. As it turns out, he had recently graduated with his doctoral degree from the University of Florida and then had completed some postdoctoral work at Johns Hopkins University. He claimed to have worked with some of the biggest names in the field. However, when the committee contacted them, these eminent researchers "vaguely remembered a brash young man who visited their laboratories on several occasions," but none would claim him as his student (McAllister, 1972, p. 19). It must be remembered that Dr. E. was trained in the late 1960s when the field was in its infancy, and it appeared that the sky was the limit as far as behavior modification was concerned. The *Journal of Applied Behavior Analysis,* the professional journal of behavior analysis, had first been published only in 1968, so there was very little research on the application of behavior principles, and there was no code of ethics for behavioral researchers or practitioners.

RECOMMENDATIONS OF THE BLUE RIBBON COMMITTEE

The investigating committee took on itself the additional responsibility of making recommendations to hopefully prevent any future systematic abuses in the name of behavior modification in the state of Florida. These included strong support for a statewide advocacy program in which staff members would be allowed to make unannounced visits to residential institutions and to collect information from key personnel as well as residents, parents, staff, and concerned citizens. In addition, the committee recommended professional peer review of all behavior programs to ensure that treatment was derived from the literature and that no procedures would be used that were considered "experimental." Experimental programs would come under standard review for human experimentation in the HRS Division of Retardation. Other recommendations of the committee included the following: (1) the prohibition of certain bizarre examples of punishment, and (2) abandoning seclusion in favor of "positive and appropriate 'time out' techniques" (McAllister, 1972, p. 31).

FOLLOW-UP

In most cases, a report such as that produced by the Blue Ribbon Committee would simply find its way to the shelves of state bureaucrats and languish with no lasting effect. Such was not the case in Florida. The Florida Association for Retarded Children (now the Arc of Florida) took up the cause of humane treatment and ultimately endorsed the notion of supporting data-based behavioral treatment, using strict guidelines, under close supervision by properly trained professionals. The Division of Retardation, under the guidance of Charles Cox, instituted reforms including setting up both statewide and local peer review committees for behavior modification programming in facilities throughout Florida.

> Charles Cox instituted reforms including setting up both statewide and local peer review committees for behavior modification programming in facilities throughout Florida.

The Statewide Peer Review Committee for Behavior Modification (PRC) then established a set of guidelines for the use of behavioral procedures, which were subsequently adopted by the National Association for Retarded Citizens (MR Research, 1976) and by the Florida Division of Retardation in the Health and Rehabilitative Services Manual (HRSM) 160–4 (May et al., 1976). The state-funded PRC proceeded to make visits to institutions around the state over the next several years, educating staff members about the guidelines and making recommendations for more ethical treatment. By 1980, the PRC reached a consensus that it was time to encourage all the institutions, group homes, and smaller residential facilities to begin networking with one another and to begin to bring some sense of professionalism to behavior analysis in Florida. The "First Florida Work Session on Behavior Analysis in Retardation" was held in September 1980 and drew nearly 300 administrators, treatment specialists, behavior analysts, and direct care staff to the two-day conference, held in Orlando. At this historic conference, a meeting was held to organize an official state association. The first annual conference of the Florida Association for Behavior Analysis (FABA) was held in 1981, again in Orlando. None other than B. F. Skinner was the keynote speaker. The formation of FABA marked a turning point in behavior analysis, not only in Florida but also in the rest of the country. It was now possible to set high expectations for behavioral treatment because leaders in the field were routinely being brought to state conferences to present their latest applied behavioral research and practitioners had an opportunity to see firsthand what others were doing in other parts of the country to solve some of the most intractable behavior problems of the day. Administrators from state government and private facilities were able to see that behavior analysis was not just some local phenomenon but rather was an approach to treatment that was legitimate, effective, and humane. The PRC, in conjunction with FABA, began the process of certifying behavior analysts via a testing program sponsored by the Division of Retardation. In 1988, FABA membership adopted the FABA Code of Ethics, the first state association to do so.

THE SUNLAND MIAMI LEGACY

In retrospect, the horrific abuses at Sunland Miami in the early 1970s were probably necessary for half-baked, unregulated behavior modification to evolve into professional, respected, behavior analysis. Without the abuses, there would have been no Blue Ribbon Committee formed to think seriously about how to protect developmentally disabled individuals from systematic abuse of behavioral procedures. The headlines resulted in the intense scrutiny of a treatment mode that was in its infancy and that needed guidelines and oversight. The pain and

> The pain and suffering of the individuals with developmental disabilities involved in the abuses amplified the need to think clearly about the ethics of treatment.

suffering of the individuals with developmental disabilities involved in the abuses amplified the need to think clearly about the ethics of treatment. Although it would have been easier to prohibit behavior modification altogether, the Blue Ribbon Committee was convinced by its two behavioral advocates, Drs. May and Risley, that a better alternative was to establish strict guidelines for treatment and to set up an infrastructure for oversight involving community citizens who would bring their values, common sense, and good judgment to evaluate behavioral treatment strategies on an ongoing basis. The notion of oversight by both human rights and peer review committees gave teeth to the public appraisal of behavior analysis. These actions, plus the development of a state-endorsed mechanism of certification, the evolution of a strong state professional organization, and its promotion of a Code of Ethics for Behavior Analysts, put in place all the necessary elements of control and management to prevent future abuses. And ethics, after all, is concerned primarily with the edict to "do no harm." In the Florida case, we saw how great harm could be done by well-meaning people and that when appropriate, comprehensive strategies were adopted, abuse was prevented. Although ethics is usually seen as an individual professional engaging in responsible behavior of his or her own volition, the Florida case suggests that responsible conduct can be encouraged by other means as well. It is certainly painful and embarrassing for a profession to undergo such public scrutiny and scorn, but it was clearly warranted in this case. Indeed, it is hard to imagine such powerful procedures as behavioral treatments being used consistently across the board in the absence of such obvious forms of oversight and control.

It is also clear that, even given these mechanisms, the behavior analyst faces numerous questions every day about the appropriateness of treatment decisions. What is fair? What is right? Am I qualified to administer this treatment? Can I do no harm? Am I taking enough data? Am I interpreting it correctly? Would my client be better off with no treatment? It is the purpose of this volume to try to elucidate the current Behavior Analyst Certification Board® (BACB) Professional and Ethical Compliance Code for Behavior Analysts to assist the behavior analyst in making right choices on a daily basis.

2

Core Ethical Principles

B ehavior analysts are part of a culture of caring individuals who seek to improve the lives of others. They carry with them a set of core ethical values that are derived from thousands of years of compassionate practices dating back to the Greeks. (Ethics comes from the Greek word *ethos,* meaning moral character.) As a field, ethics can be divided into three divisions: normative ethics, meta-ethics, and practical ethics. Although it is the purpose of this volume to focus on practical ethics in behavior analysis, we first need to discuss some basic moral principles that underlie our culture at large. These core ethical principles guide our everyday lives and play a significant role in basic decision making in the practice of our profession.

In 1998, in their book *Ethics in Psychology,* Koocher and Keith-Spiegel outlined nine ethical principles for psychologists. These principles can be applied to ethics in many areas, including psychology, the teaching of children, and the training of animals. Koocher and Keith-Spiegel's nine core ethical principles are so basic—yet often go unstated—that we listed them, following, with explanations of how they relate to behavior analysis.

1. DOING NO HARM

The expression "First, do no harm" is usually attributed to Hippocrates, a Greek physician in the fourth century B.C. Commonly written as "Do no harm," the phrase is typically referred to as appearing in the Hippocratic oath that is taken by physicians. However, there is some debate on this issue (Eliot, 1910). Hippocrates did say, "As to diseases, make a habit of two things—to help, or at least to do no harm." The Hippocratic oath states, "I will follow that system of regimen which, according to my ability and judgment, I consider for the benefit of my patients, and abstain from whatever is deleterious and mischievous."

Although no behavior analyst would knowingly do harm, it can come in subtle forms that need to be attended to carefully. One obvious example is that of a behavior analyst who is practicing outside his or her area of expertise.

> A behavior analyst who has been trained to work with adolescents accepts the case of a preschool child who is having severe tantrums at school. His initial impression is that the child is "noncompliant," and he prepares a behavior program based on extinction of tantrum behaviors plus a differential reinforcement of other behavior DRO for compliance.

Another form of "harm" might come in a more subtle case of the behavior analyst who does not develop a responsible data collection system and misses the significance of a behavior.

> A Board Certified Behavior Analyst (BCBA) consulting with a group home receives a referral for a young developmentally disabled man who is described as engaging in "self-stimulatory behavior." He asks the staff to begin data collection, which involves counting the number of incidents per day. Two weeks later he reviews the baseline data and tells staff members that they do not have a significant problem and not to worry because the behavior is occurring only two to three times per day. On his next visit, the BCBA inquires about the client, only to discover that he was taken to the emergency room with lacerations to his scalp requiring six stitches. A review of the case determined that the BCBA failed to inquire about the severity of the behaviors and failed to ask the nursing staff to perform skin ratings.

Behavior analysts often work with staff members who are not at all well versed in human behavior and who will not necessarily think to offer all the information necessary to operate ethically.

> *Herman was referred for his combative behavior when being guided toward the shower each morning in a residential facility for the developmentally disabled. He was reluctant to take a shower and showed his displeasure by pushing and shoving the staff and trying to escape. This resulted in at least two staff injuries, one in the shower itself that left the training instructor unable to work for two weeks. Clearly, this was a case of aggressive behavior that needed treatment. In light of the danger involved, the staff strongly recommended restraint as an immediate consequence for Herman's refusal to cooperate with his morning bathing routine. This program was nearly implemented when the behavior analyst inquired about how long this problem had been going on. The answer turned the treatment in a totally different direction. It turned out that Herman had previously been allowed to take his bath at night and was assisted by an aide who helped him by filling up the tub, getting just the right temperature for the water, providing his favorite towel, and in general recreating the conditions his mother used at home. When this staff member quit the facility, it was determined that Herman should take a shower in the morning, which, as we came to understand, he detested. Although it was possible that a behavior program could have been written to essentially force Herman to take a morning shower, it was determined that this would cause more harm than good. The ethical solution for this case was to train another staff member to reinstate Herman's evening bath.*

2. RESPECTING AUTONOMY

To respect one's autonomy means to promote his or her independence or self-sufficiency. Clearly, the basic procedures of behavior analysis are designed to do just this: prompting, shaping, chaining, fading, and the use of conditioned reinforcers, token economies, and prosthetic environments are all designed to change behavior in such a way that the person can deliver his or her own reinforcers rather than depend on a mediator. Clashes can occur, of course, when it is determined that someone actually prefers to keep another under his or her control. This can produce very difficult situations for the behavior analyst, who is often hired by that person.

> Molly was a cute, dimple-cheeked 4-year-old with language delay. She was receiving one-on-one therapy each day from a certified assistant behavior analyst. The therapist was making progress in teaching Molly basic sounds for common objects. The mother, who was clearly not happy with the treatment, confronted her. It seems that Molly now knew the names for milk, cookie, snack, draw, play with blocks, and a few other words and was beginning to generalize these requests to the mother. The mother's position was that Molly would get snacks only when she wanted her to have them. By learning to request these items, the mother was afraid that Molly would become pushy and demanding. "The next thing you know she will think that she can just get in the fridge and get her own drinks," said Molly's mother.

Autonomy can also bring risks that cannot always be foreseen. A behavior analyst who advocates for a person to acquire a skill that will provide greater independence has to recognize that this may put the person in harm's way.

> Marie was a geriatric patient in a nursing home. She spent most of her day in bed, refusing to participate in most activities. The goal of the facility was to encourage patients to ambulate independently when possible and to attend the wide variety of social and cultural events that were offered. The behavior analyst reviewed Marie's case and determined that she was capable of walking with assistance but got more reinforcement from refusing. After determining Marie's reinforcers, the behavior analyst arranged to make them contingent on first walking with assistance and then, after approval of the physical therapist,

walking on her own. The case was considered a success until Marie fell and broke a hip. Marie's family held the behavior analyst responsible for this accident. One family member said, "Why didn't you just leave well enough alone? She preferred to stay in bed, but you had to meddle in her affairs."

Behavior analysts often work in educational or business settings, where they consult in the areas of classroom management or performance management. In these settings, the notion of autonomy can also produce some ethical issues. For example, teachers are frequently reinforced by students who stay in their seats and follow instructions; business managers and supervisors may desire that their employees simply "follow directions" and do what they are told.

Rory supervised 15 employees in a small machine shop that fabricated specialized exhaust systems for racing cars. His employees were well paid and creative in coming up with solutions for the increasingly complex demands of their elite customers. After attending a conference on performance management, Rory contacted one of the speakers and asked for help. What he wanted was for his employees to follow the manual that he had written a few years earlier. "These young guys think they know it all. They are coming up with completely new designs and telling our customers that my methods are outdated."

3. BENEFITING OTHERS

It almost goes without saying that the primary role of behavior analysts is to benefit others in whatever setting or situation they may work. This principle can often put the behavior analyst at odds with other professionals and requires frequent checks on "who is the client?" in any given situation.

Tamara was referred to the behavior analyst by her teacher. Tamara's problem was that she caused frequent disturbances in the classroom. Her teacher, Ms. Harris, provided a data sheet showing date, time, and type of disturbance going back two weeks. Ms. Harris requested help in setting up a time-out booth for Tamara. Although Ms. Harris was the person requesting help, the behavior analyst quickly determined that Tamara was her client, and she decided to take her own data. This required several visits to the school, which was quite a distance from the rest of the behavior analyst's cases. Tamara benefited from this extra effort on the part of the behavior analyst because it was discovered that her classroom disturbances were due to a hearing problem and not "willfulness," as alleged by the teacher.

4. BEING JUST

This principle is very basic and is directly derived from the "Golden Rule" or the Ethic of Reciprocity (Ontario Consultants on Religious Tolerance, 2004). Being just means that you should treat others as you would like to be treated. This has special meaning in behavior analysis because there is some potential for the use of uncomfortable stimuli or stressful contingencies in treatment. A further refinement of the ethic might ask, "How would I like my mother or my child to be treated in similar circumstances?" Questions of just treatment arise often in behavior analysis because there is often so little known about the origins of a particular behavior, and functional relationships often assumed are yet to be determined.

A senior behavior analyst was asked to consult on the case of a client who was engaging in persistent self-injurious behavior—arm and face scratching. Ignoring had been tried without effect, and a fairly dense DRO with blocking was not proving effective either. The behavior analyst was puzzled but asked himself, "How would I like to be treated?" and realized that he had been treated for just such a behavior about two years prior. He had been diagnosed with a case of hives (his scratching looked a lot like self-injurious behavior [SIB]) and felt fortunate to receive medication rather than a DRO plus blocking. The behavior analysts' attention then turned to medical diagnosis of the client's SIB.

5. BEING FAITHFUL

Well-respected professionals attain their reputation based on the trust placed in them by others. Those who are loyal, trustworthy, and honest are sought out as dependable and reliable sources of wise counsel and effective, ethical treatment. Being truthful and honest with clients, colleagues, and administrators provides the basis for long-term relationships that make for a successful career.

> Dr. B., an experienced behavior analyst, was consulting at a residential facility for clients with behavior problems that were severe enough to prevent them from living at home or in the community. One day, as soon as Dr. B. arrived at the facility, the administrator approached him and began congratulating him on successfully treating one of the most intransient cases in the facility. After discussions with the behavior specialist and Board Certified Assistant Behavior Analyst (BCaBA), Dr. B. met with the administrator to explain that no credit was due. In fact, baseline was still under way, and the treatment plan had not yet been executed.

6. ACCORDING DIGNITY

Many of the clients we serve are not able to effectively represent themselves. They may be nonverbal or simply unable to get someone to listen to them. If their wishes are unknown and they are unable to make choices, they may become depressed and present behavior problems that come to the attention of a behavior analyst. Although it is not a "behavioral" term, low self-esteem seems to capture the essence of a person who has not been afforded dignity. As behavior analysts, our job is to make sure that every client is treated with dignity and respect. Behaviorally, this means that we would work with clients on acquisition skills to make sure that they are able to voice or signal their needs to those around them. A good behavior analyst would also push for all staff to undergo the training necessary to learn to communicate with the clients who are nonverbal. These persons should be given choices throughout the day and allowed to exercise their preferences for food, clothing, roommate, activities, and living conditions. Other more subtle ways of according dignity involve the language we use to talk to or about clients. If you want to know how Bertha feels about her treatment plan, you could ask the staff or family, or you could ask Bertha herself. Clients should be addressed by name in a friendly fashion using eye contact and a pleasant smile—the kind of treatment you expect when you are receiving services from someone in your business community.

> *Thomas was a young man with developmental disabilities who was referred for his aggressive and sometimes self-injurious behavior. The incidents seemed to occur in the afternoon, when he returned to his group home from his sheltered work setting. It often took two staff members to drag him from his bedroom to the living room, where there were group activities. Before being taken to the living room, he had to be dressed, because he was frequently found sitting in his underwear on the floor rocking and listening to music on his headset. After some considerable investigation and discussion with staff, family, nurses, and social workers, the behavior analyst prevailed in his position that Thomas should be given his choice of activities in the afternoon. He was to be offered the option of joining the group each day, but if he chose to stay in his room and listen to music, his choice was respected. Given this resolution, there was no need to develop a behavior treatment program, because the aggressive and self-injurious behavior ceased to exist.*

7. TREATING OTHERS WITH CARING AND COMPASSION

Many of the previous ethical principles relate to this ethical principle. If, as a behavior analyst, you respect the autonomy of clients, work to benefit them, and devise programs that accord them dignity, you will automatically be treating clients with care and compassion. This value also suggests not only that clients be given choices but also that interpersonal relationships should demonstrate sympathy and concern.

Terrence hated getting up in the morning to go to work. He would fight with staff members, throw shoes at them, and pull the bed covers up over his head. One staff member who reported no such reaction when she was on duty described her method of getting Terrence up. "Basically, I try to treat him like my dad, who lives with us. He's on medication just like Terrence, and I know that it makes him groggy in the morning. So, I have to show some patience with Terrence. What I do is I go in his room and say in my sweetest voice, 'Terrence, honey, it's almost time to get up,' and I open the curtains about halfway and then leave his room. Then I come back about 15 minutes later and open the curtains the rest of the way and go to Terrence and gently rub his arm and say, 'How you doin', Terrence? It's almost time to get up. We've got some fresh coffee brewing, and I've set out your favorite work clothes. I'll be back to get you in a few minutes.' Then about 15 minutes after that I come back, and, if he's not up, I turn on his clock radio and say, 'Terrence, sweetheart, it's time to get up now. Let me help you get dressed.' I know this takes extra effort. But this is the way I would like to be treated, and it's the way I treat my dad, so I don't mind. And it works. By the time I turn on the radio, he's swinging out of bed and has that little half-grin on his face that says, 'Thank you for being so understanding.'"

8. PURSUIT OF EXCELLENCE

Behavior analysis is a rapidly growing field. Behavior analysts need to stay current with new developments as well as constantly updated rules and regulations. Excellence in this profession means being aware of the latest research in the field and in your specialty and incorporating the most up-to-date methods and procedures in your practice of behavior analysis. It is a given that you will subscribe to the key journals in the field and attend your state association meeting as well as the annual meeting of the Association for Behavior Analysis International or the Association of Professional Behavior Analysts (APBA). To stay at the top of your game, you may also want to watch for specialty workshops offered in your area or consider taking graduate seminars offered at a nearby university. The Behavior Analysis Certification Board (BACB) requires BCBAs to acquire continuing education each year. Continuing education hours required by the BACB are a minimum, and the behavior analyst who wants be on the cutting edge of ABA and to maintain excellence will set aside two to four hours each week to read the latest journals and newest reference works.

Nora received her master's degree in psychology with a specialty in applied behavior analysis in the mid-1990s. Since then she has gone to a few conferences but does not find them exciting enough to maintain her interest. She was embarrassed recently at a local peer review meeting when a newly minted PhD began questioning her proposed treatment plans. She had not been aware of the latest research on functional assessment and was surprised to find that she was so out of touch.

9. ACCEPTING ACCOUNTABILITY

Behavior analysts have an awesome responsibility in analyzing the behavior of a client and then making recommendations to implement a program to change a target behavior. In pursuing excellence, you will want to make sure that everything you have done in making your diagnosis is of the highest standard. By presenting your conclusions to colleagues and other professionals, you are responsible for making sure that the proposed treatment is proper, justified, and worthy of consideration. And, when your treatments fail, you must take responsibility, accepting blame and making corrections to satisfy the consumer and other related parties. Behavior analysts who are better at making excuses than analyzing behavior do the profession no favor. Those who do not take the time to research the problem they are working on and arrive at hasty conclusions will find themselves constantly in the line of fire.

Clara had been on her job for only three months when she found herself at the center of a serious discussion at an individual education plan (IEP) meeting at one of the schools where she worked. She developed a token economy for one of the teachers to use with a student. The program involved the teacher giving the student points for quietly doing her work. Unfortunately, Clara failed to take into account the issue of quality when writing up the child's program, and now the teacher was very irritated at Clara, claiming that "she has created a monster who cares nothing for the work and just scribbles away on her papers so that she can get her stupid points." Rather than point out the obvious fact that the teacher could have easily made the decision to reward only quality work, Clara accepted responsibility, apologized to the teacher, and rewrote the program.

Behavior analysts do not begin their ethical training in graduate school. A person's ethical training begins long before the college years. Developmental psychologists would argue that individual ethical standards are fairly well set by the time a child ventures into junior high school. Personal ethical situations confront people every day, and there is probably a tendency to generalize from these everyday occurrences to professional life. Persons who advance their personal interests above others, avoid conflict, and do not take responsibility for their actions are unlikely to immediately take account of ethical standards in their profession. It is for these reasons that a Professional and Ethical Compliance Code for Behavior Analysts has been developed. It is our hope that by reviewing these principles and examining the Code carefully, behavior analysts will come to see the value in adopting a set of responsible behaviors that will advance the profession and provide respect to this important new field of behavior analysis.

3

Ethics and Whitewater Rafting

Professional behavior analysts are faced with ethical dilemmas daily. Often, these ethical conflicts seem to come out of the blue. When conflicts arise quickly and are unexpected, the behavior analyst may feel ambushed. Furthermore, some ethical situations involve hidden political traps, concealed funding implications, or serious consequences for the behavior analyst. For example, if you tell your supervisor that you cannot take a case because it is beyond your competence, you run the risk of being fired. Some quandaries, while awkward, are less complicated. They involve simple decisions about how to respond to an impromptu question: "Are you Angie's therapist? She's autistic, isn't she? I thought I recognized you from her school." Other situations require the careful weighing of options, none of which are very desirable, such as, "We can transfer Paul to a special school that is better staffed with fewer students and is more appropriate, given his aggressive behavior, but they have no behavior analysts. Or, we can keep him here where we have a BCBA and an aide, but then there is the risk to the other students . . ."

Put another way, there is a wide range of ethical situations, and some are far more complex than others. An "easy" one might look like this:

> While consulting in a second-grade classroom for "Billy," the behavior analyst is asked by the teacher what she should do about "Sarah," who sits near Billy and has a similar behavior problem.

For an experienced BCBA, this is an easy situation to handle, but a new BCaBA might see this as a serious dilemma. "I don't want to offend the teacher, we are good friends, we've gone out for coffee a few times and had drinks after work on my birthday. She's going through a rough spot with her boyfriend right now, I could just give her a few tips to help her out." This BCaBA doesn't realize that she has gradually, quietly, and not intentionally become involved in a multiple relationship (Code 1.06) with the teacher. According to the Code, she cannot consult on a client unless she has a referral (Code 2.03), but she feels subtle social pressure to be of assistance to her teacher/friend.

Here's another scenario:

> "I am a BCBA who works with children diagnosed with ASD [autism spectrum disorder]. I attend the IEP meetings at the school. At one of these meetings, the behavior specialist said, 'I recommend we try a sensory diet and a weighted vest; I think it is best for this student, since he has a sensory-processing disorder.'

For an experienced behavior analyst, the response is obvious, but a brand new BCBA would have to understand there are politics involved in dealing with other professionals and paraprofessionals they do not supervise. In this case, there is also the question of how the BCBA will start a discussion of evidence-based treatments with someone who obviously buys into a different theory altogether. These are touchy, complex ethics issues and need to be handled with care.

Here is another situation to consider:

> "I am a Behavioral tutor and go to an individual child's home to conduct sessions. The setting is the bedroom, which contains a big master bed, a twin bed sideways to it, a bathroom, and a closet. The family stays in the living room so that we may work. My client is a 5-yr old child with autism who is non-verbal. He engages in a high rate of sensory stimulation and nothing entertains or motivates him, except Play-Doh,

which he eats. This makes it impossible to have data-collection time. He started kicking the window and I stopped him, then I reinforced the stopping by turning on his movie, then he started kicking the window again making eye contact with me and laughing. After I stopped him several times he continued so the mother came in—the child got what he wanted, mom reinforced his negative behavior."[1]

This case seems more complex than the previous one since there is one more "player" involved. The behavioral tutor has to deal with both the child, who presents with serious behavior problems, and the mother, who is interfering with the treatment. Another important factor is that the therapist in this case is a "tutor," which means a person who has fairly minimal behavioral training. There must also be a supervisor involved, but this was not mentioned in the case as submitted.

After reviewing many, many ethics scenarios such as these, it occurred to us that there are at least two dimensions that must be considered when discussing ethics cases: the training and experience level of the behavior analyst *and* the complexity of the case. If there is a mismatch, such as an inexperienced therapist or tutor and a complex case, it would appear that complications can easily ensue and someone might be harmed. With this new insight, we went back and analyzed over 40 cases that were submitted at one particular ethics workshop. The issue of *complexity* of ethics dilemmas jumped out at us, and we began rating them from "easy" to "very difficult."

A USEFUL METAPHOR

As we continued to look at cases, another area in which there is a rating system involving basic to complex skills came to mind. Years ago, our family went whitewater rafting in north Georgia, and later in Colorado and Arizona. Rapids are rated on a I to VI scale of difficulty, and rafters are rated from a skill level of "None" to "Expert." Since it could be quite dangerous for an unskilled rafter to paddle Class VI whitewater (the most dangerous), the guides carefully evaluate both the rafter and the rapids and match them up conservatively.[2]

> *Class I: Very small rough areas, requires no maneuvering (Skill Level: Very basic).*
>
> *Class II: Some rough water, maybe some rocks, small drops, might require maneuvering. (Skill Level: Basic paddling skill).*
>
> *Class III: Whitewater, small waves, maybe small drop, but no considerable danger; may require significant maneuvering. (Skill Level: Experienced paddling skills).*
>
> *Class IV: Whitewater, medium waves, long rapids, rocks, maybe a considerable drop, sharp maneuvers may be needed. (Skill Level: Whitewater experience).*
>
> *Class V: Whitewater, large waves, continuous rapids, large rocks and hazards, maybe a large drop, precise maneuvering (Skill Level: Advanced whitewater experience)*
>
> *Class VI: Whitewater, typically with huge waves, huge rocks and hazards, huge drops, but sometimes labeled this way due to largely invisible dangers. Class VI rapids are considered hazardous even for expert paddlers using state-of-the-art equipment, and come with the warning "danger to life or limb." (Skill Level: Expert)*

Having put the 40 cases into categories based on complexity, we next tried to determine what factors made one case easy and another complex. We read and re-read the cases, highlighting key words and phrases and making marginal notes. The following subjective dimensions emerged:

1. There was some (minor to severe) violation of ethics code and/or client rights.
2. There was some probability of physical or psychological harm (minor to severe).
3. Solutions range from those within the authority of the behavior analyst to resolve to multiple-step solutions with a supervisor or the agency head involved.

4. There were serious conflicts between parties and agencies.
5. There were legal issues involved and/or potential lawsuits against the certificant.
6. The risk to the behavior analyst included possible firing— or worse—if the case was mishandled.

Next we examined the Level 1 cases and tried to determine if the six dimensions scaled down, which they did, for the most part. An *easy* case was one in which a relatively minor violation of a client's rights was involved; there were a minimal number of parties involved; the probability of actual harm was low; a solution could be achieved in a single step; and there were no legal issues and no estimated risk to the behavior analyst. We then proceeded to develop a behaviorally anchored rating system (BARS) for each of the levels and developed the following.

Level 1: Minor violation of ethics code and/or client rights, no physical or psychological harm; within the certificant's authority to resolve. (Skill Level: BCaBA).

Level 2: Moderate violation of ethics code and/or violation of rights, some probability of harm; is in the behavior analyst's authority to resolve. (Skill Level: BCBA).

Level 3: Serious violation of ethics code and/or violation of client's rights, increased probability of harm; is in behavior analyst's authority to resolve with cooperation/ assistance from others. (Skill Level: BCBA with at least two years' experience).

Level 4: Serious violation of ethics code and/or serious violation of client's rights, probable harm; is not in behavior analyst's authority alone to resolve. (Skill Level: BCBA with at least three years' experience).

Level 5: Serious violation of ethics code and/or serious violation of client's rights, high probability of harm, is not in behavior analyst's authority to resolve; multiple-step solution required, some politics involved, some risk. (Skill Level: BCBA-D with at least two years of supervisory experience plus one year of administrative experience).

Level 6: Serious violation of ethics code and/or client's rights and significant physical or psychological harm imminent, is not in behavior analyst's authority to resolve; multiple-step solution required, inter-agency or inter-office politics and/or legal issues involved, behavior analyst is at risk of firing—or worse—if action is taken. (Skill Level: Expert BCBA-D with at least five years of supervisory experience plus experience on Human Rights Committees or similar).

As shown in Figure 3.1, there is a matrix of categories with six levels of complexity that determine if an ethics case is complex.

Here is an example of a case that is likely to be rated a Level 5 or 6. It has all the ingredients that make it complex, including

COMPLEXITY	Ethics Code and/or client's rights violation	Probability of physical/ psychological harm (minor to severe)	Solutions within one's authority/ multiple steps required	Serious office or agency conflicts	Legal issues and/or lawsuits	Risk to BCBA
Level 1	Minor	No harm	Within authority	No conflict	No legal issues	No risk
Level 2	Moderate violations	Some probability of harm	Within authority	No conflict	No legal issues	No risk
Level 3	Serious violations	Increased probability of harm	Within authority	No conflict	No legal issues	No risk
Level 4	Serious violations	Probability of harm	Not within authority	No conflict	No legal issues	No risk
Level 5	Serious violations	High probability of harm	Not within authority; multiple steps required	Some conflict	No legal issues	Some risk
Level 6	Serious violations	Harm is imminent	Not within authority; multiple steps required	Serious conflicts	Legal issues	Serious risk

Figure 3.1 Characteristics of ethics cases and their corresponding levels of complexity

ethics violations, a high probability of harm, multiple agencies and conflicts, and risks to the client, as well as the agency and BCBA.

"In our position, we function as mandated reporters for abuse and neglect. In the event that we witness or have reasonable suspicion of abuse or neglect, we are required to report to the proper entity. After we fully disclose our intentions and future course of action to the one responsible for the abuse/neglect, my experience and that of my supervisor, has been a resulting investigation and a compromised relationship between our company and that person/organization.

"I see two major themes result from this lawful action:

"First, the investigation usually proves inconclusive with little to no actual change in the client's life due to the lack of findings. This lack of change does not help the current situation of the client.

"Second, due to the compromised relationship, the party in question terminates services. That aversive pairing can generalize to other service providers, specifically those who visit the home.

"Of course, the correlation of these results is not 100%. Our ethical code suggests that our actions remain in concordance with the law, whenever possible, with some precedents to suggest that this must not always be the case.

"With regard to this situation, what would be the proper manner of evaluating something as subjective and susceptible to predictions of events to follow? I would think that a risk/benefit ratio would help to determine the proper action. Which of our ethical codes/legal requirements throughout this dilemma would supersede the others? I see a possible situation where the abuse towards a child may be a function of the parent's need/desire to escape or avoid the problem behavior. If the incident is reported, the relationship sullied, and effective treatment removed as a result of this report, the problem behavior is likely to maintain, as is the abuse."

RECOMMENDATIONS

A number of recommendations flow from this analysis of the complexity of ethics cases. First, behavior analysts must be prepared

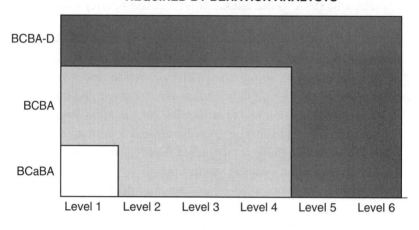

Figure 3.2 Levels of complexity and experience required by behavior analysts

for the various levels of complexity of ethical problems they will encounter on the job. Students in master's programs should be acquainted with the concept of ethics-case complexity and guided through progressively difficult dilemmas from easy to moderately difficult; they should practice devising solutions until they are fluent. They should also be trained to recognize that some ethics situations will be "beyond their pay grade" and they should seek assistance from senior behavior analysts. Behavior analysts working in organizations might want to consider holding monthly meetings to discuss ethics cases that arise to make sure they are in agreement on how to handle the complex cases. Figure 3.2 shows a proposed scheme for matching complexity of ethics cases with the training and experience level of the behavior analyst.

When a Level 5 or Level 6 ethics case is detected, the behavior analyst must be prepared for a series of discrete steps that require special skills, actual or borrowed clout, and significant fortitude. This is covered in the next chapter.

4

Analyzing Complex Ethics Cases Using a Seven-Step Model

As discussed in Chapter 3, complex ethics cases require special consideration by behavior analysts. When complex cases arise, a close and thorough analysis is needed so that clients are not harmed and the behavior analyst does not suffer in the process. The real life case here, submitted by a BCaBA, represents a situation that falls into the moderately complex category.

> *"I'm a BCaBA behavior therapist with 1 1/2 years experience. I work at a small private, for-profit school that provides educational services to children with developmental disabilities. This situation involves several of the children ages 5–7 yrs. old. I am assigned to do one-on-one therapy with children on the autism spectrum disorder (ASD). One day, an additional child was brought to me since one of the other therapists was out sick. I was not given a curriculum sheet or any instructions about the child. I was told, 'This is just for today, make it work,' which I did. But as a result, my primary student and I got nothing accomplished since it was all I could do to manage the second child. The next day I was told the same thing, 'Make it work, this is just temporary.' Again I got very little accomplished. This went on for the rest of the week. Essentially, I was just babysitting these two ASD kids. The parents of the primary child stopped me on Friday when they picked him up*

and reported that their child seemed restless and less verbal all week. They wanted to know if I knew of any problems. I lied and said that sometimes it goes like that, ups and downs, good weeks and bad weeks; they accepted my word and left. I felt horrible after this, went to the owner (who is a BCBA) and said I didn't feel comfortable with this situation. I probably shouldn't have asked, but I said, 'Are we still billing as though the children are getting one-to-one?' The owner said, 'That's a business matter, just stick to the therapy, it will work out okay.' 'What about the parents? Do they know?' I asked. The owner just stared at me and then walked away. I have the strong suspicion that the school is billing for one-on-one therapy for each child and that they have not told the parents or the insurance company of the new arrangement. What should I do? Go to the business manager? Tell the parents? Two very good BCBA's that I liked and trusted left this school six months earlier. One was the Clinical Director, and a very ethical person. I asked the owner why he left and was told, 'It's just a professional difference of opinion.'

It seems that cases similar to this are cropping up all across the country as agencies scramble with long waiting lists, too few qualified staff, and too much revenue at stake. Seemingly invisible decisions such as doubling up on clients but billing for one-on-one therapy reap great benefits and go unnoticed by nearly everyone except for the sensitive and ethical behavior analyst.

THE SEVEN STEPS

1. Is the Incident Covered by the Ethics Code?

Before you dive too deeply into the solution to a possible ethics problem, it is best to begin by making sure the problem is actually covered by the Code. This can be done by reviewing Appendix A in this text or going to BACB.com and clicking on "Ethics" on the top navigation bar. The *Professional and Ethical Compliance Code for Behavior Analysts* has a convenient two-page table of contents where you can skim the titles, looking for key words related to your dilemma. You can also scan the Subject Index at the back of this book.

For the case it would seem that several elements of the Code are relevant. Questionable Integrity (1.04) on the part of the owner is a good place to start, as well as several subsections of 2.0—Responsibility to Clients—(2.02, 2.04,

> Do you have the strength to take on the organization, the skill to deal with the other individuals involved, and the motivation to do the right thing?

2.05, 2.09, 2.10, 2.11, 2.12, and 2.13). Having established that there are serious violations of the Code involved and that you have a basis for moving forward, the next step is to understand the people with whom you will be dealing. We call them "The Players." They are also sometimes referred to as "stakeholders."

2. The Players: A) The BCBA (or BCaBA or RBT); B) The Client; C) Supervisor; D) Agency Head; E) Other Organizations

Chief among the players is you, the person who will be organizing this effort to make a decision and take steps to correct a situation that has been deemed unethical based on information obtained in Step 1. It is appropriate to do a quick check to see if you are ready for this uncomfortable state of affairs. Do you have the strength to take on the organization, the skill to deal with the other individuals involved, and the motivation to do the right thing? If you have dealt successfully with several Level 1 through Level 3 (see Chapter 3) ethics cases, then you may be ready to handle the ethics case. If you aren't ready, as long as they are not involved in the current circumstance, you can seek the counsel of trusted colleagues or your supervisor.

The next "Player" is the client. Making decisions regarding clients requires careful thinking on the part of the behavior analyst. The "Client" is often a vulnerable individual who needs protection and would benefit the most from the correction of the situation (see Glossary for the broader definition of *client*). In this example, the most immediate client was the original ASD child. There was at least one more client in this case, and that was the second child. The second child was only receiving "babysitting" services rather than language and social skills training, which the school contracted to provide. A third client in this case was the family of the original child. The family believed the child was receiving one-on-one language and social skills training. In a broader sense, the insurance company, which was largely paying for this therapeutic treatment, could be considered a *client* as well. Finally, from the perspective of the owner, the private school that hired the BCaBA was also technically considered a client in this scenario. While most of the *clients* in the case (including the behavior analyst [BCaBA]), the child, the second child, the parents, and the insurance company) were aligned in their interests, the owner had different interests, such as keeping costs down and maintaining or increasing margins.

The BCaBA did not refer to a supervisor in the case submitted, so we assume that this person was either absent (e.g., the owner did the supervising) or unresponsive. In most cases, behavior analysts will take cases such as this directly to their supervisors. Supervisors in behavioral settings should have the welfare of clients in mind and should be an ally in solving the ethical problem.

The agency head, who was the owner in this case, was a *player* in the sense that the behavior analyst had to deal with her in order to solve the ethics problem. In this case, it sounded as though the owner had not planned for emergencies or unforeseen circumstances such as a therapist being out due to illness. Further, the owner was not prepared to be upstanding on the billing with either the parents or the insurance company. She was a cunning adversary whose behavior might be difficult to change. Unfortunately, there are behavior analysis business owners in other companies who engage in the same practices.

The final player in this scenario was the insurance company. The insurance company was an outside agency that was unknowingly taking a hit with regard to billing. In cases such as this one, insurance companies should be interested in rectifying the situation, although such reports may be

> A "contingency plan" is a thoughtful and strategic analysis of what to do in the event that your first action was unsuccessful.

seen as "small potatoes" to them. Nonetheless, it would be unethical not to inform the insurance company of the breach of contract that exists with the families and the private school.

3. Contingency Plans for Ethics: Plan A, Plan B, Plan C

The concept behind this step is the possibility that your first attempt to deal with an ethics dilemma in your job may not prove successful. In this case, for example, the BCaBA spoke first directly with the owner and did not really have a plan in mind. She probably thought the owner would say, "Oh, my, has it been that long? I need to get right on that, thank you for bringing this to my attention. I'm going to talk to the parents right now." Of course, that didn't happen, and for that very reason, in complex situations such as this, we recommend having a contingency plan in place from the beginning. The contingency plan is a thoughtful and strategic analysis of what to do in the event that your first action was unsuccessful. In the case above, when Plan A (talking to the owner) failed, the BCaBA did not have a backup strategy.

A possible Plan B would have been to explain the situation directly to the parents, who had already expressed concern about their child's treatment. An option such as this is always risky to the behavior analyst since it goes directly against what she was directed to do, which was essentially babysit two clients and keep quiet. If the BCaBA talked to the parents, she could have been fired immediately for this act of defiance. This is not uncommon when dealing with ethics; doing the right thing can have negative consequences for the ethics-minded person. It is possible if the BCaBA had told the parents what was happening, they would have expressed support for the behavior analyst and advocated for her with the owner. However, this is a big unknown. Sometimes parents have a special relationship with the owner and are unwilling to stand up for the right thing. In some situations, there are other contingencies, such as both parents have jobs and don't want an interruption in services because they would then have no child care in place. In other instances, the parents' desire to do whatever it takes to support their child takes precedence. Whatever parents decide, when an ethical problem is called to their attention, they have to make some ethical decisions themselves. For example, they have to weigh being seen as troublesome parents versus leaving the school and enrolling their child somewhere else.

> In order for us to have a robust, responsible, and respectable profession, we must be aware of the conduct of other behavior analysts and be prepared to stand up for our clients' right to effective treatment.

Obviously, for every ethics dilemma, the contingency plans will be different. The contingency plans should reflect the unique circumstances of the case. There should be a method to proceed from the least-to-most intrusive interventions. Another factor that needs to be taken into account is the problem-solving repertoire of the behavior analyst and the "clout" that the person has to make things happen in the organization.

4. The Skills & Clout

Most behavior analysts entered this profession because of a strong desire to help people. For the most part, they were unaware that taking on responsibility for monitoring and maintaining ethical standards was a part of the package. But it is clear from the Code this expectation is real (see Chapter 12 for details). In order for us to have a robust, responsible, and respectable profession, we must be aware of the conduct of other behavior analysts and be prepared to stand up for our clients' right to effective treatment (2.09), and all other rights as well (Code elements 1.0–4.0).

The skills referred to in this step are described in *25 Essential Skills & Strategies for the Professional Behavior Analyst* (Bailey & Burch, 2010). The skills that are most relevant for this step include:

- Assertiveness
- Interpersonal communications
- Leadership
- Persuasion/influence
- Critical thinking
- Negotiation & lobbying
- "Think function"
- Using shaping effectively
- Handling difficult people
- Performance management
- Understanding and using power

Other skills that are not included but are very important in dealing with ethics cases are a basic understanding of (1) the law and (2) how business and government agencies function.

> The "clout" factor . . . refers to the influence of position, power, and authority to make things happen.

The "clout" factor in Step 4 refers to the influence of position, power, and authority to make things happen. In this case, the BCaBA probably had little *clout* because of her short tenure with the school and her status as an assistant behavior analyst. If she were connected somehow (e.g., one of her parents or a relative worked at the Department of Insurance Regulation or for a major insurance carrier), she would have some *borrowed clout* that could make a difference for an ethics case like this one.

Plan A Skills & Clout. Recall that the "plan" was to persuade the owner to inform parents about the situation, tell the truth about the status of their child's educational plan, beg for their understanding, and remedy the situation quickly. The BCaBA in this case operated on the spur of the moment and was not prepared to be persuasive. Some recommended skills for her Plan A include assertiveness, good interpersonal communications, leadership, persuasion/influence, and handling difficult people. Showing leadership, presenting a strong case, and being prepared for push back from the owner might have made a difference.

Plan B Skills & Clout. Plan B is to consider going directly to the parents. This would also involve good interpersonal communications skills, showing leadership, and assertiveness. In addition, in a case such as the sample case, the behavior analyst should consider "think function" when addressing the parents, i.e., understanding where they are coming from in terms of the treatment of their child. Despite the breakdown in services, the parents may not have other options, may not want to offend the owner, or may come on too strong when approaching the owner.

Plan C Skills & Clout. If the parents are not interested in dealing with the owner when told the child is not receiving services and there may have been inappropriate billing, the behavior analyst will have to decide if pushing the matter further is a good course of action. One option is for the behavior analyst to simply resign from the job and move on. Currently, there are many jobs for behavior analysts, and there is surely one that is more pro-ethics in its dealing with clients and their families (see Chapters 19 and 20 for what to look for when selecting a job). Another option is to report the fraud by the owner to the insurance company or the state insurance commissioner. This ups the ante quite a bit, and it will take some digging to understand how to do this, who to talk to, and what types of documentation are required. To proceed with this option, the behavior analyst may need to brush up on the law and do some research on insurance fraud.

5. The Risk: A) To the Client, B) To Others, C) To the Behavior Analyst

The risk to the client, which includes the ASD child and his family, under Plan B is that the school may terminate them as "trouble-makers." Depending on where they live, it might be difficult to find another placement. Or, if they do find one, the location might be inconvenient.

In the sample case (which was a real case submitted by a BCaBA), the behavior analyst was not fired for bringing up the issue to the owner. However, if she pushed Plan B, she could have found herself without a job for being insubordinate. This behavior analyst was actually a risk to the owner and the school since she could have spread the word that the owner was engaging in unethical conduct.

6. The Implementation

Plan A (which was talk to the owner) in this case basically failed. The next step would be for the behavior analyst to think carefully about Plan B (which is going directly to the parents). In your own job, if you find yourself in a situation where you have to decide if you should contact the parents of a client, there are some things to think about. Think about the time and place to meet with the parents and how to best present your case. It might not be best, for obvious reasons, to meet the parents in the lobby where they pick up their child each afternoon. You would not want to risk a dramatic scene if the owner saw you. Further, if the parents were in a rush at that time of day, you would not be able to deliver your message effectively. If you decide that contacting the child's parents is the way you need to proceed, ask the parents if there is a good time to meet for a few minutes. The parents will likely want to know what this is about, and the best advice is to simply say something like, "I have something to discuss that is fairly import-ant to me." The idea is to not tip your hand until you get to the meeting. Meeting away from the school in a quiet place is the best idea. Without being emotional, start with a statement of concern about the child and the lack of progress. Then describe clearly what transpired and the owner's response and simply wait to see how the parents respond. After that, just be supportive. Ask the parents to leave your name out of this if they decide to take action.

7. The Evaluation

As with any task that one only does occasionally, it is a good idea to keep track of what was done and how the incident turned out. This is especially important in the case of our efforts to monitor and maintain the ethical standards of our field. In any contentious arena, there is always the possibility that someone will decide to take legal action. If you are the target and you find yourself being sued, you should be prepared with detailed notes on what you did and when you did it. Having contemporaneous records of meetings, phone calls, memos, and email will show an attorney, judge, or jury that you were operating in good faith to protect others from harm and are prepared to defend your actions.

Keeping detailed notes on each ethics case you confront will also help you determine what to do the next time an issue comes up. It is neither safe nor smart to count on your memory for reporting what happened a year ago when you were asked to falsify a record or when you, as a mandated reporter, had to report a childcare worker for abuse or neglect.

> In any contentious arena, there is always the possibility that someone will decide to take legal action. If you are the target and you find yourself being sued, you should be prepared with detailed notes on what you did and when you did it.

> As a behavior analyst, you can expect to encounter somewhat complex ethical issues a few times per year.

SUMMARY

As a behavior analyst, you can expect to encounter somewhat complex ethical issues a few times per year. Having a systematic process to follow guarantees that you operate systematically and effectively on behalf of your client, yourself, and the profession. Following these seven steps will result in a deeper understanding of the factors that go into the human behavior of unethical conduct and will ensure that you always protect yourself and your clients from harm.

5

Everyday Ethical Challenges for Average Citizens and Behavior Analysts

A s they travel down the bumpy, pothole-riddled road to adulthood, children absorb the rules of their communities, religions, and cultures. Over a surprisingly short time, parents, relatives, teachers, and the occasional Scoutmaster pave the way for future ethical conduct. These unsuspecting adults may not realize that, every day, they are playing a key role in stating rules and delivering the consequences that will determine future adult behavior.

In any event, from the time people are young children, we can safely say that there is no consistent set of rules of ethical conduct for all citizens. If a junior high school student cheats on a test and does not get caught, he may come to believe that cheating is okay regardless of what his parent or religious leader says.

When students decide to enter a graduate program in behavior analysis, they are entering a world where, suddenly, the rules are different.

A pattern can develop where "don't get caught" becomes the rule rather than "don't cheat." A child who routinely fails to do her after-school chores, makes excuses, and is forgiven may grow up to be an adult who learns to make up elaborate stories about why she was late to work or why her quarterly report was sloppy and not turned in on deadline. Over time, the cumulative result of these childhood-through-adulthood experiences produces individuals with loosely formed rules, referred to as *personal ethics*. Cheating on one's spouse, lying about why you can't visit your elderly parents, and illegally using someone else's Internet connection are all examples related to personal ethics. Personal ethics can be contrasted with *professional ethics*. When students decide to enter a graduate program in behavior analysis, they are entering a world where, suddenly, the rules are different—and explicit. To understand the possible conflicts that budding professional behavior analysts face, consider the following comparisons.

FAVORS

Friends often ask each other for favors. A favor might range from sharing a DVD or watching a friend's house while she is on vacation to borrowing a lawn mower or car for a weekend. The longer the friendship, the more intimate or complex the favors can become. "Could you tell me the name of a good counselor? My husband and I are having some personal problems," or, "If my wife asks, could you tell her I went bowling with you and the guys on Thursday night?" If a citizen who is accustomed to asking for and returning favors then begins receiving in-home services from a behavior analyst three times a week, it would not be unexpected for him to also ask the behavior analyst for favors. "Could you run the therapy session for Jimmy in the car today? I have to take my older son to soccer practice." This request might sound odd, but this actually happened to one of the first author's master's degree students. Falling back on her own history of personal ethics—people do favors for each other—the student agreed. Soon it became an everyday routine. Of course, the language training was totally ineffective in the distracting backseat microenvironment of a minivan weaving through 5 o'clock traffic.

GOSSIP

If you pause briefly at the checkout counter of any grocery store, you will find yourself coming in contact with gossip—and not just any gossip, but juicy gossip, complete with in-depth, full-color, Photoshop-enhanced pictures. Between magazines at the checkout counter and reality television shows, not only is gossip one of the recognized

> The general thinking seems to be that gossip is fun and entertaining, so what is the harm?

coins of the popular cultural and commercial realm, but average citizens in our society also accept it as normal. The general thinking seems to be that gossip is fun and entertaining, so what is the harm? This attitude is so pervasive that a person refusing to participate may be seen as peculiar.

In the professional setting, behavior analysts encounter daily temptations. Consultants frequently report that parents will ask about someone else's child. "How is Maggie doing? I heard she was having some problems," a parent of another child will ask, without realizing that we cannot talk about clients or their families or reveal confidential information. To the person who wants to inquire about a client, the request seems harmless. Rather than consider the information "confidential," the person wanting to get the scoop on someone else's child views the question as just a part of the daily harvesting of bite-sized nuggets of tasty information. Talking about other people like this is gossip.

"WHITE LIES"

In an attempt to avoid conflict or censure, it has become common in our culture for people to cover up their mistakes, motives, or other personal shortcomings with "white lies." Rather than tell a friend she doesn't want to join her for coffee because she is gossipy, the sensitive person who doesn't like conflict will offer up,

"I've got to go shopping for my niece's birthday party; I'm sorry." And, of course, she will get caught. "Oh, that sounds like fun; can I join you?" Now the little-white-lying culprit will have to make additional, perhaps even more dramatic, excuses. "Well, actually, I have a lot of boxes in my car, since I have to drop off Sam's brochures at Easy Mail before I go shopping." "Oh, I can help you with that," replies the doesn't-take-a-hint friend, "We can take my new SUV; it has lots of room for boxes, and I can help you unload them." One theory says that because people so commonly use evasive tactics rather than telling the truth, they are suspicious of other people's explanations. At the other extreme, there are also plenty of people who can't read your subtle signals and will try to help you overcome every lying excuse you can offer.

APPRECIATION

Although there might be some variation from one part of the country to the other, it appears that there is a universal tendency for consumers, especially in-home clients, to give gifts to their favorite loveable, friendly, polite, kind, and gentle behavior analyst. After all, considering the behavior analyst is the lifesaver who

> Exchanging gifts creates a dual-role relationship; the client and the behavior analyst now become friends, and the BCBA is expected to return the favor at the right time.

has transformed the child and given the parents hope, it seems only reasonable to give this valued person some tangible form of appreciation. This might range from homemade cookies to leftover spaghetti ("It's my secret family recipe") or an invitation to go with the family to the beach for a weekend ("It will be fun; you can have fun with Damon and see what he is like when he sits and plays in the sand"). In the civilian world, people give gifts regularly, including cash for the doorman, hairdresser, and newspaper

professional. If standards from one's pre-behavior-analysis life are at cross-purposes with what is expected of a BCBA, they must be abandoned and replaced with our field's rather strict Professional and Ethical Compliance Code for Behavior Analysts. Furthermore, on a daily basis, the BCBA, BCaBA, and Registered Behavior Technician (RBT) will make contact with clients, paraprofessionals, and other professionals who will engage in "unethical" behaviors, possibly tempting them or even mocking them for their straight-laced approach.

The potential conflict of a history of personal ethics versus newly learned professional ethics and our Code is a worthy challenge for our field and one that is worth engaging in for the benefits and integrity that it will bring to our profession.

Two

Understanding the Professional and Ethical Compliance Code for Behavior Analysts

The Behavior Analyst Certification Board's (BACB's) Professional and Ethical Compliance Code for Behavior Analysts (the "Code") consolidates, updates, and replaces the BACB's Professional Disciplinary and Ethical Standards and Guidelines for Responsible Conduct for Behavior Analysts. The Code includes 10 sections relevant to professional and ethical behavior of behavior analysts, along with a glossary of terms. Effective January 1, 2016, all BACB applicants, certificants, and registrants will be required to adhere to the Code.

If the reader has earlier editions of this text or the Code, it should be noted that new items have been added and some of the numbers have changed in the new August 11, 2015, version of the Code.

In the following chapters, sample ethics cases from BCBAs and BCaBAs around the United States are included to illustrate the real-life problems that professionals in ABA must handle. These cases can be used to test your knowledge of the Code requirements. At the end of each chapter, you will find the first author's response to the query.

6

Responsible Conduct of Behavior Analysts (Code 1.0)

Compared to other helping professions, behavior analysis has evolved in a unique way. Our field has a relatively short history, going back only to the mid-1960s, and our roots are firmly planted in the experimental analysis of behavior. The original behavior analysts were often experimental psychologists who recognized how procedures originally developed in the animal lab could be applied to help the human condition.

The earliest applications with humans (Ayllon & Michael, 1959; Wolf, Risley, & Mees, 1964) were almost direct replications of experimental (animal laboratory) procedures. These procedures were used with populations that were abandoned by the other service professionals at the time. This was also a time in which questions about the ethics of treatment were not raised. Well-trained, responsible, experimental psychologists used their own conscience, common sense, and respect for human values to create new treatments. Based on learning theory, it was believed that these treatments might work to relieve suffering or dramatically improve the quality of life for institutionalized individuals who were not receiving any other forms of effective treatment. There was no *Professional and Ethical Compliance Code*, and there was no oversight of the PhD researchers turned cutting-edge therapists. Their work was done in the public eye with the full knowledge of parents or guardians, and a review of the work today would find little to fault in terms of ethical conduct. It was only much later that some poorly prepared and insensitive behavior analysts would run into ethical problems, creating the scandals described in Chapter 1.

Today, as a field, we have very high expectations for practicing behavior analysts, and Code 1.0 addresses the concern for overall responsible conduct. This ethics Code expresses the value system of our field, which states that those professionals who want to call themselves behavior analysts must conduct themselves in a way that reflects positively on the field—very positively, in fact.

Code 1.01 emphasizes our roots in the science of behavior (Skinner, 1953) and reminds behavior analysts that the decisions they make from day to day must be tied to this science. This is actually a very tall order, given the thousands of applied behavioral studies that have been conducted in the last 40 years. Currently, nearly two dozen journals worldwide publish behavioral research (APA, 2001), so the ethical behavior analyst has an obligation to keep in touch with quite a bit of "scientific knowledge."

Another expectation is that behavior analysts are expected to conduct their research, service, and practice "only within the boundaries of their competence" (Code 1.02). This is defined as "Commensurate with their education, training and supervised experience," but, beyond that, practitioners will have to determine whether they are indeed competent in certain subspecialties of ABA. Examples of such subspecialties include treating feeding disorders, self-injurious behavior, aggression, and destructive behaviors. Attending a workshop or a seminar on one of these specialties is not sufficient to describe oneself as competent in a subspecialty area. Having the level of expertise required to treat a behavior problem as described here would require that the behavior analyst spend several weeks on site at a clinic (specializing in the subspecialty) where treatment sessions are observed and skills are practiced with feedback from an expert mentor. Ideally, the behavior analyst would receive a certificate attesting to the acquisition of the necessary skills to deal with these potentially dangerous and life-threatening behaviors.

One more expectation, described in Code 1.03, is that behavior analysts maintain "competence in the skills they use." This is another demanding standard, given the constantly improving methodology of our relatively young field. Certificants are advised to claim and maintain competence using a conservative definition of this most important standard.

In the early years of behavior analysis, there was an emphasis on the use of aversive procedures to change behavior, which unfortunately set the stage for considerable backlash on the part of advocate and consumer groups. An "anti-aversives" movement began and still exists that has portrayed our field as prone to the use of punishment, although we have long since passed into another level of professionalism. As happens in many fields, some practitioners seem to become frozen in time with regard to their skills. It is possible even now to run into someone who got a PhD in 1975 who has not remained current with the trends in the field. Code 1.03 was meant as a wake-up call to such individuals for them to get back in touch with current standards before they hurt innocent people and damage the reputations of legitimate, up-to-date behavior analysts.

As expressed in Code 1.04, Integrity, it does not seem too much to ask of professionals that they recognize the legal code of their community and maintain high moral principles. To do otherwise is to put a stain on the good reputation of others. Even though they are not practicing behavior analysts, the community will identify you as a problem if something goes amiss. None of us wants to see a headline such as, "Behavior analyst caught dealing drugs at local high school," but that is exactly how a headline would read. As a new profession with a complex, two-part name, we are not on the radar screen of most Americans. Our goal as a profession is to gradually emerge onto the scene with a terrific reputation for truth, honesty, and reliability. What we do not want is to end up on the "Ten Least Respected Professions" list, along with journalists and government employees (BBC Radio, 1999). Advice to new behavior analysts would be to monitor your behavior, make sure that in your dealings with clients and the public your conduct is above reproach and well within the law, and be recognized by those around you as an exemplary citizen.

As a part of being a well-respected professional, behavior analysts should provide services only in the context of a professional or scientific role (Code 1.05(a)). This means that behavior analysts should refrain from casually giving advice to neighbors, friends, and relatives. This is a case where free advice is worth what you pay for it, and it can damage relationships in the future if the advice was not followed to the letter and then failed to produce results.

When providing behavioral services in a professional capacity, even though behavior analysts have been trained to use some fairly sophisticated terminology among themselves, they should keep the jargon to themselves when dealing with clients and families (Code 1.05(b)). Suggested treatment plans should be translated into plain English for clients, consumers, and other professionals, reserving the jargon for behavioral colleagues at conferences.

A major personal commitment that we ask of behavior analysts is to shed and ultimately reject any biases they may have grown up with in their families or communities. Behavior analysts should obtain the training necessary to be able to work with people of different genders, races, ethnicity, or national origin in a totally accepting and nondiscriminating manner (Code 1.05(c)). Further, they should not engage in any discrimination of individuals or groups based on age, gender, race, culture, ethnicity, national origin, religion, sexual orientation, disability, language, socioeconomic status, or any other basis (Code 1.05(d)).

Sexual harassment is a blight on our culture that will not go away. Over 26,000 charges were filed in 2014, 85% of which were made by women, with fines reaching $50 million each year to resolve conflicts (U.S. EEOC, 2014). Sexual harassment is a form of sex discrimination that violates Title VII of the Civil Rights Act of 1964. One would think that most professionals would be aware of this. However, even attorneys have engaged in this despicable form of abuse, as noted in the case of Anita Hill in her testimony against Clarence Thomas (Hill, 1998). This form of conduct includes unwanted advances, requests for sexual favors, and any form of behavior that is sufficiently severe and pervasive and produces an abusive working environment (Binder, 1992). In addition to sexual harassment, Code 1.05(e) addresses other forms of harassment, including harassment related to a person's age, gender, race, culture, ethnicity, national origin, religion, sexual orientation, disability, language, or socioeconomic status.

Even behavior analysts may develop problems in their personal lives. Chronic illness, a messy divorce, or alcohol addiction can bring almost anyone down, and, as in the case of any professional, your obligation is to make sure that personal issues do not interfere with your ability to deliver quality services (Code 1.05(f)). This is probably best handled via the "trusted colleague" model in which you develop a relationship with a person on whom you can rely to be straight and honest with you on a range of matters that affect your professional life. If you in any way feel that you might not be fulfilling your obligations to your clients or your workplace, it is time to have a heart-to-heart talk with a trusted colleague to determine his or her perceptions and to help you sort out your options. Some of those will probably involve taking a leave of absence for a period of time while you get your life in order. During this time, you need to make sure that you have made other arrangements with other behavior analysts to cover your clients and sit for you on committees.

Effective behavior analysts wear many hats in their communities, and it is easy for them to encounter situations where a conflict of interest might arise. Ideally, behavior analysts will avoid any situation that can result in a multiple relationship or conflict of interest (Code 1.06(a)). Such conflicts come about because busy, effective behavior analysts who have a full client caseload might also have other responsibilities such as serving on the peer review committee, being an elected representative of their state association, or possibly having some responsibility with their local parent-teacher organization. More personal conflicts of interest can arise when a neighbor asks for help with a child behavior problem or a visiting relative clearly needs help resolving a personal issue. A behavior analyst who is a government employee elected to a position with a state organization might find that the position the organization adopts is at odds with his or her employer. Behavior analysts who freely give advice to a relative run the risk of alienating that person if the behavioral program does not work or their advice is contrary to what a school psychologist, counselor, or other professional recommended. The best solution is to avoid such situations on the front end, but the Code requires the behavior analyst to resolve these situations before any harm is done (Code 1.06(b)). Further, behavior analysts should be open and quick to inform clients about the potential harmful effects of multiple relationships (1.06(c)).

Surprisingly, one of the most frequent questions about the Code centers around the giving and receiving of gifts. Behavior analysts who do a good job and are professional and reliable soon become important to the families that they serve. Before long, many families will want to give the behavior analyst a gift, have the BA over for dinner, or invite the BA to a family party or celebration. Code 1.06(d) states that behavior analysts do not accept or give gifts, because this constitutes a multiple relationship. Having the parents/guardian party sign a "Declaration of Professional Practice" in which the expectations are described before services begin is a good way to lay the groundwork for ethical service provision.

As our profession has grown over the past 40 years, behavior analysts have increasingly been respected for their skills and have moved into positions of authority, where they wield some considerable power and influence. Whereas in the beginning they served only as therapists or unit directors, many behavior analysts are now chairs of psychology departments, superintendents of large residential facilities, or owners of major consulting firms. In such positions, even the most ethically sensitive behavior analysts may find that they can call the shots without anyone else's approval. The PhD president of a consulting firm can direct his or her master's level consultants to advocate a certain procedure, to promote overbilling, or to encourage snooping on the competition while on the job. We would hope that the ethical master's level consultant would resist such pressure, but the differential in power allows supervisees to be exploited if care is not taken to prevent this. Supervisors could extract favors from students in exchange for a good grade in a practicum, and, theoretically, behavioral faculty could do the same. Or, as has been occasionally reported, students may offer favors for a good grade. Behavior analysts should never exploit persons over whom they have supervisory, evaluative, or other authority such as students, supervisees, employees, research participants, and clients (Code 1.07). Thus, parties on both sides need to be equally aware of the potential for exploitation when one person is in control, even if the person is a behavior analyst.

1.0 RESPONSIBLE CONDUCT OF BEHAVIOR ANALYSTS

Behavior analysts maintain high standards of behavior of the profession.

This simple statement contains a great deal of meaning for professionals in our field. The "high standards" include honesty, integrity, reliability, confidentiality, and trustworthiness. Unstated here is the assumption that these values will carry over into the behavior analyst's off-duty time. This extends to other professions as well. Physicians, architects, school psychologists and a host of other professionals are all expected to demonstrate their honesty and integrity whenever they are in public; to do otherwise is bad for business and puts a black eye on the profession. The case here pertains to maintaining high standards of behavior.

• • • • • • • •

CASE 1.0 EXPOSED

"Katie is the single mother of a child with autism who had visited several different behavior analytic service providers before deciding on a particular service provider. A few weeks after

making the decision about which behavior analyst would be selected to provide services, Katie was at a local fair and saw Marilyn, one of the service providers she had interviewed but ultimately decided not to use. Marilyn looked up and greeted Katie loudly, and then exclaimed, 'Katie! What happened? I thought when you visited my autism clinic we had a deal. . . . Why didn't you choose me?' Katie felt uncomfortable about the exchange, especially because she had not mentioned to people in her community that her child had autism. She muttered something about finances and then hurried out of the fair."

• • • • • • • •

1.01 RELIANCE ON SCIENTIFIC KNOWLEDGE (RBT)[1]

Behavior analysts rely on professionally derived knowledge based on science and behavior analysis when making scientific or professional judgments in human service provision, or when engaging in scholarly or professional endeavors.

@2015 Behavior Analyst Certification Board, Inc. All rights reserved. Reprinted by permission. The most current version of this document is available at www.BACB.com.

One of the primary characteristics of behavior analysis is our reliance on scientific evidence as a basis of our practice. In particular, we value single-subject design studies that clearly demonstrate functional control of behavior and which additionally point to effective interventions that are also evaluated carefully with clinical data. Although we might seek input from family or caregivers during an intake process, the behavior analyst depends on objective data that are sufficient to allow a data-based conclusion.

• • • • • • • •

CASE 1.01 BOO FOR THE HOME TEAM

"Anthony is a BCBA who works in the home of a child whose parents strongly believe in FC, or facilitated communication (AKA 'supported typing'). Anthony uses a typing machine and

physical prompting to guide a child (who is in the third grade and nonverbal) to generate language-related responses. Anthony justifies his work by saying, 'I don't look at the screen.' A BCBA at the school has tested the student and has demonstrated that he is clearly prompt-dependent and produces no intelligible responses on the device on his own. Should this BCBA be reported to the Board?"

• • • • • • • •

1.02 BOUNDARIES OF COMPETENCE (RBT)

(a) All behavior analysts provide services, teach, and conduct research only within the boundaries of their competence, defined as being commensurate with their education, training, and supervised experience.

(b) Behavior analysts provide services, teach, or conduct research in new areas (e.g., populations, techniques, behaviors) only after first undertaking appropriate study, training, supervision, and/or consultation from persons who are competent in those areas.

Behavior analysis is much more widely known now than it was several years ago. The pressure is mounting in many quarters to expand our evidence-based procedures into areas where there is very little research. The risk of doing this is that, absent proper training and supervision, it is likely that some harm will come to the client and the agency will be held liable. Behavior analysts may find it useful to cite and explain element 1.02 to their employers if pressured to provide treatment beyond their boundaries of competence.

• • • • • • • •

CASE 1.02 PEDOPHILIA PROFESSIONAL

"I am writing about an individual recently added to my case-load at a residential facility. The individual is 18 years old, has an Axis I diagnosis of Autism, an IQ under 70, and exhibits behaviors associated with pedophilia. He will target younger children (regardless of gender), attempt to remove their clothes,

and will attempt to make contact with the child's genital area. These behaviors have been observed toward younger peers both here on campus and in the community. Over the past couple of years, the frequency and intensity of these behaviors have increased significantly. I do not have any experience addressing behaviors such as this one that are potentially dangerous and socially sensitive in nature, but I am being pressured to do an assessment and provide treatment."

• • • • • • • •

1.03 MAINTAINING COMPETENCE THROUGH PROFESSIONAL DEVELOPMENT (RBT)

Behavior analysts maintain knowledge of current scientific and professional information in their areas of practice and undertake ongoing efforts to maintain competence in the skills they use by reading the appropriate literature, attending conferences and conventions, participating in workshops, obtaining additional coursework, and/or obtaining and maintaining appropriate professional credentials.

The rationale behind this requirement is to encourage all behavior analysts to remain current with the legitimate research in our field. One key expression here is "appropriate literature," which we take to mean peer-reviewed, evidence-based research that is current and relevant. Failure to keep up can result in the application of procedures that have been shown to have serious limitations or, possibly, hidden dangers. Behavior analysts should also attend conferences and workshops to enhance their skills.

• • • • • • • •

CASE 1.03 MINDFUL MEETING

"At my job, I am required to attend in-service training on a regular basis. Recently, we were instructed to participate in a workshop on Mindfulness and were told that we would receive 3-hours of CEU credit since the instructor was a BCBA-D. The gist of the training was that behavioral interventions were inferior to

Mindfulness methods. This individual presented some research but it seemed full of holes compared with JABA studies that I've read. I feel guilty about claiming my 3-hours of credit for this, what should I do?"

• • • • • • • •

1.04 INTEGRITY (RBT)

(a) Behavior analysts are truthful and honest and arrange the environment to promote truthful and honest behavior in others.

(b) Behavior analysts do not implement contingencies that would cause others to engage in fraudulent, illegal, or unethical conduct.

(c) Behavior analysts follow through on obligations and contractual and professional commitments with high quality work and refrain from making professional commitments they cannot keep.

(d) Behavior analysts' behavior conforms to the legal and ethical codes of the social and professional community of which they are members.

(e) If behavior analysts' ethical responsibilities conflict with law or any policy of an organization with which they are affiliated, behavior analysts make known their commitment to this Code and take steps to resolve the conflict in a responsible manner in accordance with law.

This element of the new ethics Code really represents the foundation of all others. It is greatly expanded from the previous Guidelines and pulls together all of the important values that we think are essential to maintain the credibility of our field. Subsection (b) seems timely, since many agencies now see ABA as a gold mine that can generate a bonanza for owners if they can just get the BCBAs to go along. Subsection (d) reminds everyone that we exist in a community of legal guidelines and laws and must be constantly aware of the need to follow these existing regulations.

Subsection (e) should guide the behavior analyst in those incidents where it appears that an employer or supervisor is urging an illegal or unethical course of action.

• • • • • • • •

CASE 1.04 QUESTIONABLE INSURANCE BILLING

"While consulting with a teacher at a local school, I was asked to conduct an observation of a child in his classroom. When I inquired about billing, I was told to bill under a different client name (in the same classroom) for a child for whom I was not rendering services. I was told that the other client's insurance provides him with 'unlimited hours.' I stated that I would not bill for a client for whom I was not providing service, as that would be not only unethical but also illegal. The policy of this company is to first see how many hours the client's insurance will pay for, and bill the maximum amount of time for that client, regardless of the client's needs."

• • • • • • • •

1.05 PROFESSIONAL AND SCIENTIFIC RELATIONSHIPS (RBT)

(a) Behavior analysts provide behavior-analytic services only in the context of a defined, professional, or scientific relationship or role.

The intent of this element is to discourage behavior analysts from freely giving advice to friends, neighbors or relatives. A "defined" relationship generally means a verbal or written contract that specifies duties and responsibilities as well as the term of the relationship, description of wages, and other considerations.

(b) When behavior analysts provide behavior-analytic services, they use language that is fully understandable to the recipient of those services while remaining conceptually systematic with the profession of behavior analysis. They provide appropriate information prior to service delivery about the nature of such services and appropriate information later about results and conclusions.

It is generally understood that behavior analysts must be at least bilingual to be effective; we must speak our complex technical language to communicate with each other and speak in plain English (or other language appropriate to the client) when dealing with clients or their caregivers.

(c) Where differences of age, gender, race, culture, ethnicity, national origin, religion, sexual orientation, disability, language, or socioeconomic status significantly affect behavior analysts' work concerning particular individuals or groups, behavior analysts obtain the training, experience, consultation, and/or supervision necessary to ensure the competence of their services, or they make appropriate referrals.

Many behavior analysts are now working in urban or other environments where people from a wide variety of cultures are in need of behavioral services. In such settings, it is necessary for the behavior analyst to be very aware of such cultural and ethnic differences. When necessary, the BA should call on someone with the proper cultural expertise to expedite his or her services.

(d) In their work-related activities, behavior analysts do not engage in discrimination against individuals or groups based on age, gender, race, culture, ethnicity, national origin, religion, sexual orientation, disability, language, socioeconomic status, or any basis proscribed by law.

Examples of discrimination include not interviewing or hiring employees over 40 because it is thought they cannot perform their duties or refusing to give employees time off for their religious holiday. Another example of discrimination is sex discrimination, where women are paid 77% of what men do for the same type of work.

(e) Behavior analysts do not knowingly engage in behavior that is harassing or demeaning to persons with whom they interact in their work based on factors such as those persons' age, gender, race, culture, ethnicity, national origin, religion, sexual orientation, disability, language, or socioeconomic status, in accordance with law.

While it is highly unlikely that behavior analysts would engage in such practices, posting cartoons or making comments about certain races or religions is absolutely out of bounds. Also in the category of entirely inappropriate are email jokes or stories passed around via the Internet about people with disabilities or language impairments.

(f) Behavior analysts recognize that their personal problems and conflicts may interfere with their effectiveness. Behavior analysts refrain from providing services when their personal circumstances may compromise delivering services to the best of their abilities.

Unfortunately, with easy access to illegal drugs and the wholesale encouragement of the use of alcohol as a social lubricant, some in the professions succumb to these temptations, and, subsequently, their work as a behavior analyst suffers. Professionals should engage in self-monitoring and make other arrangements to have their work covered by other qualified professionals when necessary. Behavior analysts should also arrange to have their work covered whenever stress, a change in a life situation (e.g., break-ups, divorce, death in the family), or other conflicts negatively affect their professional performances.

• • • • • • • •

CASE 1.05 DRUG SPECULATION

"I work as a consulting BCBA and I provide home-based services for a school district. Recently, it has been reported to me (by clients and colleagues) that the school district's BCBA 'has a serious drug problem.' I interact with him rarely and do not have any evidence of this, though I am concerned that illicit drug use—or perceived drug use by consumers and colleagues—is a violation of our ethical guidelines, in that it is (1) in violation of state laws and (2) does not represent our

field well. What's the best way for me to proceed, given that I don't interact with this individual a great deal? That is, how should I proceed given that I've only heard rumors?"

• • • • • • • •

1.06 MULTIPLE RELATIONSHIPS AND CONFLICTS OF INTEREST (RBT)

(a) Due to the potentially harmful effects of multiple relationships, behavior analysts avoid multiple relationships.

(b) Behavior analysts must always be sensitive to the potentially harmful effects of multiple relationships. If behavior analysts find that, due to unforeseen factors, a multiple relationship has arisen, they seek to resolve it.

(c) Behavior analysts recognize and inform clients and supervisees about the potential harmful effects of multiple relationships.

A multiple relationship for a behavior analyst could arise if he or she is involved in a professional capacity while also in some other role with an individual. An example of this would be the behavior analyst who is providing therapy services or supervision and is also in a close friendship with the client or client's family. The primary concern is that in such a situation, the behavior analyst would have his or her objectivity impaired. For example, a behavior analyst who became friends with her client's parents might find it difficult to give the parents bad news on an assessment. Befriending clients or their families, supervisees, or research participants can create the impression of favoritism. This can be damaging to the BA's working relationship with other clients and supervisees.

• • • • • • • •

CASE 1.06(C) CLIENT AS EMPLOYEE

"A few months ago, we hired someone for our Case Management Department. This employee is responsible for case assignment,

securing funding for our clients, and acting as a liaison to the insurance companies. She has turned out to be a fantastic employee and in her short time with us, she has made a significant impact in her administrative position. Unfortunately, she just received news that her 3-year-old son has autism and is in need of ABA services. We understand that she cannot receive services from our company, as that would be a direct violation of the Code. Therefore, we have prepared a list of other ABA companies that have built a reputation of providing high quality service. Is there anything else we can do to help her?"

• • • • • • • •

(d) Behavior analysts do not accept any gifts from or give any gifts to clients because this constitutes a multiple relationship.

One of the most frequently asked questions about the new Code involves this element, which prohibits the acceptance of gifts from clients. We interpret this to also include food and services. The goal, of course, is to prevent the development of a dual relationship between the behavior analyst and her clients, since staying for dinner or going to a client's birthday party starts to look like a friendship relationship. While many people have a hard time accepting this idea, even a token gift or a cupcake can begin a slippery slope toward that relationship. The concern here is that the client may expect a favor in return at some point, and the behavior analyst's judgment about the case could easily be compromised.

But why not *any* gifts of *any* value? In some professions, there is an understanding that *small* gifts (i.e., value less than $10) do not present a problem unless they lead to "manipulation" (Borys & Pope, 1989), which we interpret to mean there is an expectation of some reciprocation, which then produces the aforementioned slippery slope. Even token gifts given to behavior analysts may have some subtle impact on their professional judgment at a later time; a gift is symbolic of appreciation for services rendered in a kind and considerate way, so it would be a hard-hearted individual indeed who would not feel the need to exercise a little flexibility at some point in the future regarding billing, signing a waiver, or attesting to the person's good character. Furthermore, by setting some upper limit to the value of a gift puts the behavior analyst in the position of having to estimate the asking cost (retail or whole-sale?) of the item ("Is this really less than $5.00 worth of candy?" "I know these flowers cost more than $10," and "You got it on eBay for $5? Surely this is worth $100"). Once trying to determine the value of a gift becomes part of the practice, the BA must face the uncomfortable situation of returning certain gifts (because they exceeded the limit) to some clients but not to others.

It is often pointed out that, in some cultures, refusing a gift is considered rude at worst or very poor manners at best, but these are normal circumstances where a family is receiving a *guest*. A behavior analyst coming to work with a child in the home of the client is not a guest, any more than a plumber or electrician would be a guest, and it seems nonsensical to expect these tradespeople to bring gifts or accept them. In developing the initial relationship with an in-home client, it is paramount that the behavior analyst use the Declaration of Professional Practice (Bailey & Burch, 2011, p. 261) wherein the "culture" of behavior analysis is explained: "We are in your home to provide treatment to your child; we are not guests and do not expect to be treated as such. We have to abide by professional practices in our country. Please do not offer us food or drink or expect that you should give gifts or tokens of appreciation. We derive all of our rewards from the improvements that your child will show as a result of treatment, and an occasional 'thank you' is more than enough."

• • • • • • • •

CASE 1.06(D) THERE YOU GO

"One of my graduate students was working for a big agency that actually had a policy of employees NOT accepting gifts from families. Our student, however, was getting pressured

from a family to accept token gifts. She politely resisted for a long time, but then her supervisor told her, 'Oh, just go ahead and accept the gift, let's not upset the parents any further.' The student accepted the gifts. Several months later, something happened that soured the parents with the graduate student and the agency and the parents filed a complaint with the agency that the student accepted the gift against company policy!"

• • • • • • • •

1.07 EXPLOITATIVE RELATIONSHIPS (RBT)

(a) Behavior analysts do not exploit persons over whom they have supervisory, evaluative, or other authority such as students, supervisees, employees, research participants, and clients.

In some settings, behavior analysts exercise considerable power because of their authority as president of the company, CEO, or clinical director or simply by virtue of the fact that they are the only BCBA in the building. In this latter capacity, behavior analysts have the authority of the pen, since their signature is required on a lot of paperwork that goes to funding agencies and insurance companies. In university settings, there are sometimes situations where faculty members use their authority to keep students from reporting unwanted advances. The intent of 1.07 is to keep behavior analysts from exploiting others.

• • • • • • • •

CASE 1.07(A) THE MANIPULATIVE BCBA

"I work at a center where none of the program coordinators who do behavioral treatment are BCBAs or BCaBAs, nonetheless they are required to send their paperwork to a BCBA. The BCBA has never seen any of the clients except for an hour or so at intake, knows nothing about their history or behaviors, and never reviews what the program manager's reports. However, the BCBA signs the forms as though he did the work.

I feel this BCBA is taking advantage of us since we do all the work, receive no supervision, and he takes all the credit. This just doesn't seem fair."

• • • • • • • •

(b) Behavior analysts do not engage in sexual relationships with clients, students, or supervisees, because such relationships easily impair judgment or become exploitative.

For some, the temptation is great to take advantage of their superior employment position with others, particularly male supervisors with young female supervisees or older behavior analysts with teenage clients. Such assignations are repugnant and illegal. They are also unethical, since the young client or supervisee feels helpless to do anything for fear of being fired or dismissed.

(c) Behavior analysts refrain from any sexual relationships with clients, students, or supervisees for at least two years after the date the professional relationship has formally ended.

Because of a rash of reported sexual relationships between male behavior analysts and female clients (usually a single mother of a child client), it became necessary to make the stricture about refraining from such relationships perfectly clear. The case here is a clear example of how such unethical conduct can ruin lives.

• • • • • • • •

CASE 1.07(C) DATING MOM

"The following information has been reported to me by a student's parents. Upon accepting a referral to see the student approximately one year ago, the BCBA invited the mother to come work for him, which she did. Approximately three months ago, the student's parents reported to me that they were getting a divorce. The student's father volunteered that the impetus for the divorce was his wife was having an affair with the BCBA.

> *The student's mother volunteered that the BCBA was her cur-rent 'boyfriend.' The student's mother reported that the BCBA provides professional/advocacy services to her free of charge. The student's mother has requested that the BCBA be invited to an upcoming Planning and Placement Team (PPT) meet-ing during which he is to act in a professional capacity pro-viding advocacy for the student. I have contacted our agency director regarding my concerns relating to ethical stan-dards of conduct on the part of this BCBA. In short, I am concerned that there are several conflicts of interest (i.e. employer-employee; personal relationship) that make the BCBA's professional involvement in this case potentially harmful to the student. I am looking for advice as to whether my concerns are valid in this case and, if so, how to proceed in addressing them."*

• • • • • • • •

(d) Behavior analysts do not barter for services unless a written agreement is in place for the barter that is (1) requested by the client or supervisee; (2) customary to the area where ser-vices are provided; and (3) fair and commensurate with the value of behavior-analytic services provided.

The previous edition of the Guidelines cautioned against "bartering with clients," and that position is maintained in the new Code, but with these new stipulations. This practice may become unethical if either party begins to feel cheated by the arrangement. A behavior analyst who is working with a child whose parents own a restaurant may agree to provide services in exchange for regular dining out opportunities. This could go sour if the behavior analyst gets tired of the food, or the parents/owners may feel cheated if the behavior analyst starts inviting friends to join her for the free meals. Such an arrangement is full of conflicts of interest by both parties, and such arrange-ments should probably be avoided unless no other payment option is available.

RESPONSES TO CASES

CASE 1.0 EXPOSED

As a BCBA, Marilyn violated the confidentiality of her client in public. Even though she was at a public event and Katie was not her client, Marilyn (the BCBA) is required to respect the privacy of others.

CASE 1.01 BOO FOR THE HOME TEAM

Anthony is not relying on scientific evidence to guide his practice. FC was exposed in the '90s as invalid, and nearly a dozen scientific and professional organizations, including the Association for Behavior Analysis: International, have since discouraged its use. Anthony could be reported to the Board for this unethical activity, since the BCBA at the school has already tried to dissuade him from supporting FC.

CASE 1.02 PEDOPHILIA PROFESSIONAL

The purpose of this admonition is to (1) prevent mistreatment of the client and (2) prevent behavior analysts from being accused of misrepresenting their qualifications. Even attempts at an assessment could cause arousal and possible adverse affects on the behavior analyst and others in the vicinity. If something like this happened, it would quickly come to light that the behavior analyst (BA) was not qualified to provide treatment. The BA could lose his or her job or land in the middle of a malpractice lawsuit. The best advice is for BAs is to tell their supervisors they do not feel comfortable handling such cases. This case should be referred to someone who is qualified to take such dangerous and specialized clients. The BA should also mention the exposure the organization has to litigation in the event treatment at the facility goes bad. Another option is sending out a call to colleagues asking if anyone knows a behavior analyst with sufficient background in pedophilia who might be able to take this case.

CASE 1.03 MINDFUL MEETING

While this training might have been approved for CEU credit, it does not appear to meet the intent of this element of our code of ethics. Mindfulness might be a suitable method to help people feel calmer or more relaxed after a stressful day; however, the notion that mindfulness could substitute for well-established and documented behavioral treatments is a stretch. Since you did not pay for the CEUs, you could keep a clear conscience by not including these hours in your accounting for the year. If the course was particularly irrelevant and made negative claims about behavior analysis, you should notify the Board.

CASE 1.04 QUESTIONABLE BILLING

This is clearly a case of insurance fraud. The agency (consulting firm) is insulating itself from responsibility by having the behavior analyst manipulate the paperwork. Reporting this incident to the insurance company (in writing) would seem to be a required response under 1.04. Leaving the company could follow shortly thereafter.

CASE 1.05 DRUG SPECULATION

Our ethics code does not allow the reporting of second-hand information. Only those who have witnessed the illicit use of drugs can make the call. The most appropriate action that you can take is to go to those who have reported this to you and encourage them to first approach the person directly and see how he responds. This may be just the push he needs to get help. However, if he does not respond appropriately or does not provide an acceptable explanation, it may be appropriate for you to report this to the proper authorities, including the Board.

CASE 1.06(C) CLIENT AS EMPLOYEE

It was good judgment to help the employee find another agency to provide treatment for her child. This might be an awkward situation for her, since she now has a comparison with the way that your agency operates, and it may be difficult to satisfy her. In another case, a local private school that faced a similar situation decided it was acceptable for it to provide behavioral services to an employee's child. All went well for a few weeks, but when the employee/parent began asking questions about treatment, billing, and qualifications of staff, the situation quickly turned bad. The employee eventually quit her job, took her child out of the program, and now has nothing good to say about her former employer.

CASE 1.06(D) THERE YOU GO

This is a classic example of what can happen when professionals allow themselves to second-guess the ethics Code. There are numerous other examples where behavior analysts innocently engaged in "friending" their clients, only to get bitten for their kindness.

CASE 1.07(A) THE MANIPULATIVE BCBA

This BCBA is acting unethically in not engaging in proper oversight of the individuals who are doing the ABA work; this could be reported to the BACB. Code 5.0 is also being violated in several respects, and that should also be included in your report.

CASE 1.07(C) DATING MOM

The best course of action is to meet individually with the BCBA as soon as possible to explain his multiple, serious violations of the ethics Code and ask him to have another person represent the child at the meeting. File a complaint with the BACB detailing the situation and making a formal grievance against the BCBA for multiple violations of conflict of interest.

7

Behavior Analysts' Responsibility to Clients (Code 2.0)

In the early days, when our field consisted of experimental psychologists applying the principles of behavior to "subjects" they encountered in the residential units of state institutions, there was no question about where the responsibility lay; it was clearly with the employer. These pioneer behavior analysts most often had no training in clinical psychology. They believed that behavior could be changed using procedures derived from learning theory. The "client" (although that term was not used initially) was their employer. In some cases, the parents of a child were the "clients."

It was not until 1974 that issues of a client's "right to treatment" would surface as an issue in the landmark *Wyatt v. Stickney* (1971) case in Alabama. In this case, it was argued that institutionalized mental patients had a right to receive individual treatment or be discharged to the community. Although the case really did not have anything directly to do with treatment per se (e.g., it dictated increases in professional staff, improvements in the physical plant, and how many showers a patient should receive per week), it blasted the term *right to treatment* into the legal arena and put all psychologists,

> *Wyatt v. Stickney* (1971) put behavior analysts on notice that a paradigm shift had occurred.

including behavior analysts, on notice that a paradigm shift had occurred. In behavior analysis, we immediately became sensitive to the possibility that our "client" might be harmed by our procedures, and in a short period of time, "clients' rights" were the new watchwords. The original trial judge, Frank M. Johnson, Jr., set forth what later became known as the Wyatt Standards. This case set a precedent and put all mental health and retardation professionals on notice that their services had to be delivered in humane environments where there were sufficient qualified staff members and individualized treatment plans, and that the treatment had to be delivered in the *least restrictive* environment.

> Following the *Wyatt* decision, it was clear that you had a responsibility to the person on the receiving end of treatment.

Following the Wyatt decision, if you were assigned to work with a client in a residential facility, it was clear that you had not only an obligation to the facility to do your best work but also a responsibility to the person on the receiving end of the treatment to make sure he or she was not harmed. There was concern in the beginning that "behavior specialists" (they were not yet called behavior analysts) would manipulate "client" behavior just for the convenience of the staff, such as punishing clients who were incontinent so that staff members would not have to change their diapers. Over time it became evident that, ethically speaking, it was only right to consider the needs of the actual client along with anyone else who might be affected by the procedures (e.g., staff, parents or guardian, other residents). This immediately made the behavior specialist job far more difficult. By the end of the 1970s, behavior analysis was becoming more prevalent and visible, and behavior analysts found themselves working with other professionals on "habilitation teams" to determine the right treatment for clients. Thus, the beginning of issues concerning consultation and cooperation with other professionals arose. In addition, there began to be differentiation of the roles of the entities, and concerns developed about "third party" involvement. If a client (first party) hires a behavior analyst (second party), presumably there is no conflict of interest, and the client can fire the behavior analyst if he or she is not satisfied with the services.

> In the late 1980s, the Association for Behavior Analysis convened a blue-ribbon panel of experts to reach consensus on right to treatment.

Likewise, the behavior analyst will do his or her best to satisfy the client's needs so that the behavior analyst will be paid for his or her services. This arrangement has built-in checks and balances. But if the behavior analyst is hired by a third party (e.g., a facility) to treat the behavior of one of its residents (first party), there is a presumption that the behavior analyst will work to satisfy the needs of the third party to keep his or her job. The Code addresses this issue in some detail in 2.04.

By the 1980s, behavior analysis was much more visible in mental retardation treatment circles and was accepted by many as a viable strategy for habilitation. It was around this time that the further trappings of service delivery had to be accommodated. It was clear that clients had rights (both under the U.S. Constitution and the Wyatt standards) and that everyone, including the behavior analyst, had to respect them and certainly to be informed of them prior to treatment. Furthermore, with behavior analysis approaching the mainstream of accepted approaches, other protections had to be put in place. Clients had a right to privacy, and arrangements had to be made to protect their privacy and confidentiality. Records had to be stored and transferred in a way that maintained these rights, and behavior analysts had the same obligation as other professionals to obtain consent to disclose the information.

By the late 1980s, the time had come for behavior analysts to speak out on the issue of right to treatment, and the Association for Behavior Analysis (ABA) convened a blue-ribbon panel of experts to reach some consensus on the topic. A consensus was reached and ultimately approved by the governing body of the ABA that essentially stated that clients had a right to a "therapeutic environment" where their personal welfare would be of paramount importance and where they had a right to treatment by a "competent behavior analyst" who would conduct a behavioral assessment, teach functional skills, and evaluate the treatments. The ABA panel finally concluded that clients had a right to "the most effective treatments available" (Van Houten et al., 1988). This reference to *effective* treatments set the stage for behavior analysts to redouble their efforts to make a direct connection between the published research and the application of empirically tested interventions.

Code 2.0 provides a clear and detailed list of the obligations that behavior analysts have if they undertake to treat any client using behavioral procedures. By accepting these responsibilities and taking them seriously, we can guarantee that our clients will receive the first-class treatment they deserve and that, as a profession, we will have demonstrated our respect for their rights even as we provide state-of-the-art behavioral interventions.

2.0 BEHAVIOR ANALYSTS' RESPONSIBILITY TO CLIENTS

Behavior analysts have a responsibility to operate in the best interest of clients. The term client as used here is broadly applicable to whomever behavior analysts provide services, whether an individual person (service recipient), a parent or guardian of a service recipient, an organizational representative, a public or private organization, a firm, or a corporation.

We use the term "client" in behavior analysis because we have a long-term interaction with the people we serve; this is opposed to "customers," who would typically be considered one-time or short-term consumers. Because of our specialized training, we are uniquely qualified to operate in the best interest of clients. We can help them increase their potential with our intimate understanding of functions, antecedents, motivation, and consequences and design programs that will assure all of our clients have the best lives possible.

2.01 ACCEPTING CLIENTS

Behavior analysts accept as clients only those individuals or entities whose requested services are commensurate with the behavior analysts' education, training, experience, available resources, and organizational policies. In lieu of these conditions, behavior analysts must function under the supervision of or in consultation with a behavior analyst whose credentials permit performing such services.

As discussed in Code 1.02, we take seriously the notion that our clients deserve the best from us as professionals, and, therefore, we must limit ourselves to work not only within our boundaries of competence (education, training, experience) but also with the resources necessary to produce effective improvements in behavior. To do otherwise would be unethical. When a behavior analyst has the resources to provide treatment but feels unqualified to do so, assistance should be requested from the behavior analyst's supervisor. The nature of the assistance may be finding someone who can provide the necessary consultations and supervision. One example is self-injurious behavior (SIB). Unless a behavior analyst has been given specific training in how to treat this difficult and potentially dangerous behavior, it is essential to get a BCBA with the necessary expertise involved with the case. It is not appropriate to simply try to generalize from a graduate school practicum where some aggressive students were observed on the school play yard. A brief search for key words "self-injury" or "SIB" in *JABA* is a good place to start to find an expert on this topic.

2.02 RESPONSIBILITY (RBT)

Behavior analysts' responsibility is to all parties affected by behavior-analytic services. When multiple parties are involved and could be defined as a client, a hierarchy of parties must be established and communicated from the outset of the defined relationship. Behavior analysts identify and communicate who the primary ultimate beneficiary of services is in any given situation and advocates for his or her best interests.

We make a distinction between the person we are treating and the source of funding; a behavior analyst might be hired by a school district to do functional behavioral assessments of students, but the *client* in this case is the student who receives the assessment and her family, who will receive the report. The behavior analyst is working on behalf of, and watching out for, the best interests of the most vulnerable person, who in this case is the child. It is important to spell this out in the beginning to the organization that hires you. We recommend the Declaration of Professional Practice (Chapter 18) to assist with this.

• • • • • • • •

CASE 2.02 PERILS OF CONTRACTING WITH A SCHOOL DISTRICT

"I was hired by a school district as an independent contractor to complete an FBA for a student. I have provided the report to the district. The district is required to provide the report to the family two days prior to the meeting. The family of the student is now requesting the report from me directly. Our typical policy is that we provide any documents requested by a client within 24 hours of the request. The district has told me I am not to provide the report directly to the student's family. Any advice would be much appreciated. Thank you for your assistance."

• • • • • • • •

2.03 CONSULTATION

(a) Behavior analysts arrange for appropriate consultations and referrals based principally on the best interests of their clients, with appropriate consent, and subject to other relevant considerations, including applicable law and contractual obligations.

An "appropriate" consultation for our field would generally be understood to mean a referral to another evidence-based field compatible with behavior analysis. An example of this would be referring a client with an obsessive-compulsive disorder (OCD) to a psychiatrist. "Appropriate" consent means that the client is informed of the process by which other professionals are recommended and given information on their qualifications. Referrals to your friends or relatives are inappropriate and unethical due to potential conflicts of interest. In these situations, it is standard practice to provide two or three names so the client can choose with whom they wish to work.

(b) When indicated and professionally appropriate, behavior analysts cooperate with other professionals, in a manner that is consistent with the philosophical assumptions and principles of behavior analysis, in order to effectively and appropriately serve their clients.

Behavior analysts often work with other professionals in a team made up of a physician and/or nurse, social worker, occupational therapist, physical therapist, speech therapist, and so on. Some beginning behavior analysts, upon first entering this arena, are surprised to learn that some of these other professions do not hold the same philosophical assumptions that we do. While we are staunchly evidence-based, other disciplines may be theory bound. While we rely almost exclusively on single-subject designed studies, they trust group statistical data. As behavior analysts, we assume that behavior is malleable and can be changed if we can find the right antecedents, motivating operations (MOs), and contingencies. In contrast, other approaches emphasize genetic or personality variables or theories, which have a weak empirical base. Most of us are quick to ask, "Do you have data to support that?" which can be off-putting or even threatening to others. Before those from other persuasions will cooperate with us, it is necessary to develop some rapport and let them know you respect their point of view (Bailey & Burch, 2010). Being a good listener during meetings and providing reinforcement and support of any ideas they have which *are* compatible with ABA will go a long way toward improving cooperation when you are ready to present your proposed intervention.

2.04 THIRD-PARTY INVOLVEMENT IN SERVICES

(a) When behavior analysts agree to provide services to a person or entity at the request of a third party, behavior analysts clarify, to the extent feasible and at the outset of the service, the nature of the relationship with each party and any potential conflicts. This clarification includes the role of the behavior analyst (such as therapist, organizational consultant, or expert witness), the probable uses of the services provided or the information obtained, and the fact that there may be limits to confidentiality.

In a recent case when a behavior analyst was contracted by the school district to do an FBA on a student (who had very high rates of tantrums and head banging), it would have been appropriate under 2.04 to inform those school officials of their relationship with the family. To operate in the best interest of the child, the behavior analyst would need to first obtain permission from the parents and then provide the report directly to the family, with a copy to the school district when it is completed.

(b) If there is a foreseeable risk of behavior analysts being called upon to perform conflicting roles because of the involvement of a third party, behavior analysts clarify the nature and direction of their responsibilities, keep all parties appropriately informed as matters develop, and resolve the situation in accordance with this Code.

Behavior analysts are occasionally asked to testify in custody cases where a divorce is imminent. The questions being raised are who should have custody of the child and will the behavior analyst who provides daily treatment testify for the mother or the father?

If you find yourself in this situation, hopefully you will find solace in our data-based methodology. For example, if you have been training either or both parents to implement training, then you may have data on their effectiveness. As to the broader question, "Who do you believe is the better parent?" this is beyond the scope of our practice, and you would be totally honest and say something like, "I'm sorry, that is beyond the scope of my expertise." All parties should be informed of your position on this matter ahead of time so there are no surprises at a deposition or in the courtroom.

(c) When providing services to a minor or individual who is a member of a protected population at the request of a third party, behavior analysts ensure that the parent or client-surrogate of the ultimate recipient of services is informed of the nature and scope of services to be provided, as well as their right to all service records and data.

The key term in this element of the Code is "protected population." It refers to those individuals in our culture who require additional support or protection and includes prisoners, minors, those experiencing diminished capacity, and the mentally or physically challenged.[1] Basically, this is a reminder to behavior analysts who work with protected populations in residential settings that there should be an attempt to contact the parents or client-surrogates and keep them informed (i.e., procedures and data).

(d) Behavior analysts put the client's care above all others and, should the third party make requirements for services that are contraindicated by the behavior analyst's recommendations, behavior analysts are obligated to resolve such conflicts in the best interest of the client. If said conflict cannot be resolved, that behavior analyst's services to the client may be discontinued following appropriate transition.

Here is an example of just such a situation. Be sure to read the outcome at the end of the chapter.

• • • • • • • •

CASE 2.04(D) MERGER BLUES

"The behavioral organization I work for is beginning to work with another company that provides rehabilitation services such as OT, PT and Speech. My company wants to collaborate with them so that we can become a 'One Stop Shop' for all of our clients' autism treatment needs. In addition, our BCBAs are being asked to identify clients who may benefit from these additional therapies and suggest to their parents that they should be assessed by the OT/PT/SLP. I have expressed my concern that our clients have a right to effective treatment and some of the therapies that we may begin to provide at our center are not evidence-based. After looking deeper into the treatments that this organization provides, I found that they implement sensory integration, therapeutic listening, astronaut training therapy, sensory diets, and others. I've been told by both my director (who is a BCBA) and the owner of the other organization that when we begin to collaborate and work together we will see that we are all doing similar things with our clients; we just call them by different names. My director has tried to put my mind at ease by saying that my clients may only receive 1 hour of other therapies each week and they will still be getting at least 10 hours of ABA each."

• • • • • • • •

2.05 RIGHTS AND PREROGATIVES OF CLIENTS (RBT)

(a) The rights of the client are paramount, and behavior analysts support the client's legal rights and prerogatives.

(b) Clients and supervisees must be provided, on request, an accurate and current set of the behavior analyst's credentials.

(c) Permission for electronic recording of interviews and service delivery sessions is secured from clients and relevant staff in all relevant settings. Consent for different uses must be obtained specifically and separately.

(d) Clients and supervisees must be informed of their rights and about procedures to lodge complaints about professional practices of behavior analysts with the employer, appropriate authorities, and the BACB.

(e) Behavior analysts comply with any requirements for criminal background checks.

Some of these items (2.05 (b, c, d)) should be included in a Declaration of Professional Services (see Chapter 18). When the rights and prerogatives of parents (2.05 (a)) are not respected, there can be a huge backlash, as shown in this case.

• • • • • • • •

CASE 2.05 (A–D) INFURIATED PARENTS

"My wife and I have an 11-year daughter who is autistic. A behavior analyst hired by the public school system treated our child without our knowledge or consent for a 12-week period. We found out about this inadvertently when a crumpled monthly progress note was found in our daughter's lunch box. There is no mention of ABA therapy in our child's IEP, and no mention in the published notes of team meetings during the time the behavior analyst was treating her. We were not advised of the treatment plan or direct services inflicted on our child. Further, we were not included in the assessment process and we did not receive assessment results. When confronted, the therapist informed us that he did not need to include parents in the implementation of his services. He said that his contract with the public school system constituted the legal authority to treat our daughter and that he had engaged in no legal or ethical impropriety. The Director of Special Education told us, 'The methodology and specifics for treatment is entirely the prerogative of the school.' The therapist is a BCaBA. The 'supervisor' for the therapist, a BCBA-D, states that supervision occurs over the phone, every couple months for less than an hour. The supervisor further claims all of this is routine and acceptable treatment. We are appalled and infuriated. We believe any treatment in the absence of full legal informed consent is unethical and illegal. Treatment with this level of secrecy is indicative of a serious abuse

potential. Have you any suggestions as to how we might get somebody to address this?"

• • • • • • • •

2.06 MAINTAINING CONFIDENTIALITY (RBT)

(a) Behavior analysts have a primary obligation and take reasonable precautions to protect the confidentiality of those with whom they work or consult, recognizing that confidentiality may be established by law, organizational rules, or professional or scientific relationships.

(b) Behavior analysts discuss confidentiality at the outset of the relationship and thereafter as new circumstances may warrant.

(c) In order to minimize intrusions on privacy, behavior analysts include only information germane to the purpose for which the communication is made in written, oral, and electronic reports, consultations, and other avenues.

(d) Behavior analysts discuss confidential information obtained in clinical or consulting relationships or evaluative data concerning clients, students, research participants, supervisees, and employees, only for appropriate scientific or professional purposes and only with persons clearly concerned with such matters.

• • • • • • • •

CASE 2.06 (D) PRYING PARISHIONERS

Dr. Elizabeth C. was a BCBA-D who worked with a number of children in her small community. Dr. C. most often provided treatment in the children's homes after school. Two of Dr. C.'s clients, Jason and Jessica, were a brother and sister. Their alcoholic father was in and out of the home, and the father had abused their mother in the past. Dr. C. attended a church where several members of the congregation knew the family. They cared very much about the children and would ask how they were doing. These caring people would often tell Dr. C.

what they knew about the family, and they would ask how the
children were getting along in school and what kinds of things
she worked on when she went to the home. The women from
the church donated clothing to the family in the past, and they
always had the children on the list to receive Christmas gifts
from the church.

• • • • • • • •

(e) Behavior analysts must not share or create situations likely to result in the sharing of any identifying information (written, photographic, or video) about current clients and supervisees within social media contexts.

This addition to the Code is intended to protect the confidentiality of clients in the modern "Wild West" atmosphere of social media. Behavior analysts understandably become close to the clients with whom they work, and with the craze for posting "selfies" everywhere, they often forget it is inappropriate to "out" clients on Facebook, Instagram or other social media pages.

2.07 MAINTAINING RECORDS (RBT)

(a) Behavior analysts maintain appropriate confidentiality in creating, storing, accessing, transferring, and disposing of records under their control, whether these are written, automated, electronic, or in any other medium.

Behavior analysts cope with a lot of paper assessments, memos, email, and other documents. They increasingly use electronic media to record data and produce monthly, quarterly, or annual reports. A reliable method for keeping information about clients confidential is absolutely essential. As a behavior analyst, you cannot leave paperwork lying around your apartment or in your car, where anyone dropping by to see you or catching a ride might see client information. Particularly critical is the use of passwords known only to you for accessing electronic information that you might have on a desktop computer, laptop or iPad. One thought to keep in mind involves a worst case scenario: If someone who wished to do you harm came across your confidential client records, would they be able to access these? Client records should be treated with more care than expensive jewelry.

> (b) Behavior analysts maintain and dispose of records in accordance with applicable laws, regulations, corporate policies, and organizational policies and in a manner that permits compliance with the requirements of this Code.

It is important to be up to date on state and federal laws regarding the maintenance and destruction of client records. Depending on the types of records, this might range from one to seven years or more. Be sure to check the laws in your state and with your agency to learn the specific policies that pertain to client records in your area. The worst case scenario for this element involves you being taken to court over a client you served several years prior. If this happened, would you be able to defend yourself by producing and using your records?

2.08 DISCLOSURES (RBT)

> Behavior analysts never disclose confidential information without the consent of the client, except as mandated by law, or where permitted by law for a valid purpose, such as (1) to provide needed professional services to the client, (2) to obtain appropriate professional consultations, (3) to protect the client or others from harm, or (4) to obtain payment for services, in which instance disclosure is limited to the minimum that is necessary to achieve the purpose. Behavior analysts recognize that parameters of consent for disclosure should be acquired at the outset of any defined relationship and that this is an ongoing procedure throughout the duration of the professional relationship.

It should be noted that "consent" means *written* consent. This is one form of documentation that comes under Code 2.07. There are a few other terms here that will require interpretation on your part. In (1), "needed" professional services will require an understanding of all services your client needs to ensure a good quality of life. This might include nursing, physical therapy, counseling or any other professional service that appears relevant. Under (2), "appropriate professional consultations," this might mean bringing in a person, for example, who specializes in feeding disorders or self-injurious behavior. In a rare case under (3) where law enforcement must be called in to protect the client or other individuals from injury, it would be important to provide information about the client to assure that he or she is treated with care. Finally, (4) alludes to instances where invoices to an insurance company or government agency may require divulging certain minimal descriptive or diagnostic information. It is recommended that these disclosures be the "minimum necessary," and all of these conditions should be spelled out in a Declaration of Professional Services (see Chapter 18) at the onset of treatment, with occasional reminders during the course of treatment.

2.09 TREATMENT/INTERVENTION EFFICACY

(a) Clients have a right to effective treatment (i.e., based on the research literature and adapted to the individual client). Behavior analysts always have the obligation to advocate for and educate the client about scientifically supported, most-effective treatment procedures. Effective treatment procedures have been validated as having both long-term and short-term benefits to clients and society.

The right to *effective* treatment in this code item refers to an early position paper by Van Houten et al. (1988). This paper was in response to a movement in developmental disabilities to stress a client's "right to treatment." Leaders in our field felt it was important to stress the term *effective*, since that was a distinguishing characteristic of our emerging behavioral science. It is assumed that the "research literature" referred to here is *our* behavior analytic work that meets the requirements of the original Baer,

Wolf and Risley (1968) paper, *Some current dimensions of applied behavior analysis*. That is, as behavior analysts, we are advocating the use of that research which comes out of the tradition of operant conditioning beginning with Skinner's *Behavior of Organisms* (1938). The simple fact that a procedure is published in just any journal does not mean that it meets this requirement. There is a clear expectation that behavior analysts will use behavior analytic procedures published in peer-reviewed, behavior analytic journals with high standards. Here is an example of the culture clash that can happen when these views meet in one family.

• • • • • • • •

CASE 2.09 (A) CLASH OVER EFFECTIVE TREATMENT

"I have a five year old client who is mostly nonverbal. The client's speech/language pathologist (SLP) is using Floortime and her own adapted version of PODD (Pragmatic Organization Dynamic Display) to teach functional communication in the school. I am the client's home based BCBA and my team is teaching him the PECS (Picture Exchange Communication System). His vocalizations are emerging, but highly restricted. It is difficult to read through all the research available on PODD as an effective, evidence based functional communication system, even when it is used with procedural integrity. I have always understood from my BCBA colleagues that Floortime is not research based. I am conflicted in terms of guiding my parents because of the SLP at school. She has basically defined PECS as a simple manding procedure and applied behavior analysis (ABA) as only Discrete Trial Training (DTT). Question 1: Ethically how should I proceed? Question 2: Is there research within the scope of ABA that supports Floortime or PODD as effective teaching methodologies?"

• • • • • • • •

(b) Behavior analysts have the responsibility to advocate for the appropriate amount and level of service provision and oversight required to meet the defined behavior-change program goals.

Admittedly, we do not have a well-worked-out science of determining the precise amount and level of treatment that is correct for every client. However, we do have a rich research literature that provides guidance. Behavior analysts are expected to be well acquainted with the behavioral literature and apply the findings to their daily practice. Here is an example.

• • • • • • • •

CASE 2.09 (B) "BILL THE MAXIMUM HOURS"

"The policy of my company is to first see how many hours the client's insurance will pay for, and bill the maximum amount of time for that client, regardless of the client's needs. For example, clients who presented with MINIMAL SKILLS DEFICITS, for whom it is clinically appropriate to recommend only a few hours a week of therapy, would ALWAYS receive the maximum number of hours allotted by the insurance company (sometimes 20-hours per week), despite clinical recommendations. When I questioned this system, I was told, 'It doesn't matter. Insurance is paying for it.' I observed one session with a client, a 5-year-old boy with a diagnosis of Asperger's Disorder. He was receiving 'feeding therapy' at the clinic from a BCaBA. When I inquired as to what goals she was working on, she stated that the client had met all of his feeding goals, but, since insurance pays for this therapy, the company asked her to continue to see him regularly."

• • • • • • • •

(c) In those instances where more than one scientifically supported treatment has been established, additional factors may be considered in selecting interventions, including, but not limited to, efficiency and cost-effectiveness, risks and side-effects of the interventions, client preference, and practitioner experience and training.

This item makes it obvious why behavior analysts need to be constantly aware of the ongoing research in our field. There are so many procedures from which to choose and so many decisions to make that it can be dizzying at times. Just weighing the factors of cost-effectiveness vs. risks (including side effects), for example, requires an incredible amount of professional decision making.

(d) Behavior analysts review and appraise the effects of any treatments about which they are aware that might impact the goals of the behavior-change program, and their possible impact on the behavior-change program, to the extent possible.

This code item can be interpreted to mean that as a behavior analyst, it is necessary to know if there are any other treatments being implemented with the client and what the evidence shows; here is an example.

• • • • • • • •

CASE 2.09 (D) DO YOU BELIEVE IN MIRACLES?

"I have been working with a 5-year old girl and her parents for about 1.5 years now. In addition to the ABA services I provide in the home, the family is very interested in biomedical treatments. Last fall, during one of my sessions, the father gave her something that I had not seen before and told me it was Magic Mineral Solution (MMS). Once I got home, I read about MMS and what the FDA had to say about it. I also could not find any peer-reviewed studies suggesting the effectiveness or safety of this product. I became concerned at that point and emailed the child's mother. I mentioned how as a behavior analyst, I am trained to do a lot of research and only use treatments that are evidenced-based, best-practice interventions for our clients. I sent her a link to an article that suggested it was a scam and also sent a link to the FDA's commentary about MMS: http://www.fda.gov/Safety/MedWatch/SafetyInformation/ SafetyAlertsforHumanMedicalProducts/ucm220756.htm

"I also mentioned, 'I would highly recommend speaking with her doctor about it. I'm not a doctor and don't know a lot about this product. However, I do know to follow what

peer-reviewed research says is effective, and this product has a lot of the qualities of what one might consider to be a "fad" treatment for autism."

• • • • • • • •

2.10 DOCUMENTING PROFESSIONAL WORK AND RESEARCH (RBT)

(a) Behavior analysts appropriately document their professional work in order to facilitate provision of services later by them or by other professionals, to ensure accountability, and to meet other requirements of organizations or the law.
(b) Behavior analysts have a responsibility to create and maintain documentation in the kind of detail and quality that would be consistent with best practices and the law.

When it comes to documenting their work, behavior analysts should be the exemplars at record keeping. Our standard is that we take data on what we do and most often graph that data so that it can be shown to others. If there is an area of weakness, it is most likely in the non-data department. This code item reminds us that intake interviews, phone conversations, and notes from meetings need to always be documented for later use. Given the litigious nature of our current culture, it is probably wise to create a paper trail for each and every client. Of course, another more likely use of your documentation would be if you needed to transition a case to another behavior analyst for some reason. Begin by thinking of the material you would like to receive if someone transferred a client to you, and you will understand the need for this standard.

2.11 RECORDS AND DATA (RBT)

(a) Behavior analysts create, maintain, disseminate, store, retain, and dispose of records and data relating to their research, practice, and other work in accordance with applicable laws, regulations, and policies; in a manner that permits compliance with the requirements of this Code; and in a manner that allows for appropriate transition of service oversight at any moment in time.

(b) Behavior analysts must retain records and data for at least seven (7) years and as otherwise required by law.

This is a strict requirement because of (1) the nature of the security required for client data and (2) the time requirement. In many cases, the protection and retention of client data will be the job of the company or agency where the behavior analyst works. However, if you are a solo provider, be prepared to purchase secure, locking file cabinets as soon as you set up business and develop an exacting filing system for efficient retrieval of documents.

2.12 CONTRACTS, FEES, AND FINANCIAL ARRANGEMENTS

(a) Prior to the implementation of services, behavior analysts ensure that there is in place a signed contract outlining the responsibilities of all parties, the scope of behavior-analytic services to be provided, and behavior analysts' obligations under this Code.

(b) As early as is feasible in a professional or scientific relationship, behavior analysts reach an agreement with their clients specifying compensation and billing arrangements.

One easy way to ensure that all parties are aware of the nature of your services and your billing practices is to use a Declaration of Professional Services (discussed in Chapter 18). This document can be used to document initial agreements if there is some question later.

(c) Behavior analysts' fee practices are consistent with law and behavior analysts do not misrepresent their fees. If limitations to services can be anticipated because of limitations in funding, this is discussed with the client as early as is feasible.

(d) When funding circumstances change, the financial responsibilities and limits must be revisited with the client.

2.13 ACCURACY IN BILLING REPORTS

Behavior analysts accurately state the nature of the services provided, the fees or charges, the identity of the provider, relevant outcomes, and other required descriptive data. It appears, however, that some unscrupulous behavior "therapists" are operating in our communities; see the case here.

• • • • • • • •

CASE 2.13 BILLING NIGHTMARE

"My daughter was receiving ABA therapy from a board certified behavior therapist. The therapist was billing our insurance company for services my daughter never received. The therapist is an in-service provider, and by law, all ABA therapy is covered by the insurance company. I have asked the therapist for explanations and clarifications, but she has refused me any recourse, telling me to take my daughter home. She recently sent me an invoice by certified mail and has threatened debt collection. I am trying to make sense out of how many hours she has billed me for, but all the information I have are the units of codes billed to the insurance."

• • • • • • • •

2.14 REFERRALS AND FEES

Behavior analysts must not receive or provide money, gifts, or other enticements for any professional referrals. Referrals should include multiple options and be made based on objective determination of the client need and subsequent alignment with the repertoire of the referee. When providing or receiving a referral, the extent of any relationship between the two parties is disclosed to the client.

The purpose of this code item is to prevent a "payola" style scandal in our field such as the one that hit the music industry back in the 1950s. This involved commercial bribes to radio disk jockeys to play certain songs more frequently than others to increase record sales. By restricting a behavior analyst from receiving any "enticements" for a referral and requiring that we suggest multiple options, this greatly reduces any contingency for "kickbacks" in our field.

2.15 INTERRUPTING OR DISCONTINUING SERVICES

(a) Behavior analysts act in the best interests of the client and supervisee to avoid interruption or disruption of service.

While this is the ideal, real-world circumstances may occasionally intervene, as shown here.

• • • • • • • •

CASE 2.15 (A) JUSTIFIED

"We are working with a family where the father is not wanting us to use reinforcers that we have determined to be effective based on a reinforcer assessment. As a result, we are struggling to find other effective means of reinforcement. In addition, the father enters the therapy room every time his daughter is upset. We have discussed with the child's mother how this is impeding sessions. We have also tried to meet with the father multiple times but he will not make himself available. We feel the client is not benefiting from our service, but the mother has insisted that she is seeing the child make gains as a result of the interventions we are implementing. We want to ensure we are proceeding with providing services in an ethical and responsible way. From an ethical perspective, what type of pre-termination services would be appropriate and/or what is the best way to approach terminating services in this situation if this is the recommendation?"

• • • • • • • •

(b) Behavior analysts make reasonable and timely efforts for facilitating the continuation of behavior-analytic services in the event of unplanned interruptions (e.g., due to illness, impairment, unavailability, relocation, disruption of funding, disaster).

Unplanned interruptions of service are by definition difficult to handle. In particular, behavior analysts who are solo providers will have a difficult time in the event they are suddenly incapacitated by illness or accident. The best plan of action for these professionals is to have a colleague available to fill in on short notice. This means that the colleague will need permission to read client files and talk to the clients. In addition, the behavior analyst should be certain that the substitute is competent to take on the client caseload.

(c) When entering into employment or contractual relationships, behavior analysts provide for orderly and appropriate resolution of responsibility for services in the event that the employment or contractual relationship ends, with paramount consideration given to the welfare of the ultimate beneficiary of services.

In this code element, two key phrases stand out. The first is "orderly and appropriate," which we take to mean that considerable time and thought have been given to how one discontinues services. This would include initial meetings to discuss the circumstances that have arisen, and then follow-up meetings to see if some resolution is possible. If this is an employee who is "just not working out," and if training and counseling have failed, the agency, in order to prevent the client from lapsed services, will need to plan for coverage. The second phrase, "paramount consideration," can be interpreted to mean that management will not take precipitous action without regard to the client's need for continuous services.

(d) Discontinuation only occurs after efforts to transition have been made. Behavior analysts discontinue a professional relationship in a timely manner when the client: (1) no longer needs the service, (2) is not benefiting from the service, (3) is being harmed by continued service, or (4) when the client requests discontinuation. (*See also, 4.11 Discontinuing Behavior-Change Programs and Behavior-Analytic Services.*)

In some cases, where a client has shown progress and no longer needs therapy or where, despite several revisions of the program, no progress is being shown, the behavior analyst will need to make the client aware of the situation and present a plan for "discontinuation." Some clients become very attached to their therapist and refuse to accept that services need to be phased out because of the progress shown. If a client makes the decision that they wish to discontinue services, this process would likely be accelerated to meet their needs. The behavior analysts involved should make an effort to help the client find other professional services under such circumstances.

(e) Behavior analysts do not abandon clients. Prior to discontinuation, for whatever reason, behavior analysts: discuss service needs, provide appropriate pre-termination services, suggest alternative service providers as appropriate, and, upon consent, take other reasonable steps to facilitate timely transfer of responsibility to another provider.

"Abandon" is a harsh term that suggests the client was abruptly discharged with no notice, recourse, or assistance provided. This is highly unlikely in the consumer-oriented behavior analysis services we provide, but even a hint of discontinuation can cause a major ruckus, as shown here.

• • • • • • • •

CASE 2.15 (C, D, E) ACCUSED OF ABANDONMENT

"We were just notified yesterday by a parent of a child with autism that she intends to file a complaint against us with the BACB related to negligence and abandonment. The notification of the impending complaint occurred after we recently initiated a termination process for our current ABA direct services. We began providing services to this student in June and intend to conclude our services in October. We provided formal notice of our termination in September but we initiated discussions about our concerns with the parent in mid-August. We have had ongoing problems with this case that we have attempted to solve including

conflict of interest, dual roles, as well as a parent's request for ABA practices that are not matched for this child's needs. We are willing to explore the option of staying involved longer than our one-month notice in order to facilitate a successful transition to another BCBA. However, we hesitate given the ethical implications of the already-referenced concerns that we have been unable to remedy. As a first step, we intend to immediately respond directly to this parent to offer continued collaboration relative to facilitating a transition to another agency and/or individual professional who is best matched for the needs of this child as well as his mother. For example, we could suggest program recommendations about local options including working with BCBAs who are employed full time at his current placement if this is the most ethical response. We have a few creative recommendations relative to meeting this child's needs but these would warrant our being involved longer in order to verify the receiving agency/district has the trained staff and professionals in place. Is it wise to stay longer given our ethical concerns?"

• • • • • • • •

RESPONSES TO CASES

CASE 2.02 PERILS OF CONTRACTING WITH A SCHOOL DISTRICT

Following the district's guidance does not seem to be in the client's best interest; our ethics code requires that we consider the client's (the family in this case) interest paramount. It appears that the school district's policy is to give the family the least amount of time possible to analyze the report and prepare a response to present at the meeting. The most ethical action in this case would be for you to quickly provide the report to the family so they have adequate time to prepare their response and possibly

Behavior analysts always support the rights of clients and operate in their best interests; they are not hired guns available to the highest bidder.

seek legal counsel in this important matter. Behavior analysts always support the rights of clients and operate in their best interests; they are not hired guns available to the highest bidder. If you do provide the family with the report, you will likely be terminated by the school district and receive no further work from them, so be ready for that righteous consequence.

CASE 2.04 (D) MERGER BLUES

The author of this question rallied the support of the other BCBAs in the organization and prepared a letter to the Board of Directors protesting the merger of her behavioral organization with an organization that supported non-evidence-based procedures. They were successful in slowing down the merger and limiting the use of non-evidence-based procedures.

CASE 2.05 (A-D) INFURIATED PARENTS

The parents appealed their case all the way to the State Department of Education, which then scheduled an IEP where the parents were present. It was decided at this meeting there was no reason to use these state-provided behavioral services for this child, who is now in a private school where she is not exhibiting any serious behavior problems.

CASE 2.06 (D) PRYING PARISHIONERS

Behavior analysts have an obligation to respect the confidentiality of those with whom they work. When asked about the children, Dr. C. should politely tell anyone who asks that she cannot discuss her work with her clients. She should then politely change the subject.

CASE 2.09 (A) CLASH OVER EFFECTIVE TREATMENT

Question: 1. Ethically, how should I proceed?

It will be difficult to convince the SLP to drop what she is doing with PODD and use your system. It would be appropriate for you to explain to the parents your rationale for using PECS and to discuss the data that supports its use.

Question: 2. Is there research within the scope of ABA that supports Floortime or PODD as effective teaching methodologies?

There is no substantial research (as defined by behavior analytic single-subject design methodology) that shows that Floortime is an evidence-based procedure, so you should not feel any pressure to use this fad treatment. For PODD, there was one "study" that was published in 2007, and it clearly did not meet behavior analysis research standards.

CASE 2.09 (B) "BILL THE MAXIMUM HOURS"

Undoubtedly, this practice is unethical, but it is also illegal and fraudulent. The behavior analyst protested the practice of billing the maximum hours whether or not they were needed both verbally and in writing to the company. She also reported the company to the insurance company and, following that, she immediately resigned from her position.

CASE 2.09 (D) DO YOU BELIEVE IN MIRACLES?

The behavior analyst has gone above and beyond the call of duty in an attempt to handle this case responsibly. She provided a thorough warning for the parents about the product. If the behavior analyst had noticed deleterious effects on the child or her behavior, it might have been necessary to take additional steps, but she did everything called for in the ethics Code. If the child developed symptoms as a result of long-term usage of the product or if her behavior began to change in a negative way, it would be time to bring this up again to the parents. At that point, the behavior analyst could make the call as to whether she wanted to continue to work with the child. Some parents are so desperate for a full recovery that they have adopted a "Try anything" and "What can it hurt?" attitude. Behavior analysis students should be taught to be critical thinkers when it comes to fad treatments. The behavior analyst in this case was cautious, careful, and a credit to our profession.

CASE 2.13 BILLING NIGHTMARE

This is clearly a case of unethical conduct as well as a violation of law. This should be referred to the Department of Consumer Protection or the Department of Insurance Regulation in your state.

CASE 2.15 (A) JUSTIFIED

This situation is fairly common, and problems can arise when both parents do not agree about specific aspects of treatment. The behavior analyst attempted to coordinate the parents and involve the father to no avail.

Before giving notice of termination, there are several things to consider. Was a Declaration of Professional Services used at the beginning when the parents first asked for ABA? If so, did it include a clause about the requirement for total cooperation with the behavioral plan? And was there a discussion about conditions for program success that preclude implementation? Also, were termination criteria included? If all of these steps were taken, there should be one more (documented) attempt to set up a meeting to discuss these issues. If both parents won't attend, it is time to begin the termination process. It should be made clear to the parents that the reason for termination is a lack of client improvement. Two final steps are to cite the specific code items to the parents and then refer them to someone else for services. In this case, the services might include family counseling in order to bring the parents around to the idea that they need to work together if their child is to move ahead.

Note: This case ended with the family terminating services due to a lack of funding.

CASE 2.15 (C, D, E) ACCUSED OF ABANDONMENT

The behavior analyst should begin the transition process immediately, making sure to keep all communications in writing and to maintain these documents in case they are needed later. The most ethical response is to help the parent find an agency or solo BCBA who has the skill set to work with this child. The parent should be given at least three suggested referrals. In a case such as this one, it is usually better to make a clean break.

8

Assessing Behavior (Code 3.0)

It is a bedrock principle of behavior analysis that it is necessary to "take a baseline" before any treatment is contemplated. The reasons are not so obvious to outsiders, and the methodology by which it is accomplished is out of the reach of most other professions. For us, taking a baseline means many things, including the following:

- A referral has been made of a behavior that is problematic to a significant person.
- The behavior is observable and has been operationally defined in some manner that allows quantification.
- A trained observer has visited the setting where the behavior occurs and has documented the occurrence and the circumstances under which it occurs (this indicates that the referral is legitimate, that the problem is measurable, and that the behavior may or may not require treatment, depending on what the graphs of the data show).

> Behavior analysts do not work on rumor or hearsay. They want to see the problems for themselves.

Behavior analysts do not work on rumor or hearsay. They want to see the problem for themselves, to get some sense of the variability from day to day, and to determine if there is any trending; and, finally, they want to understand the circumstances under

The astute and ethical behavior analyst will take enough baseline to ensure that there is indeed a problem that needs solving.

which the behavior occurs and to get some sense of the function of the behavior.

"This kid is driving me crazy, he is constantly out of his seat, talking with the other children, and he never completes an assignment that I hand out. I spend all my time sending him back to his seat and telling him to sit down." This referral from a very frustrated third-grade teacher would be the stimulus for a behavior analyst to go to the classroom and observe exactly what is going on. The teacher, meanwhile, was thinking that she would like to get this "brat" out of her classroom. Although the assistant principal, school counselor, or school psychologist might immediately start giving the teacher some advice on what to do or schedule a battery of IQ and personality tests, the behavior analyst insists that some assessment of the behavior occur first. How much time is the student out of his seat? What was the stimulus for this behavior? What kinds of assignments are given, and how many does he actually complete? The behavior analyst will also be interested in knowing what kind of prompts the teacher uses for each of the behaviors and what type of reinforcement she currently uses to maintain the behavior (if any). Another question that might come up has to do with the appropriateness of the class assignments for the student. Is there any chance that they are too difficult or that the instructions are inadequate? And, finally, the behavior analyst, while observing the referred student, will also be assessing the physical environment and the degree of peer involvement in this child's behavior; is there any chance that the student has vision or hearing problems or is simply distracted by irritating peers? The astute and ethical behavior analyst will take enough baseline to ensure that there is indeed a problem that needs solving and will have some

The concept of limiting conditions is critical to an understanding of how behavior analysis works.

preliminary ideas as to the variables that might be operating. One final point is that these baseline data will be graphed and used in an evaluation of treatment effects. Imagine how this would work if there was no rule about taking a baseline first. The behavior analyst would have to rely on an untrained, possibly biased person's estimate of the frequency of the target behaviors, would have to take this person's opinion of likely causal variables seriously, and would have no basis for evaluation of any suggestions made. Viewed in this light, it is downright unethical to operate in this fashion, yet this scenario is probably the mode for what passes as behavior consulting in America by nonbehavioral "professionals."

In ethics Code 3.0, Assessing Behavior, the Code clearly specifies what goes into a behavioral assessment and further (in Code 4.0) includes an even broader obligation to explain to the client (e.g., the teacher, principal, and parents) the conditions necessary for the intervention to work (4.06) and those that might prevent it from being properly implemented (4.07). If the ethical behavior analyst determines what the controlling variables are using a functional assessment (see Iwata, Dorsey, Slifer, Bauman, & Richman, 1982, for the original study on this method), he or she is obligated to spell this out for the clients and to explain the limiting conditions for treatment. This latter concept, limiting conditions, is critical to an understanding of how behavior analysis works in applied settings. To take a simple example, if we want to use a reinforcer to strengthen the *sitting-in-seat behavior* of the third-grader described earlier, we have to find out what is the reinforcer. If, for some reason, we are not able to find a reinforcer, then this limiting condition has been exceeded. Or, if we discover what the reinforcer is but are not allowed to use it, or if the teacher refuses to use the reinforcer even if we know what it is, we have exceeded the limiting conditions of treatment. If the reinforcer is some sort of snack (discovered through a reinforcer assessment) but

> As a behavior analyst, you have an obligation to explain your data in plain English or other relevant language.

the teacher "doesn't believe in using snacks," then it will be difficult to change this child's behavior through this means. Or if the behavior analyst determines that a daily report card is the best solution for the child but the parents refuse to cooperate by delivering contingent reinforcers at home, we have run headlong into a limiting condition of treatment.

As a final note on assessment, it is so important that behavior analysts explain to the client what the data mean (probably using actual working graphs to illustrate the key points) that this point is included in the Code. There, in Code 3.04, it is clearly stated that as a behavior analyst, you have an obligation to explain the baseline data, functional assessment, reinforcement assessment, or other forms of behavioral data collection to the client, in plain English or other relevant language, so he or she can understand what is involved. This includes, of course, the results of any interventions to show actual measured effects of what was tried and what worked. Besides keeping the client, guardian, or advocate apprised of our interventions, this requirement also probably serves some public relations function. It teaches the client that what we do is transparent and understandable, that we are objective in our approach, and that we use data for decision making. One hoped-for result is that clients and client-surrogates so educated will begin to ask questions of other professionals about the basis for their interventions. One important requirement is to seek a medical consultation (Code 3.02) in cases where a behavior may be a result of a "medical or biological variables." Most well-trained behavior analysts have been doing this for years, but now this is made explicit in our new ethics Code.

3.0 ASSESSING BEHAVIOR

Behavior analysts using behavior-analytic assessment techniques do so for purposes that are appropriate given current research.

This code item is a reminder that the assessments we employ are not for the purposes of determining IQ, personality traits, or the prediction of successful outcomes. Practitioners should resist any pressure to extrapolate from these narrow but highly useful assessment tools to do anything other than provide a very accurate picture of some aspect of behavior, whether it be social, academic, or language skills. If an employer or institutional manager applies pressure to perform tests outside of your comfort zone, feel free to refer them to other professionals who perform such duties, such as school or clinical psychologists.

3.01 BEHAVIOR-ANALYTIC ASSESSMENT (RBT)

(a) Behavior analysts conduct current assessments prior to making recommendations or developing behavior-change programs. The type of assessment used is determined by client's needs and consent, environmental parameters, and other contextual variables. When behavior analysts are developing a behavior-reduction program, they must first conduct a functional assessment.

The primary reason for conducting an assessment is to determine the current repertoire of the client so that effective interventions may follow. Skill acquisition assessments will help the therapist understand where the client stands relative to others of the same chronological age and may also point toward priorities in training. Unstated, but assumed, is that the assessment has been properly developed so as to be valid and reliable. There has been a great deal of work done in the past decade on functional assessments that can be done quickly and with consistent results. The primary function of a functional behavior assessment (FA or FBA) is to find out the conditions under which the behavior is most likely to occur or not occur rather than to label the client.

In the next case, the questioner wants to know if the assessments being done are appropriate.

• • • • • • • •

CASE 3.01 TESTING SCOPE OF PRACTICE

"I have been working with a BCBA who has completed some graduate work in clinical psychology; however, he did not finish the degree and does not have any licensure or certification outside of the BCBA. I have recently reviewed one of the BCBA's FBA reports that was conducted with insurance funding for ABA services. I have some concerns both about the use of the funding and also about the scope of practice under the BACB. Here are the concerns:

1. *There were several psychological assessments conducted during the FBA including the Developmental Profile-3, the Parent Stress Inventory, and the PDD Behavior Inventory. The client is 15-years old and all assessments were conducted through parent interview. The DP-3 is only normed and standardized on children from birth to 12. The assessments do not provide any additional insight or information about the targeted problem behavior (SIB and aggression).*
2. *The client has a history of suicidal threats and acute depressive disorder. The targeted problem behavior assessed included SIB (hand to head hitting) and verbal aggression (these behaviors were not observed during the assessment). The client was placed on a 48-hour hospitalization as a result of these threats. The BCBA told the parent that these behaviors were common in high-functioning individuals on the autism spectrum and discussed how depression presents differently in adolescents than it does in adults.*

"My questions are:

1) When you are conducting an assessment under the BACB certification and with funds for an ABA assessment, is it ethical to include testing that is psychological in nature and does do not add information about the function, intensity, or level of problem behavior be included?
2) Would you consider this practice outside the scope of the BCBA?

"I did discuss my concerns with the individual. I said that I was concerned both about how the funding was used and that the practice seemed to be outside the scope of the BCBA and more in the scope of practice of a licensed psychologist. The individual disagreed. If this is outside the scope of practice, what additional steps would you take to address this issue?"

• • • • • •

(b) Behavior analysts have an obligation to collect and graphically display data, using behavior-analytic conventions, in a manner that allows for decisions and recommendations for behavior-change program development.

Since behavior analysis is a data-based field, it is no great challenge for behavior analysts to collect data. However, there are

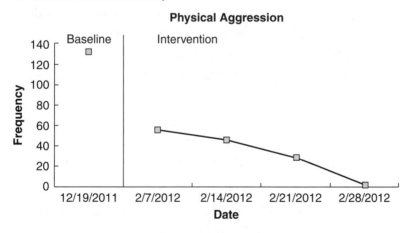

Problem Behavior Summary

Figure 8.1 This graph of client data was presented in the case of K.G. v. Dudek in Federal Court in March 2012.

sometimes difficulties in presenting the data in such a way that it can be easily understood by non-behavior-analysts. Figure 8.1 is a graph presented at trial in Federal court to illustrate the impact of behavioral services.

Serious students who are interested in methods of data presentation will enjoy Edward Tufte's (1983) *The Visual Display of Quantitative Information*. This is a classic work in the world of data graphics and a must read for serious ABA professionals.

3.02 MEDICAL CONSULTATION

Behavior analysts recommend seeking a medical consultation if there is any reasonable possibility that a referred behavior is influenced by medical or biological variables.

Behavior analysts are often called upon to provide consultation on behaviors that may not be entirely operant in nature. These include responses that are due to medications the clients are taking or to some medical or biological variable. A client who is waving her hand in front of her eyes may be doing so for attention or for automatic visual stimulation. Scratching at the skin can be caused by sunburn, poison ivy, certain foods, or medication allergies. This code item reminds the behavior analyst to consider all reasonable possibilities as to these types of non-operant variables when handling cases such as these, since treating them with consequences could be not only unethical but also disastrous to the client.

• • • • • • • •

CASE 3.02 SEARCHING FOR A NEW FUNCTION

"I'm looking for some guidance regarding a case in my school. I am working with a 2-year-old child with severe behaviors. In the past, the functions avoidance (from demands made in the home and classroom) and attention were quite clear and our intervention procedures (antecedent manipulations and extinction)

have been effective. About a month ago, his behaviors started to change. This happened around a time when a lot of things changed in his environment (i.e., parents separating, new school). He's presenting with behaviors now that are not decreasing and our original methods are not effective. These newer behaviors seem to occur across all environments. I have observed them in school and in his home, and another observer has reported them at his other school. These behaviors still seem to be socially mediated some of the time, but they also appear to partially be maintained by automatic reinforcement. Since the function is no longer clear, we are planning to conduct an FA. Additionally, given that these behaviors seem to have a more automatically reinforcing component and involve his head (e.g., head-banging, head-shaking), I recommended the family see a neurologist for further testing and scans. Would it be unethical for me to proceed with the FA without these results? I worry that it could take a while to get an appointment and results, and I don't think we can wait that long to intervene."

• • • • • • • •

3.03 BEHAVIOR-ANALYTIC ASSESSMENT CONSENT

(a) Prior to conducting an assessment, behavior analysts must explain to the client the procedures(s) to be used, who will participate, and how the resulting information will be used.

(b) Behavior analysts must obtain the client's written approval of the assessment procedures before implementing them.

As discussed in Case 2.05, it is essential for behavior analysts to gain permission from parents, or other authorized caregivers, to do an assessment. Further, the behavior analyst must explain who will be conducting the assessment and how the results will be used. This simple straightforward requirement can be clouded somewhat by organizations such as clinics or school districts, which require a blanket approval for all evaluations at the onset of services. The intent of this code item is to give control over the information to the caregivers who are responsible for the client and to hold the behavior analyst responsible for assuring that this process is kept intact.

3.04 EXPLAINING ASSESSMENT RESULTS

Behavior analysts explain assessment results using language and graphic displays of data that are reasonably understandable to the client.

The following case is an example of how this works. A parent who wanted an independent assessment of her child's behavior at school contacted a BCBA. The child was reporting headaches; the mother contacted the school and was told by the principal, "We have no idea about what might be causing her headaches, perhaps you should take her to a doctor." The mother contacted the school and told the principal when the behavior analyst would be arriving. Here is the BCBA's description of the subsequent events.

• • • • • • • •

CASE 3.04 EXPLAINING ASSESSMENT PROCEDURES

"I observed for nearly two and a half hours and then presented my report to the parents the next day. What I saw in Jenny's classroom was a high rate and intensity of self-injurious behaviors. I immediately began taking a frequency count; I observed 359 head hits in 2-hrs 25-min. In addition, there was a lack of evidence-based teaching strategies being utilized. I looked at records the teacher provided and found a history of prolonged ineffective interventions. There was a current behavior plan that actually appeared to be eliciting and maintaining the behaviors. I advised the parents that considering the high level self-injurious behavior, the student should probably not attend school until a crisis management plan was in place. We needed to prioritize their daughter's well being. After speaking with the family, I then contacted the Chair of the IEP team and explained that further observations would not be conducted due to concerns regarding the student's safety and said that I would, within a few days, provide a final report for the team to review."

Due to the urgency of these findings, it was not deemed necessary to produce a graph, but this chart summary tells it all.

• • • • • • • •

Summary: From 8:30AM – 11:55AM (2 hours and 25 minutes), the student hit her head 359 times, with 28 minutes of behavior not accounted for.
- 179/hour
- 2.99/minute

Figure 8.2 Chart summary from a BACB's report on a child with SIB.

3.05 CONSENT-CLIENT RECORDS

Behavior analysts obtain the written consent of the client before obtaining or disclosing client records from or to other sources, for assessment purposes.

Behavior analysts who are actively engaged in working with clients may occasionally come under pressure to reveal client information to a school district or another professional in their agency. This code item is designed to remind behavior analysts and give protection from this pressure, since it requires written consent of the client or the individual's guardian. Note that a "blanket" agreement at the beginning of school for any and all assessments is not adequate to preserve this protection in the case of behavioral assessment.

• • • • • • • •

CASE 3.05 RELUCTANT TO SHARE

"I was contacted by a parent to conduct an FBA on her child in the home and the classroom. There are some issues with non-compliance, aggression, and off task behavior. When the mom saw the data, she said she was not sure she wanted it as part of her daughter's permanent record. Now the BCBA for the school district is pressuring me for the data saying that since the child attends their school, the data belongs to them. They have also contacted my agency head, who said, 'We have always shared our data with the school district. We have a big contract with them, what is the problem?'

What should I do?"

• • • • • • • •

RESPONSES TO CASES

CASE 3.01 TESTING SCOPE OF PRACTICE

It is inappropriate for a BCBA without the proper credentials to be doing psychological testing. And further, under 3.0, it is clear that behavior analysts use behavior-analytic assessments rather than psychological tests. Psychological tests simply do not provide the kind of information needed to provide behavioral treatment.

Follow up: The organization terminated the BCBA's employment. The BCBA was also reported to the Behavior Analyst Certification Board for activity outside the scope of behavioral practice.

CASE 3.02 SEARCHING FOR A NEW FUNCTION

In considering a case like this, the predominant ethical question is: What is in the child's best interest? In this case, the child's best interest would be served by eliminating any medical variable that might be operative. If there were no medical issues, then the development of an effective behavioral treatment based on a new FA would be the next step. It is not in the child's best interest to do any behavioral interventions that could increase his risk of harm in the meantime, so the safest strategy would be to try and protect the child by using response blocking while at the same time reducing any requests or demands to a minimum and continuing to use attention as a reinforcer.

Note: The behavior analyst sent the following communication one month after the initial question was submitted.

"After a meeting with my clinical team and the parents, we decided to wait for the results of the neurologist appointment. We put various antecedent manipulations in place during this time to prevent any of the behaviors from occurring and to keep the child safe. These were based on common antecedent situations that often triggered the child's behavior (this was for approximately 3-weeks as we waited for the appointment). The neurologist indicated that there were no medical issues and encouraged the family to proceed with whatever behavioral approach that we recommended. We had parents sign consent to conduct the FA and we proceeded with a formal FA, as well as a more natural one in the classroom given that many behaviors occurred during group activities (with many safety measures in place to protect the child and others around him). The FA indicated that the function

was access and we proceeded with a very intensive intervention plan to address this. We also got approval from the Early Intervention program for an increase in ABA in the home, and put his head teacher at the school on those hours to ensure consistency and proper training of the parents. As a result of these steps, the plan was successful and the child no longer presents with any of these interfering behaviors. The components of the behavior plan have been faded out and he is functioning more independently and success- fully in the classroom and at home. We are very happy with the results."

CASE 3.04 EXPLAINING ASSESSMENT PROCEDURES

The parents decided to take the behavior analyst's advice and requested an IEP meeting, while keeping their daughter home in the interim. A meeting was held in which the parents brought an advocate and the behavior analyst presented a summary of the findings, as well as suggestions on what was necessary for the student's safety. The parents requested private placement at a center with the training and levels of support necessary to address the behaviors as well as teach the student skills that would prepare her to be successful returning to a less restric- tive environment. After discussing several options, the IEP team decided that a placement transfer was in the best interest of the student and approved the parents' request.

The strategy with the private placement was that since the public school was not going to pay for a behavior analyst to be involved on site, get- ting the child placed at a specialized ABA school would facilitate behavior analysts overseeing her programming. Then the services of the behavior analysts could be included in a transition plan back to the public school.

The child's mother emailed the behavior analyst as the child was being transferred and commented, "Personally, I have a been a wee bit wary of ABA due to some encounters with older models and thinking, but the strength of ethics and character that you have has truly been a pleasure to experience."

CASE 3.05 RELUCTANT TO SHARE

Under this code item, the behavior analyst must respect the wishes of the parent. The parent may have had a bad experience with the school district over-sharing information in the past. This code item also protects behavior analysts from being pressured by agencies.

9

Behavior Analysts and the Behavior-Change Program (Code 4.0)

Early in the evolution of the field, behavior analysts had a modus operandi of carrying out behavior-change programs that could be described encouragingly by supporters as "fluid" and by detractors as "making it up as they went along." In the beginning, behavior programs were just extensions of laboratory procedures, with adaptations for humans and the settings they occupied. Nothing was written down, and there was no formal approval process. Data were always collected, usually with precision and consistency, and the results were so novel and amazing that all of those involved would marvel at the effects they were seeing with these primitive procedures. With

> The pioneers of behavior analysis quickly realized that these were not just experiments in behavior change but rather a totally new form of therapy.

success came recognition of the seriousness of the mission these early leaders had undertaken. The pioneers of behavior analysis soon realized that these were not just experiments in behavior change but rather a totally new form of *therapy*—data based to be sure, but therapy nonetheless. In Code 4.01, it is clear the obligation of those who want to call themselves behavior analysts must remain conceptually consistent with the behavior analytic principles of our field (Baer, Wolf, & Risley, 1968; Miltenberger, 2015) and avoid appeals to theories other than learning (Skinner, 1953). As the field of behavior analysis evolved, behavioral treatment required an extra level of care, consideration, thoughtfulness, and responsibility. It

> As the field of behavior analysis evolved, behavioral treatment required an extra level of care, consideration, thoughtfulness, and responsibility.

became apparent that better record keeping would be required. By the mid-1980s, behavior analysis practitioners were fully in compliance with standards of the time, which required that the client, or a surrogate, actually approve the program in writing before it was implemented. Along with the changes in behavioral treatment, as advances in applied research were made, the limiting conditions of behavioral procedures became apparent, and it was incumbent on therapists to describe these conditions to consumers.

This increased responsibility and accountability also meant that other protocols must be followed as well, such as using least restrictive procedures, avoiding harmful consequences (including both reinforcers and punishers), and involving the client in any modifications to programs that might be made along the way. Skinner (1953) had always been against the use of punishers, but it took the field of behavior analysis some time to codify our objectives on this. It was the vetting of the original BACB Guidelines for Responsible Conduct, which evolved into the current ethics Code, that finally resulted in a concise and cohesive position (4.08): "Behavior analyst recommends reinforcement rather than punishment whenever possible." The essence of this aspect of the Code is to inform consumers and to remind behavior analysts that, as a field, we are primarily interested in developing behavior change programs that teach new, appropriate, adaptive behaviors using nonharmful reinforcers whenever possible (4.10).

In the new Code, 4.01 makes clear that behavior analysts design behavior-change programs that are consistent with behavior-analytic principles. When compared with other forms of treatment, this

A great deal of "clinical judgment" goes into the decision of when to stop treatment.

presents one of the most unique and valuable features. Ongoing, objective data collection helps the behavior analyst understand the effect of treatment, and the consumer is able to make an ongoing evaluation of the worth of the treatment as well.

At the onset of a behavior change program, most of the focus is on finding just the right treatment and implementing it correctly, under safe conditions. One additional requirement for behavior analysts is that some consideration be given to the termination criteria (4.11). Basically, we need to ask, "When will we stop treatment?" It is presumed that termination comes when the consumer's behavior has been sufficiently changed to warrant cessation, but what is the criterion? There is a great deal of "clinical judgment" involved in this decision, and of course the client or his or her surrogate must also be involved. By requiring that some thought be given to what level of behavior change is desired, the Code prevents open-ended treatment that goes on and on. If the behavior analyst is treating self-injurious behavior (SIB), for example, he or she must indicate, and get approval for, some level of acceptable behavior change. "Zero SIB for two weeks" might be one such goal. Or, if the behavior change program involves an adaptive behavior, the goal might state, "Carl will be able to completely dress himself, without any assistance, for three consecutive days." As often happens, the client or the client's surrogate might at that point decide to terminate treatment, or, as often happens, another goal might be set, such as, "Carl will be able to ride the bus independently for one week" or "Carl will be able to complete a full work day with no SIB or inappropriate behavior."

4.0 BEHAVIOR ANALYSTS AND THE BEHAVIOR-CHANGE PROGRAM

Behavior analysts are responsible for all aspects of the behavior-change program from conceptualization to implementation and ultimately to discontinuation.

This simple, powerful statement makes clear that we, as behavior analysts, "own" the entire process of behavioral treatment for our clients. We do not borrow psychoanalytic, theory of mind, sensory integration, or other theoretical concepts about the "causes" of behavior; we develop our own interventions based on *behavior analysis* research, and we are prepared to follow through until the client is discharged.

4.01 CONCEPTUAL CONSISTENCY

Behavior analysts design behavior-change programs that are conceptually consistent with behavior-analytic principles.

"Conceptually consistent" means consistent with operant learning theory, which began with B.F. Skinner's landmark publication of *The Behavior of Organisms* in 1938. The conceptual basis for operant learning theory was updated in the classic *Some Current Dimensions of Applied Behavior Analysis* by Baer, Wolf and Risley (1968). The consistency of this approach continues to unfold in research published in the *Journal of Applied Behavior Analysis* (*JABA*). As a behavior analyst, you will no doubt encounter proponents of other approaches, as shown by this example.

• • • • • • • •

CASE 4.01 FACILITATED COMMUNICATION IS BAAAACK

"Facilitated communication (FC) appears to be making a comeback in my community. Several parents have raised questions about why we are not using it. Apparently there is a new age of FC and proponents have corrected some of

the controversies around it. An example is not looking at the screen, the child must show intent to push a key. It 'looks' more convincing that the child is typing. However, after exploring FC myself and practicing it the way therapists are taught to use this technique, I'm still not convinced. And of course, parents who are supporters would argue that because I'm not a 'believer' the child senses this and will not type for me! They also argue that I should look at the keyboard, 'To make sure I am making sure they are typing what they are looking at.' My argument is if the information is truly coming from the child, I do not need to look at the keyboard because unconsciously, I may predict what letter should come next and subtly move the child's hand to that letter. Any advice would be helpful!"

• • • • • • • •

4.02 INVOLVING CLIENTS IN PLANNING AND CONSENT

Behavior analysts involve the client in the planning of and consent for behavior-change programs.

It is extremely important for behavior analysts to be in tune with the values of individual clients and their concept of treatment at the outset of communications. Since it is possible for conflicts to develop, it is best to be perfectly clear about your conceptual framework and methods. In this statement from the parents of an autistic child, it would seem evident that they have strong opinions that may clash in some ways with our methods.

• • • • • • • •

CASE 4.02 FRANK DISCUSSION OF VALUES

"Regarding Methods ... There are some that I find more troubling than others, but in the end, the thing I care about more than anything else is: Is it helping my child? Is she learning? Is she safe? Will the short-term gains be at the cost of long-term pain and even trauma? What is this doing to her self-esteem? Is respectful interaction being modeled? Is she being humiliated, shamed, made to

feel badly for the way her brain processes information? Do teach-
ers and therapists believe my daughter has the ability to learn? Do
her teachers believe she is capable and are they giving her the tools
she needs to flourish and be all that she can be? Is she assumed to
be competent or is she being forced to prove her competence? Is
she being taught the same equation, story, concept and terms over
and over? Is she seen as a human being with the same rights as
any other person? Would YOU want to be treated the way you are
treating and teaching this person?"

• • • • • • • •

4.03 INDIVIDUALIZED BEHAVIOR-CHANGE PROGRAMS

(a) Behavior analysts must tailor behavior-change programs to the unique behaviors, environmental variables, assessment results, and goals of each client.

One of the most difficult tasks the behavior analyst faces is extrapolating from published research methods to procedures that will work with an individual client. Although we have high-quality single-subject design studies by the thousands, it is still necessary to make numerous adaptations to fit a client's unique assessment findings, behavior repertoire, setting, and goals of the parents, teachers, etc. Even a small difference in procedure can mean a behavior program might not work or could produce negative side effects. For example, a DRO of 15 seconds might work fine for one child but prove very frustrating to a second child and be totally ineffective for a third. The same goes for reinforcers to be used, who implements the treatment, and what else is happening in the environment. A compliance program for a 6-year-old would look totally different than an instruction-following program for a 4-year-old, and so on.

(b) Behavior analysts do not plagiarize other professionals' behavior-change programs.

Copying a program, even one of your own, to use with another client is considered plagiarism, and it is unethical. Cookie-cutter programs for multiple clients are bad enough when generated by an overloaded, too busy behavior analyst and even worse when deliberately pushed by an agency, as illustrated here.

• • • • • • • •

CASE 4.03 CUT, PASTE, REPEAT

"My ethical question is in regard to individualization and operationalization to each specific client. I just recently got my BCBA certification and I now am faced with a dilemma as to how to proceed from an ethical standpoint, as I do not want to risk my certification. At my company, the behavior plans for each client are cut and pasted with the exception of a (too) brief description of the behavior. All other antecedent and consequence intervention strategies are copied and pasted and are all the same. They include a generic version of all possible interventions (token systems, first/then contingencies, etc.) but little to nothing specified to the client."

• • • • • • • •

4.04 APPROVING BEHAVIOR-CHANGE PROGRAMS

Behavior analysts must obtain the client's written approval of the behavior-change program before implementation or making significant modifications (e.g., change in goals, use of new procedures).

Code 3.03 states that it is necessary to gain consent from the client in order to conduct an *assessment*; this approval process also applies to the development of the program and for any major modifications. The bottom line for behavior analysts is keeping the client informed about all phases of behavioral treatment and to actively solicit their approval before moving on.

4.05 DESCRIBING BEHAVIOR-CHANGE PROGRAM OBJECTIVES

Behavior analysts describe, in writing, the objectives of the behavior-change program to the client before attempting to implement the program. To the extent possible, a risk-benefit analysis should be conducted on the procedures to be implemented to reach the objective. The description of program objectives and the means by which they will be accomplished is an ongoing process throughout the duration of the client-practitioner relationship.

The purpose of having clients approve the *objectives* of the behavior-change program is to assure they understand the goals, methods, and timeline and are not disappointed with the results. Parents can be so eager for their sons or daughters to have normal language restored that they are often disappointed when, after six-months of therapy, the child is only saying short phrases instead of complete sentences. In establishing objectives, it is probably wise to be conservative so that a client does not become disenchanted with the overall treatment plan if progress is not rapid. The "risk-benefit analysis" (discussed in detail in Chapter 16) has as its purpose to disclose any potential risks of treatments so that clients do not feel blind-sided by unexpected effects.

4.06 DESCRIBING CONDITIONS FOR BEHAVIOR-CHANGE PROGRAM SUCCESS

Behavior analysts describe to the client the environmental conditions that are necessary for the behavior-change program to be effective.

Experienced behavior analysts know that there are circumstances required for any behavior-change program to be successful. First among those is the cooperation of the clients. Next, are there any safety considerations? Are the necessary resources available (including time and qualified person power) to implement the program? Other obvious variables are finding a strong reinforcer and getting permission to control reinforcers so they remain powerful and effective.

4.07 ENVIRONMENTAL CONDITIONS THAT INTERFERE WITH IMPLEMENTATION

(a) If environmental conditions prevent implementation of a behavior-change program, behavior analysts recommend that other professional assistance (e.g., assessment, consultation or therapeutic intervention by other professionals) be sought.

(b) If environmental conditions hinder implementation of the behavior-change program, behavior analysts seek to eliminate the environmental constraints, or identify in writing the obstacles to doing so.

If the condition that is interfering with the implementation of a behavior-change program is a lack of support, it is usually necessary to have another meeting to explain the need, establish a retraining program, and try again. If this approach fails, it may be time for other strategies, such as family counseling, as a way of bringing some unity to the treatment.

• • • • • • • •

CASE 4.07 NO FOLLOW-THROUGH

"We have been providing behavioral services for a 7-year-old boy diagnosed with Asperger's for approximately one year. In the past, we have observed behaviors of aggression (throwing himself on floor and banging his head as well as biting of others), fabrication (telling people that the therapist hurt him or called him names) and inappropriate comments that he will harm others. Although in the past the child engaged in inappropriate comments to others, he has never made any such comments/threats about hurting himself. Throughout therapy, we have attempted to provide parent training to the mother; however, she has not been able to comply with this requirement (she has missed training sessions in the past). However, she has not informed the behavior analyst that she is willing to attend parent training. We are concerned of the lack of parent follow through in addition to the fact that the environment is not

equipped to secure the child's safety. We are also not confident that the parent will heed our recommendations if we advise for a more restrictive setting that will ensure safety during the implementation of behavior analytic techniques. We have reviewed our ethical Code with respect to this situation and feel that it will be very difficult to implement sound behavior analysis while ensuring the child's safety. Therefore, we are considering referring the case to a more restrictive setting. Is there anything else you would recommend we do in this situation to ensure that safety of everyone involved?"

• • • • • • • •

4.08 CONSIDERATIONS REGARDING PUNISHMENT PROCEDURES

(a) Behavior analysts recommend reinforcement rather than punishment whenever possible.

It is well established that punishment can produce troublesome side effects (Cooper, Heron, & Heward, 2007, pp. 336–338) and that other strategies should almost always be used first. While there could be some life-threatening situations where punishment as a first option would be necessary, this would be extremely rare. Some of the effects of punishment include the reliable production of escape and avoidance responses and emotional reactions that could be dangerous. Occasionally, and regrettably, there will be a rogue behavior analyst who is not complying with this code item.

• • • • • • • •

CASE 4.08 PUNISHMENT FIRST

"We have been presented with behavior intervention plans written by a BCBA who gives presentations about punishment based procedures as an acceptable first step in programming. We're now seeing evidence of his practice through these plans and through troubled professionals and consumers. For example, in some plans we've seen he has recommended manual labor such as stacking firewood as a punisher. If the child

does not comply after the punishment procedure, then there may be something else aversive that is recommended, such as a cold shower. I'm not sure how to best handle this situation as it pertains specifically to this BCBA. We tell the families and practitioners that these recommendations are not best practice and make other recommendations as best we can. Sometimes we can simply just recommend an alternative BCBA. What troubles me in addition to these recommendations is that this person has a prominent role as a university faculty member at an accredited BCBA program. He speaks regularly at local workshops and conferences, and holds a position on the executive committee of our state ABA chapter."

• • • • • • • •

(b) If punishment procedures are necessary, behavior analysts always include reinforcement procedures for alternative behavior in the behavior-change program.

In order to argue that punishment procedures are necessary, the behavior analyst first needs to make sure that an appropriate functional assessment (3.01) has been conducted. Without knowing the controlling variables, punishment can simply be aversive control rather than a behavior-change plan. If alternative behaviors can be identified, then reinforcers for these behaviors probably can be found as well.

(c) Before implementing punishment-based procedures, behavior analysts ensure that appropriate steps have been taken to implement reinforcement-based procedures unless the severity or dangerousness of the behavior necessitates immediate use of aversive procedures.

Some examples of severe or dangerous behavior include SIBs such as hand biting, head banging, eye poking, or cutting, as well as aggressive behaviors such as attacking others, throwing furniture, or breaking windows. Even in these cases, a review of research in *JABA* will probably provide ideas for effective procedures. Finally, the ethical behavior analyst will always want to consider the possibility of medical or biological factors, which may elicit such dangerous behaviors, as suspected in the previous example in Case 3.02.

(d) Behavior analysts ensure that aversive procedures are accompanied by an increased level of training, supervision, and oversight. Behavior analysts must evaluate the effectiveness of aversive procedures in a timely manner and modify the behavior-change program if it is ineffective. Behavior analysts always include a plan to discontinue the use of aversive procedures when no longer needed.

Aversive procedures can be volatile and produce unpredictable and unwanted side effects. In the rare situations when aversive procedures are used, extra precautions must be put in place to protect the client and others in the area (including staff) from harm. Only behavior analysts who have been specifically trained in the use of aversive procedures should be involved with their administration, and certainly staff must require extra monitoring to assure safety.

· · · · · · · ·

CASE 4.08(D) FORCE-FEEDING

"We had a client who was beginning 'food expansion therapy,' which started with force feeding of sliced strawberries. This resulted in the child vomiting, and then the food was re-presented again. Non-certified staff did this force-feeding. I also witnessed one occurrence of a non-certified supervisor training a therapist (at the assistant level) on this. One staff did deliver vocal praise and tickles, and changed the client's shirt after vomiting. However, I am concerned that beginning a procedure that is so intensely . . . aversive for the child may harm the success of expanding non-preferred foods into the client's diet. The child did not appear malnourished during my time with this agency."

· · · · · · · ·

4.09 LEAST RESTRICTIVE PROCEDURES

Behavior analysts review and appraise the restrictiveness of procedures and always recommend the least restrictive procedures likely to be effective.

A "restrictive procedure" is defined as "A practice that limits an individual's movement, activity or function; interferes with an individual's ability to acquire positive reinforcement; results in the loss of objects or activities that an individual values; or requires an individual to engage in a behavior that the individual would not engage in given freedom of choice."[1] Based on this definition, we would conclude that a mechanical restraint is likely the most restrictive, with timeout probably rated as less restrictive. A response cost procedure, while still a punisher, has little to no restrictiveness involved. This code item then, directs behavior analysts to (1) use the least restrictive methods (Cooper et al., 2007, p. 350) that (2) do not interfere with the client's ability to contact reinforcers and (3) provide the client freedom of choice. Obviously, this is a complex formula that needs to be negotiated any time an aversive or restrictive procedure is contemplated.

4.10 AVOIDING HARMFUL REINFORCERS (RBT)

Behavior analysts minimize the use of items as potential reinforcers that may be harmful to the health and development of the client, or that may require excessive motivating operations to be effective.

There was a time when various forms of tobacco were used as reinforcers with adult clients in residential settings. This was a time when smoking and using dip or snuff were acceptable and prevalent in the culture. People were allowed to smoke in restaurants and bars, on airplanes, in movies, and in other public places. Most facilities are now nonsmoking, with policies of "no tobacco in any form," so this is less of a problem. Behavior analysts must be concerned about the health and welfare of our clients when searching for potentially powerful reinforcers. Long gone are the days when clients in residential settings could be deprived of food or water for long periods so as to make both of these necessary items potent reinforcers.

4.11 DISCONTINUING BEHAVIOR-CHANGE PROGRAMS AND BEHAVIOR-ANALYTIC SERVICES

(a) Behavior analysts establish understandable and objective (i.e., measurable) criteria for the discontinuation of the behavior-change program and describe them to the client. (See also, 2.15(d) Interrupting or Discontinuing Services.)

To make objective criteria very clear for clients, many behavior analysts use the VB-MAPP Guide (Sundberg, 2008). When objectives are met, the behavior program may be discontinued. This assessment tool looks at performance across 18 areas and allows the assessor to score the child from 1 to 5 (5 being optimal). An objective of "Works Independently on Academic Tasks" could be made specific and understandable by stating, "Works independently on academic tasks for at least 10 minutes without adult prompting to stay on task."[2] Another language-based objective to meet transition criteria might be, "Intraverbal: Answers four different rotating WH questions about a single topic for 10 topics (e.g., Who takes you to school? Where do you go to school? What do you take to school?)[3]

(b) Behavior analysts discontinue services with the client when the established criteria for discontinuation are attained, as in when a series of agreed-upon goals have been met. (See also, 2.15 Interrupting or Discontinuing Services.)

While this code item is quite clear, there are times that other contingencies, often economic exigencies, come into play, and a behavior analyst can "behave badly" by disregarding the needs of a client, as shown here.

• • • • • • • •

CASE 4.11(B) MISPLACED PRIORITIES

JD is a behavior analyst who passed her BCBA exam during the time that the situation here was happening.

"One of JD's clients (JD is a BCBA), Andrew, has been offered a government-funded intensive behavioral intervention program

by the local service provider. The parents therefore notified JD that Andrew will be no longer need JD's services at the end of the month. JD reminded the family that when they started, they signed a contract that required a month's notification before the client could terminate services. JD said this month's notice had to be given before the 3rd day of any month, otherwise the notice would be taken for the remaining days of that current month as well as a month after that. The parents are confused at this policy (even though they signed it) but when they resist, JD starts to become aggressive and sounds angry. The parents do not want to burn the bridge with JD in case they wish to continue with services after they are finished with the government service. JD admits to a colleague that she is aware of the fact that if the clients leave she has no legal basis to her termination notice, but she is worried about the loss of income that would result from this client leaving so quickly before she has found another client. Therefore, she continues to press the parents to stay for the agreed period, and insinuates that she will take legal action against them if they do not."

• • • • • • • • •

RESPONSES TO CASES

CASE 4.01 FACILITATED COMMUNICATION IS BAAAACK

It is disturbing to hear that this long and fully discredited method is coming back to haunt families and ABA, as well. There is not much behavior analysts can do about parents attempting to use FC in their own homes (except try to educate them), but, surely, they cannot force behavior analysts to use this in ABA therapy.

CASE 4.02 FRANK DISCUSSION OF VALUES

It is the position of our field that parents are always included at the beginning of treatment. We would ask parents (or anyone else) not to judge our profession by the missteps of one person. We are evidence-based therapists who feel uncomfortable with vague terms like, "humiliated, shamed, made to feel badly for the way her brain processes information." We know which procedures work based on previous research, and we know how to tailor these procedures to individual clients. We bring good, humane values along with our scientific orientation. We also bring a healthy dose of skepticism to those approaches that are loaded with humanitarian beliefs, warm fuzzy terminology, and oozing with compassion but have not a stitch of data to support their claims.

Ideally, the parent's statement would be submitted at the time decisions were being made as to whether or not the child should receive behavioral services to determine if the treatment team members feel that they can meet this standard and are willing to be judged, perhaps harshly, if they do not meet it. Certainly, the treatment team could describe for the parent values and characteristics of behavior-analytic treatment. One problem with the parent's statement is the subjective requirements that could be easily interpreted one way or another by someone with strong personal views.

CASE 4.03 CUT, PASTE, REPEAT

This code item could not be clearer: Plagiarism of any sort is unethical, and with good reason. Our approach to treatment is solidly based on the concept of individualization of treatment. A program that is successful with one child with aggressive tendencies simply will not work with another, since the causal variables are no doubt quite different. It is absolutely inappropriate to cut and paste a treatment plan for one client and pretend that it will suit someone else with a similar behavior. Such a plan will no doubt fail, and there will be precious waste of time and resources trying to figure out the reasons for a lack of success. When a behavior analyst sees this occurring, the Professional and Ethical Compliance Code for Behavior Analysts should be shown to the appropriate administrator of the company. The behavior analyst should point out the ethics violation and provide a rationale for this position. If this is met with resistance, respond with, "Please don't ask me to violate my code of ethics; I could lose my certification." A follow-up email to document that this was discussed with the administrator is also a good idea.

CASE 4.07 NO FOLLOW-THROUGH

The first author advised the behavior analyst to inform the parents that it would be necessary to start reducing services, as it was not possible to have success in this environment. Here is what the behavior analyst wrote back a few weeks later: "As recommended, I spoke to the parents of this child yesterday and made a recommendation for a more restrictive setting. As expected, the stepfather stated that they did not feel that it was necessary to place the child in this type of setting as he was simply doing things for attention. *I attempted to explain the complications of delivery of services without the appropriate supervision and assured him that the child's safety was our main concern. I also referred the family to a psychologist who works with other children on the spectrum for further care.*

P.S. Two months after this communication.

"After reading your comments, we heeded your advice and attempted to fade services. I made a personal visit to both parents and explained that due to the lack of agreement on a treatment plan as well as the challenges that we were facing in providing efficacious treatment, we felt that it was best to fade services, at least for the time being until the court situation was settled. The parents stated that instead of losing services, they would rather come to an agreement with us of what they needed to do in order to keep the services. Upon this request, we drafted a contract explicitly delineating what we needed to continue services. Some of the requirements were open communication between all parties (hence any emails must be sent to all parties) so that everyone was informed of everything at the time of the actual communication, meetings with all parties present, and agreement on treatment.

"We are happy to state that both parents immediately agreed and signed the contract. They even stated that the fear of losing therapy for their son actually prompted them to communicate better and to work things out."

CASE 4.08 PUNISHMENT FIRST

As a first step, The BACB should be notified in writing with specifics provided.

The easiest solution to deal with this person's intervention plans is to stamp them, "REJECTED due to violation of ethics Code 4.07" and return them. With regard to the "troubled professionals and consumers," behavior analysts who are seeing questionable practices could have a short paragraph prepared for distribution that educates these professionals and consumers. The wording could be similar to, "We understand that you may have seen behavior programs that stress the need for punishment as a first treatment. We want you to know that this is considered unethical practice according our BACB Professional and Ethical Compliance Code . . ."

Finally, in a case where the "punishment first" therapist is on a faculty, a letter could also be sent to the department chair and dean pointing out these outrageous violations of the BACB Professional and Ethical Compliance Code. A copy of the letter sent to the BACB should be attached.

Follow up: This faculty member's contract at the university was not reinstated when it came up for renewal.

CASE 4.08(D) FORCE-FEEDING

This element of the Code requires an "increased level of training, supervision, and oversight" if aversive procedures are used with clients. Force-feeding surely qualifies as an aversive procedure, so this is an obvious case of unethical conduct that threatens the safety of the children. The behavior analyst needs to act quickly to prevent harm by approaching the supervisor, administrator, and, if necessary, local authorities, pointing out the danger of inexperienced, untrained staff with this method. The behavior analyst should also file a complaint with the BACB.

CASE 4.11(B) MISPLACED PRIORITIES

The behavior analyst in this case clearly has lost her way, since she is more worried about loss of income than she is about helping her clients. This unethical and unprofessional conduct is harmful to the parents and reflects badly on our field. A behavior analyst who has firsthand knowledge of this situation is required by the Code to approach this individual and try to educate her about the values of our profession and, if a client-friendly resolution is not achieved, this should be reported to the BACB.

10

Behavior Analysts as Supervisors (Code 5.0).

Providing high quality, hands-on supervision is the most critical aspect of developing new professionals in any field. Supervision has taken on enhanced importance since the BACB required eight hours of training that follows the very complete Supervisor Training Curriculum Outline (BACB, 2014a). The BACB also established a requirement for three hours of continuing education (CEU) per certification cycle requirement.

This section of the code requires behavior analysts to take full responsibility when they are functioning as supervisors. They must operate only within their areas of competence. Additionally, behavior analysts who are supervising others must not take on more supervisees than they can effectively handle.

While it is common for supervisors to delegate client-related tasks such as observation and data collection, intake interviews, administering functional analyses, writing behavior plans, and more, the Code now makes it very clear that supervisors must carefully determine whether supervisees are ready to perform these tasks "competently, ethically, and safely." If they are not, training must be provided

> **Providing high quality, hands-on supervision is the most critical aspect of developing new professionals in any field.**

to bring supervisees up to speed. Furthermore, supervisors now have a responsibility to "design" the supervision and training process, which means it has to be planned in advance and supervisees have to be provided with a written description of how the supervision will be carried out. Before the current standards for supervision were developed, "supervision" could be described topographically, e.g., "I'll meet with you once a week in my office." Under the new guidelines, supervisees should expect to receive frequent direct observation and be given precise and timely feedback in such a way that it actually *improves* their performance. The final new requirement is that supervisors must include some system for evaluating *their* effectiveness. This renewed emphasis on effective supervision is refreshing and demanding and bodes well for future classes of supervisees.

5.0 BEHAVIOR ANALYSTS AS SUPERVISORS

When behavior analysts are functioning as supervisors, they must take full responsibility for all facets of this undertaking. *(See also 1.06 Multiple Relationships and Conflict of Interest, 1.07 Exploitative Relationships, 2.05 Rights and Prerogatives of Clients, 2.06 Maintaining Confidentiality, 2.15 Interrupting or Discontinuing Services, 8.04 Media Presentations and Media-Based Services, 9.02 Characteristics of Responsible Research, 10.05 Compliance with BACB Supervision and Coursework Standards.)*

After just a few years' experience as BCBAs, many behavior analysts are promoted to "supervisor" level and will begin working with newly trained professionals. For some, all they receive is a new title and a bump in salary, since it is assumed they learned all about supervision in graduate school. Very few new supervisors will receive anything more than an eight-hour training, with no follow-up on site to see if their new skills generalized. And yet, our Code now requires these newly minted supervisors to "take full responsibility for all facets of this undertaking," which includes avoiding conflicts of interest, avoiding exploitation of others, respecting the rights of clients, avoiding breaches of confidentiality, preventing the ill-timed interruption of services, and avoiding all types of exposure in the media. And, if the supervisors were involved in research, that is covered as well. Finally, supervisors must make sure that they and their supervisees are in compliance with the ethics Code.

Some examples of behaviors related to effective supervision are prompting supervisees to engage in relevant clinical skills, observing them while they are performing those skills, and identifying in writing or video recording anything that needs improvement. Next, supervisors need to prioritize the corrective steps that need to be taken, starting with safety issues and continuing on through ethics and problems with skill acquisition or behavior reduction and observing the supervisee's affect and how it might impact the client. Supervisors should be particularly aware of any repeated errors since the previous feedback session and determine if supervisees are able to maintain and generalize newly learned skills from one client to the next.

During the feedback session, the supervisor needs to make sure that the supervisee takes notes and is responsive to the corrective feedback given. In addition, supervisors should model appropriate behavior and ask the supervisee to demonstrate the correct behavior. It goes without saying that the supervisor should be using shaping and errorless learning during these sessions. Follow up appointments should be scheduled (to repeat the previous sequence) within two weeks to determine if the supervisee has responded to the corrective feedback.

• • • • • • • •

CASE 5.0 LAZY SUPERVISOR

"My question is about my supervisor. I am a grad student and I work 10-hours per week in a school. I met her on the phone before the first day of my assignment, she asked me a few questions and then told me where to meet her a couple of days later in one of the classrooms. I arrived early for the 1:00 pm

meeting and waited and waited but she never showed. As I was headed to the main office to sign out, my cell rang, 'So how did it go?' I told her I was waiting for her and that 'I didn't do anything' since I wasn't sure what to do. She said, 'Oh, I should have mentioned that I was running late, I guess I forgot to call you. Let's try again on Thursday. Just go in the classroom and introduce yourself to the teacher and have her point out Allie, she's the problem child, gotta run.' I heard from her two weeks later and asked if she was going to observe me, 'No, not now, I've got a lot going on, just put your supervision papers in my mailbox at the school and I'll sign them for you.'

• • • • • • • •

5.01 SUPERVISORY COMPETENCE

Behavior analysts supervise only within their areas of defined competence.

The key term in this element is "defined competence," which is not operationalized at present. A *competent* behavior analyst would be one who has the necessary knowledge, skills, and ability to perform routine tasks in the general areas of our field, including discrete trial training (DTT), classroom management, consulting with clients who have developmental disabilities in their homes and residential settings, and delivery of standard autism training services (including intake, initial informal observations, setting of objectives, gaining necessary permissions, etc.) in clinic, school, and home settings. These skills are taught in most graduate programs, and someone with this experience and background should be able to handle routine supervision tasks—in those areas. However, if one of their supervisees is assigned to work with a client with a life-threatening feeding disorder or dangerous self-injurious behavior, not only may that therapist not be competent to take the case, but the supervisor may also fall short. In behavior analysis, competence is defined by the types of specific training and supervision that our professionals have had either in graduate school or sometime later. This might include participating in a series of workshops conducted by an expert, followed by a practicum experience at a specialized center for treatment and research. Receiving a certificate of completion of training from such a model program would provide the necessary *defined competence* that is called for in this code item.

5.02 SUPERVISORY VOLUME (NEW)

Behavior analysts take on only a volume of supervisory activity that is commensurate with their ability to be effective.

This new Code element focuses attention on outcome of supervision rather than the process. We interpret "effective" to mean that supervisors "show improved performance on the part of each supervisee." Simply meeting with supervisees and having discussions is not sufficient; supervisors have to manage their time and utilize their shaping skills in such a way that their trainees show demonstrable improvements in their skill set.

It is difficult to specify a precise number of supervisees that one supervisor might be responsible for, since some supervisors also have administrative duties and cases of their own to manage. For example, in some organizations, one person is designated as the full-time supervisor; in others, the senior staff members supervise part time. To approximate some degree of parity, we will assume a supervisor who works in the supervisory capacity 15 hours per week. A standard schedule would be to observe and meet with each supervisee individually at least one hour per week and then have a one-hour group meeting for all of them together. If the supervisor had 10 supervisees to manage, this would amount to a total of 11 hours per week, with some time left over for travel, handling paperwork such as scheduling, writing memos and reports, analyzing data, reviewing video tapes, and preparing training and role-play sessions, as well as dealing with emergencies and conflict resolution.

The supervisor's ability to be effective might include the following outcomes: all supervisees receive their regularly scheduled one-on-one observations and feedback sessions, no supervisees have any complaints lodged against them, and a satisfaction survey of supervisees and clients would indicate at least an "8" on a 10 scale, where 10 is Outstanding. A more refined measure of effectiveness might include data on client progress that was rated as "at or above" the expected or projected rate of success.

Some variables that would affect this standard formula would include the status of the supervisees and the difficulty of their cases; a new supervisee with a difficult case load would obviously require more time than a BCaBA with years of experience working with relatively easy clients.

5.03 SUPERVISORY DELEGATION

(a) Behavior analysts delegate to their supervisees only those responsibilities that such persons can reasonably be expected to perform competently, ethically, and safely.

(b) If the supervisee does not have the skills necessary to perform competently, ethically, and safely, behavior analysts provide conditions for the acquisition of those skills.

These two elements complement one another: supervisors only delegate those responsibilities at which supervisees can succeed, and if the individual is not ready to perform specific tasks related to behavior programming independently, it is the supervisor's job to provide the necessary training. There is a presumption here that the supervisor has observed the supervisee sufficiently—live, through videotape, or via role-play—to understand the supervisee's strengths and weaknesses and to make the necessary adjustments. A good rule of thumb is *assume nothing*.

• • • • • • • •

CASE 5.03 CONFUSED

"Annie is a BCBA working in a new center that boasts two BCBA's, several BCaBA's, 30 children, and a state of the art environment. One client, Gloria, has been with the center for

several months. She has made some good progress but is still largely non-verbal. She is able to ask for a few things vocally, but she also uses an electronic PECS (picture exchange communication system). The parents told the BCBA that Gloria makes vocal sounds that they find annoying, and they wanted to know if there's anything that can be done about it. Annie recommended a procedure she knows has become popular in the research, although she has never used it before—Response Interruption and Redirection (RIRD). She was excited that she had an answer to this problem so she implemented RIRD right away with her team of therapists.

"When the other BCBA in the program saw the RIRD implemented, she noticed that the staff seemed to be applying the procedure differently. Some seemed to be applying it to vocalizations that were appropriate, and others were only applying it to vocals that were repetitive or non-functional. When this BCBA asked the direct service staff about the program, two of the four instructors on Gloria's team called it a 'vocal imitation' program. They did not seem to understand the purpose of it. Lastly, the data showed that all of Gloria's vocal mands and other vocal/verbal behaviors have been decreased since the onset of the RIRD. When the other BCBA asked Annie about what the research says on using RIRD on early vocal learners, Annie replied, 'I don't know . . . I haven't read it.'"

• • • • • • • •

5.04 DESIGNING EFFECTIVE SUPERVISION AND TRAINING

Behavior analysts ensure that supervision and trainings are behavior-analytic in content, effectively and ethically designed, and meet the requirements for licensure, certification, or other defined goals.

This requirement makes clear that behavior analysts use behavioral procedures when it comes to training and supervision. We are behavior analysts; that is what we teach, and those are the methods that we use to teach behavior analysis. As pointed out in Case 1.03, it is inappropriate for behavior analyst supervisors to teach *mindfulness* or other such non-behavior-analytic methods to their supervisees. By restricting the scope of training to ABA, we are essentially guaranteeing that supervisees will be reading about and learning exclusively evidence-based procedures.

> ## We are behavior analysts; that is what we teach, and those are the methods that we use to teach behavior analysis.

• • • • • • • •

CASE 5.04 UNPLANNED CONTINGENT MASSAGE

"Ryan has been engaging in high frequencies of hair pulling. He pulls his own hair and the hair of others. Katie, a BCBA, told the staff to start using ABC (Antecedent-Behavior-Consequence) narrative recording. After several weeks, the other BCBA on staff noticed that the staff were massaging Ryan's head and hands as an intervention for hair pulling. The BCBA looked over the data and saw that the frequency of the behavior did not seem to be decreasing. The graph showed that if anything, the frequency of Ryan's hair pulling increased over several weeks since the start of the intervention. No one seemed to be concerned about this. The parents approached the center to say that hair pulling was also occurring at the school that Ryan attended half the day. The teachers at the other school were complaining, especially because Ryan pulled the hair of the children in his class. When the other BCBA approached Katie about this, Katie replied that she was certain the intervention was working because she had not seen as much hair pulling during her observations, and the staff were not complaining as much."

5.05 COMMUNICATION OF SUPERVISION CONDITIONS

Behavior analysts provide a clear written description of the purpose, requirements, evaluation criteria, conditions, and terms of supervision prior to the onset of the supervision.

In the same way that we expect behavior analysts to provide written descriptions of behavior programs to clients, they should similarly present a supervision contract describing what is expected of supervisees prior to the supervision experience.

• • • • • • • •

CASE 5.05 NO BRIEFING

"I was assigned to a new case over the phone. I was told what school to go to, which classroom and the time I should arrive. 'I'll send you the behavior program as an email attachment later today,' wrote my supervisor. The email never arrived even though I left a voice message and sent two text messages to my supervisor. I reported to the appointed school and classroom on time as directed, approached the teacher, identified myself, and asked if she had a student for me. She pointed to a boy in the back row who had his head on his desk and was sobbing. I really didn't know what to do so I just sat next to him and tried to provide some comfort."

• • • • • • • •

5.06 PROVIDING FEEDBACK TO SUPERVISEES

a) Behavior analysts design feedback and reinforcement systems in a way that improves supervisee performance.

b) Behavior analysts provide documented, timely feedback regarding the performance of a supervisee on an ongoing basis (See also, 10.05 Compliance with BACB Supervision and Coursework Standards.)

The best practice in ABA for training and supervision is behavior skills training (BST) (Chapter 24, Bailey & Burch, 2010). This basically involves explaining or modeling the desired behavior, giving the supervisee an opportunity to demonstrate the skill, followed by corrective[1] or positive feedback. "Timely feedback" should be specified as occurring in minutes rather than hours after the demonstrated performance. For example, the supervisor observes the supervisee from 3:00–3:30 p.m., takes notes or videos the session, and then meets immediately thereafter, from 3:30–4:00 p.m., to discuss and provide feedback, give time for questions, engage in role-play and practice, etc. Depending on the status of the supervisee and the nature of the case, this would occur on a weekly or biweekly basis.

• • • • • • • •

CASE 5.06 AWKWARD SITUATION

"On Wednesday I met with an individual that I supervise. She submitted a time log detailing a variety of fieldwork activities for the two-week period. Some of her activities included reading a variety of texts. When questioned about a particular text listed in the time log, it became very apparent to me that she did not do the 4.5 hours of reading that was documented for the particular text. We discussed this in a calm and professional manner, but she displayed outward signs of 'panic' when she realized that she was caught falsifying her fieldwork time log. After taking the rest of the day to think about it, she informed me that she plans to find another BCBA to provide the remainder of her supervision. Of course, I am comfortable with terminating our supervision contract but I have several concerns related to what my ethical obligations are in this situation. I feel that I should report the supervisee's behavior to someone, but I'm unsure if that is appropriate in the supervisory role. I believe that it is important that she never falsifies any documentation ever again, but I don't think she should be prevented from pursuing her certification if she successfully completes the remainder of her fieldwork in an ethical manner."

• • • • • • • •

5.07 EVALUATING THE EFFECTS OF SUPERVISION (NEW)

Behavior analysts design systems for obtaining ongoing evaluation of their own supervision activities.

This new code item sets a new standard for supervisors. Three approaches appear to be appropriate. First, if supervisors have followed code item 5.05, they will have specified in writing what is expected of each supervisee, including some sort of timeline for meeting goals, e.g., "By the end of three months Jane will be able to . . ." So, for each individual, the supervisor will compare the supervisee's repertoire at the beginning and end of the three months and determine how much progress has been made. Then, a final accounting can be established, e.g., "Jane has met 95% of the goals that were identified for her in the area of DTT." If the supervisee has not met the objectives, the supervisor has to take responsibility and review her methods of supervision by asking questions such as, "Is my feedback given quickly enough?" "Is the feedback individualized?" "Am I including enough role-play and practice?" Effective supervision will involve the supervisor adjusting supervisory behaviors if supervisees are not learning skills and achieving goals.

Second, most supervisors could benefit from occasional feedback from another supervisor who is asked to observe the supervisor or view a video of a supervision session. The supervisor's boss would also be an appropriate person to observe and give feedback, since this person will be doing the annual performance review on the supervisor.

Third, and finally, the supervisor should conduct regular evaluations from supervisees, asking questions like, "Was my frequency of observations sufficient to meet your needs?" "Did you feel you benefited from our feedback sessions?" "Please rate my use of positive reinforcement during the feedback meetings on a 1–5 scale," and other social validation questions that would appear to be appropriate. These rating forms should go to the supervisor's boss who would then include them in the supervisor's annual evaluation.

In order to qualify as a "system," the supervisor would need to make sure that any or all of these methods were carried out systematically, that data were retrieved and analyzed and that modifications to supervision practice were modified accordingly.

RESPONSES TO CASES

CASE 5.0 LAZY SUPERVISOR

This supervisor's conduct is irresponsible to the point of being unethical. This needs to be reported to her supervisor and perhaps to the BACB. A person who is this busy should not be accepting an assignment as a supervisor. This supervisor needs to do the right thing and explain to her supervisor that she has too many other activities and responsibilities to serve as a proper role model and supervisor for junior behavior analysts who are in need of guidance and instruction.

CASE 5.03 CONFUSED

For starters, behavior analysts should not be implementing any procedures that they have not thoroughly researched. Any new technique will have constraints and limitations as to implementation, and some of those might involve side effects. Annie not only did not have any real knowledge of RIRD, but she did not train the staff or monitor their use of it. This was totally irresponsible. In this example, we see what happens when this sort of haphazard implementation goes into place, which is the exact reverse of what is desired. Further, any gains the client might have shown earlier can be reversed.

CASE 5.04 UNPLANNED CONTINGENT MASSAGE

Katie started off on the right foot by asking the staff to start with an ABC narrative recording. Sadly, however, she was not monitoring the situation with Ryan at all, and her line staff started giving him head and hand massages as a way of calming him. This suggests that they were not trained to watch for reinforcing consequences. Katie did not monitor the data, which showed that hair pulling was on an uptrend and generalizing to other settings. This series of violations of 5.04 should not go unnoticed in the organization and could be reported to the BACB.

CASE 5.05 NO BRIEFING

It should never happen that a supervisee receives instructions for a new case over the phone. This is both unprofessional and unethical. The "clear written description of the purpose, requirements, and evaluation criteria" would most likely be in a Word (or similar) document that each supervisor would have to share with new supervisees at the onset of new case assignments. The supervisor and supervisee would then meet face to face and discuss the details of the assignment and the conditions of supervision.

CASE 5.06 AWKWARD SITUATION

There is some question as to whether using assigned readings for supervision hours is ethical. Many supervisors will assign readings to students but do not count the time reading as supervision hours. In addition, it would appear that the supervisee could have been terminated on the spot for lying about completing her assignment (a violation of 1.04 Integrity). For a situation such as this, the supervisor should consider herself a mandated reporter and inform the BACB about the incident and indicate that she terminated the individual on the spot.

11

Behavior Analysts' Ethical Responsibility to the Profession of Behavior Analysis (6.0)

Behavior analysis, although growing rapidly as a profession, is still a very small field when compared with other related areas such as social work or clinical psychology. For the most part, we are not yet on the radar screens of most Americans, and, based on our past experience, we know that unethical conduct by a small number of persons can reflect badly on our whole field. If we are to gain the trust of the public, we must set a very high standard of moral and ethical conduct for ourselves. To be an ethical behavior analyst means not only upholding this ethics Code for your protection and the protection of your clients but also preserving and enhancing the reputation of behavior analysis in general. In discussing the behavior analysts' ethical responsibility to the profession, section 6.0 of the Code states that each of us has an "obligation to the science of behavior and profession of behavior analysis." This no doubt includes the nine core ethical principles discussed in Chapter 2 as well as those values inherent in a behavioral approach. In addition to honesty,

> If we are to gain the trust of the public, we must set a very high standard of moral and ethical conduct for ourselves.

fairness, taking responsibility, and promoting autonomy, behavior analysts also promote the value of objective, reliable data in determining treatment effectiveness, in using that data in decision making, and in focusing on individual behavior as our primary focus of study. Behavior analysts value novel assessments, effective

> We believe in optimizing each individual's worth, dignity, and independence and in developing the repertoires necessary to accomplish these goals.

nonintrusive interventions, and the production of socially significant changes in behavior that have worth to the individual and to society. We believe in optimizing each individual's worth, dignity, and independence and in developing the repertoires necessary to accomplish these goals. It is sometimes necessary to remind our colleagues of these basic values, and this Code element provides this occasion.

Additionally, Code 6.0 is a prompt to all behavior analysts to promote our methodology and findings to the public (Code 8.01) and a reminder to ourselves to occasionally review the Code so we are well aware of the standards that have been set. A somewhat onerous task involves monitoring other professionals (or paraprofessionals) in our community to make sure that they do not advertise themselves as certified when they are not. This vigilance is

> It is basically unethical to turn a blind eye to those claiming to be BCBAs when they are not.

warranted, considering the harm that could be done to clients by practitioners who are not properly trained. The additional harm to the reputation of our field should something happen to a client is also a constant worry to those who work hard to maintain high standards. It is basically unethical to turn a blind eye to those claiming to be BCBAs when they are not.

How one "discourages" these noncertified individuals is not spelled out in the Code, but presumably contacting the Behavior Analysis Certification Board would be a first step; another might involve contacting the Association for Behavior Analysis International (ABAI) or your local state association for advice and assistance.

6.0 BEHAVIOR ANALYSTS' ETHICAL RESPONSIBILITY TO THE PROFESSION OF BEHAVIOR ANALYSIS

Behavior analysts have an obligation to the science of behavior and profession of behavior analysis.

The "obligation" referred to here means that behavior analysts put our science, our technology, and our profession above all other methodologies. We have one world-view and one perspective; we support science and the practice of science. Behavior analysis does not permit multiple world-views or multiple explanations of behavior. From this outlook, other explanations of behavior contradict our science-based approach. Accepting this obligation is not difficult for those who received their undergraduate, master's or PhD degrees in behavior analysis, but it can present quite a dilemma for those who were originally trained in some other field, especially if that other field was not evidence-based.

• • • • • • • •

CASE 6.0 STANDING UP FOR BEHAVIOR ANALYSIS

"I am working with a family that has chosen to use multiple interventions that are not evidence-based. Interventions include creeping and crawling, masking (breathing into a bag to increase carbon dioxide intake), massaging the hands, using Nuk brushes to massage the inside of the mouth, and having the client smell different scents. These interventions are to be done dozens of times throughout the day. I have discussed the use of evidence-based practice with the student's mother. I gave her the national autism standards and discussed other research

findings on the interventions. I let the mother know that I could not support the interventions she was using. We are currently working with the student three hours a day and we implement a verbal behavior program. The student's mother wants to implement the alternative program throughout our sessions, and she is very upset and frustrated that we are not supportive of the techniques. I have been clear that I do not support these alternative interventions. I have also made the mother aware I have implemented evidence based interventions. I am unsure if it is ethical for me to continue with the case as the mother continues to move in this direction. I also want to be mindful and respectful of the family's decisions. I am unsure if it is unethical for me to leave the case because I disagree with their choice of additional programming. Please advise!"

• • • • • • • •

6.01 AFFIRMING PRINCIPLES (RBT)

a) Above all other professional training, behavior analysts uphold and advance the values, ethics, and principles of the profession of behavior analysis.

This code item reinforces the position taken in 6.0 that we expect behavior analysts to support our field above any other approaches. The values of behavior analysis include a rock solid commitment to the study of socially significant, individual human behavior and to a methodology for changing that behavior to the betterment of the individual and society. We take seriously the seven dimensions of ABA as outlined by Baer, Wolf, and Risley (1968) in their guiding principles: our field is applied, behavioral, analytic, technological, relevant to our conceptual system, effective, and produces behavior change that proves to be durable over time and across settings (generality). Our primary commitment is to the study of learned behaviors (those acquired through operant conditioning) and the use of positive reinforcement strategies to effect change. We eschew hypothetical concepts that supposedly affect behavior but for which there is no demonstrated empirical evidence. Single subject designs with clear experimental control provide the empirical evidence that is the foundation of behavior analysis. In the following case, we see some behavior drift that raises questions about this individual's commitment to behavior analysis.

• • • • • • • •

CASE 6.01(A) ETHICAL TO USE REIKI?

"After managing a parent-training program for the last eight years, I have significantly expanded my counseling skills through research and practice. While I have found that parents are extremely motivated by the change they see in their children, they also have barriers that keep them from implementing treatment plans. The biggest barrier I have encountered is parental stress. Stress from finances, lack of services, lack of family support, and grief.

"In an effort to help counsel these families, I became very interested in mindfulness and started to intensively research its application. When I stumbled upon an intervention called Reiki, I was skeptical but intrigued. My background taught me to seek out research to validate any new intervention. After researching Reiki, I discovered that it is a Japanese technique for stress reduction and relaxation that also promotes healing. It is used to decrease stress, anxiety and pain in several populations.

"My friends and colleagues found it amusing that a behavior analyst would take an interest in something so seemingly 'non-behavioral.' After explaining the research that was available on Reiki and showing them how it worked, they encouraged me to think of ways that this could be applied to decrease the stress in parents that have children with special needs.

"This brings me to my ethical question. Some behavior analysts in the field have frowned on the idea of a BCBA providing these types of services. It has been said that providing these services is unethical, as there is not enough research to support it and it takes advantage of a vulnerable population. My intention is not to use Reiki as a treatment for autism. My preference is to work with the parents, but I have not said 'no' when the parents have asked me to try it on their children.

"I feel strongly that science can only progress when people think outside of the box. That said, I understand the importance of data in science, and only proceeding with interventions that can bring forth no harm. I have collected data on the application of Reiki with each individual I have treated. For those who maintain treatment, there has been a decrease in their stress and anxiety levels over multiple appointments. I feel there is enough evidence to examine the use of this intervention with parents. While I find this work fascinating, I am a behavior analyst first and foremost. I do not want to put my BCBA or my standing with ABAI in jeopardy and be lumped into the group of people providing services professionals in the field do not find acceptable!

"I am looking for guidance on this matter: is it unacceptable considering my certification and licensure, for me to provide this service in this limited manner (i.e., stress reduction for parents)? If you tell me that it is inappropriate for someone to represent themselves as a BCBA and do this, I am willing to discontinue providing this service, or alternatively, remove the letters BCBA from my business cards."

• • • • • • • •

b) Behavior analysts have an obligation to participate in behavior-analytic professional and scientific organizations or activities.

This next code item gives strength to the push for constant self-improvement as a professional; it is now an "obligation" rather than "strongly encouraged," as in the previous Guidelines. The basic idea is that professionals in ABA should stay in close touch with new developments in the field. Reading journals, attending conferences, and going to workshops is the best way to stay informed and connected, but some find this difficult.

• • • • • • • •

CODE 6.01(B) ISOLATED

"In my country it is quite difficult to participate in behavior-analytic professional activities since these are rarely offered. Most

professional meetings and conferences don't offer the audience any new knowledge because no one is conducting research about ABA here. We have limited resources for research and even less for travel. As a result, most presenters report only about their current clinical work, which doesn't evolve much over the years."

• • • • • • • •

6.02 DISSEMINATING BEHAVIOR ANALYSIS (RBT)

Behavior analysts promote behavior analysis by making information about it available to the public through presentations, discussions, and other media.

The intent of this code item is to encourage behavior analysts to translate their work into a form that makes it easily consumable by the public. We have acknowledged for years that our technical vocabulary is not helpful in communicating with clients, advocates, and average citizens who could benefit from knowing more about our principles and procedures. As you will see in this next case, however, there needs to be some consideration given to who will use the information provided and how they will use it.

• • • • • • • •

CASE 6.02 A LITTLE KNOWLEDGE . . .

"I spend the majority of my time training other professionals outside of our field in the principles of applied behavior analysis. While the dissemination of knowledge is a wonderful thing for our field, I sometimes fear that without enough training, these individuals could potentially do more harm than good for not only children on the spectrum but also for the field of behavior analysis as a whole. Do you think there is any truth to the saying that, A little behavior analysis is more dangerous than no behavior analysis at all, in the context that people may not be correctly applying the techniques they are being trained in? Or, once some nonbehavioral professionals get a little bit of information about our techniques, they think they are ready to use them."

• • • • • • • •

RESPONSES TO CASES

CASE 6.0 STANDING UP FOR BEHAVIOR ANALYSIS

The behavior analyst is not required to continue ABA therapy under these circumstances. Basically, it will be impossible to evaluate treatment results because of the simultaneous application of these untested, unproven fad treatments. With multiple interventions, contingencies, and therapies going on at once, there is no way to determine which interventions resulted in progress or failure. It appears that the behavior analyst has done everything possible to educate the family. The behavior analyst should (and is obligated to) give the family notice and help them find someone else to provide treatment. This could be difficult, under the circumstances.

CASE 6.01(A) ETHICAL TO USE REIKI?

Alternative approaches to the understanding of behavior are ubiquitous and wildly popular among typical citizens. Advocates of these practices shout their enthusiasm for these exotic and sometimes mysterious-sounding schemes and declare themselves cured of whatever ailed them. In this case, the behavior analyst was seeking a solution to parental stress and "stumbled upon" Reiki, which is a "Japanese technique for stress reduction and relaxation that also promotes healing. It is administered by 'laying on hands' and is based on the idea that an unseen 'life force energy flows through us and is what causes us to be alive.'[1] *Since Reiki is clearly not an evidence-based procedure (using our definition) and is not conceptually consistent with ABA, it is not appropriate for a behavior analyst to be using it as a part of an ABA practice. This service should be discontinued, and any references to it should be removed from the behavior analyst's ABA business cards and website.*

CODE 6.01(B) ISOLATED

Even if you are in a country that does not have many behavior-analytic conferences, it is still possible to stay up to date by reading journal articles and communicating with other behavior analysts via the Internet. There are quite a few webinars that cover topics in our field. Probably the best resource outside of the United States for behavioral meetings and workshops is the European Association for Behavior Analysis (http://www.europeanaba.org).

12

Behavior Analysts' Ethical Responsibility to Colleagues (Code 7.0)

Behavior analysts have, in their vast catalog of work to be done, a clear set of responsibilities to their colleagues. A new responsibility (7.01) that has been added in our updated Code is that we have an "obligation to promote an ethical culture" in our work environments and to educate those around us about the ethics Code (see Chapter 20 for one way to do this).

If you are a practitioner or therapist, you may be concerned about possible ethical violations that you have learned about first- or secondhand. It should be understood that attending to a situation like this

Unethical colleagues can damage not only their reputation but also yours.

does not make you a "busybody" or "snitch." Most of us have been culturally conditioned by parents and teachers to "mind your own business," and, in your private life, this is a pretty good rule to follow. How others conduct their private lives really *is* their own business, unless, of course, it affects your life in some way. This is basically the situation you tackle when you believe that a behavioral colleague has violated the Code. It becomes your business by virtue of the fact that unethical colleagues can damage not only their reputation but also yours. It is in this vein that Code element 7.02 is written, to encourage you, despite how uncomfortable it may make you feel, to bring the issue in question to the attention of the person and seek a resolution. Ideally, the individual will quickly see the error of his or her ways, apologize, and correct

> ## If you find that a client's rights have been violated . . . you must do whatever is necessary to protect the client.

the situation with appropriate action. It is not your job to dictate the action but rather to serve as a "trusted colleague" for the person on behalf of the field and possibly the client who may have been involved.[1] In this role, you should seek an ethical solution to the problem and then fade from the picture as quickly as possible. This works most of the time. However, it might happen that the colleague stubbornly resists recognizing the problem or refuses to do anything about it.

If you find that a client's rights have been violated, or there is "potential for harm," you must do whatever is necessary to protect the client, including contacting "relevant authorities." In some cases the situation may qualify as meeting the "reporting requirements" of the BACB, and it will be necessary for you to submit a formal complaint.

7.0 BEHAVIOR ANALYSTS' ETHICAL RESPONSIBILITY TO COLLEAGUES

Behavior analysts work with colleagues within the profession of behavior analysis and from other professions and must be aware of these ethical obligations in all situations. *(See also, 10.02 Behavior Analysts' Ethical Responsibility to the BACB.)*

In general, people prefer to avoid conflict, and behavior analysts are no exception. For this reason, Code 7.0 can make even a strong behavior analyst somewhat squeamish. Most of the time, the first reaction to an apparently unethical act is to be incensed, especially if the unethical behavior of another professional affected a client's right to treatment, confidentiality, or safety. But when you are confronted with an ethics violation, calm and caution must rule the day. First, you have to be sure that you are operating with firsthand

> When behavior analysts become aware of ethical violations, doing nothing to correct the problems can serve no good purpose.

evidence. For example, hearing a rumor about an alleged abuse such as, "She yelled at him and then spit in his face!" is not something you can operate on yourself. If you heard this from a teacher, you should tell the teacher it is his or her duty to report the incident, but you cannot. If you see an abuse, you must report it. If you overhear a conversation where a colleague is talking about a client and using the client's name, you are justified in approaching the colleague, not to confront or accuse but to clarify and try to understand what happened. If your observation was correct and the person admits the action, you have an obligation to try to educate the individual about the relevant guidelines. When behavior analysts become aware of ethical violations, doing nothing to correct the problems can serve no good purpose.

7.01 PROMOTING AN ETHICAL CULTURE (RBT, NEW)

> Behavior analysts promote an ethical culture in their work environments and make others aware of this Code.

As our profession matures, a growing number of behavior analysts are moving from being an employee of a company to clinical director, president, or CEO. In this capacity, they are able to create company policies that include references to ethics standards and the ethics Code. Further, with the new code item 7.02, there is now a directive to do this. Here is an example of a statement from the CEO of a behavior analysis company to his employees.[2]

CASE 7.01 ESTABLISHING AN ETHICAL CULTURE IN AN ABA BUSINESS

"Ensuring that you behave ethically is paramount to your success as a behavior analyst, however, engineering the environment in which you work to evoke ethical behavior in others can help create and maintain a culture of ethics. This means that as a behavior analyst you are not only responsible for your own ethical behavior, but also for encouraging other professionals in our field to evoke behavior from a similar response class. Inspiring others to uphold the standards of our profession can create an atmosphere such as this. This motivation is oftentimes generated by utilizing behavior analytic technologies to create contingencies that reinforce honest and principled behavior within the workplace. Behavior analysts can establish these contingencies in a variety of ways from discussing ethics during supervision to constructing evaluations that prioritize ethical competencies. Even by simply praising appropriate verbal behavior emitted by staff around the office can have a salient effect. Promoting cultural expansion can be a daunting task, so organizations can benefit from assigning a behavior analyst to act as an ethics officer to help communicate their vision. This professional would assist by providing training to others on the intricacies of the ethical code and by helping to coach colleagues and administrators through unique and/or challenging ethical dilemmas."

7.02 ETHICAL VIOLATIONS BY OTHERS AND RISK OF HARM (RBT)

(a) If behavior analysts believe there may be a legal or ethical violation, they first determine whether there is potential for harm, a possible legal violation, a mandatory-reporting condition, or an agency, organization, or regulatory requirement addressing the violation.

The process of acting on an ethical violation begins with a determination as to whether the situation actually constitutes a legal or ethical violation. For possible legal violations, the behavior analyst would need to consult local and state statutes. To determine if there is an ethical violation, this Code or some other relevant professional code should be examined to make the determination.

• • • • • • • •

CASE 7.02(A) DOUBLE BREACH

"A therapist under my supervision informed me that she recently went on a job interview with another agency. When the therapist told the interviewing agency where she works, the interviewing manager said disparaging things about the owner of the company for which we work. The interviewer told the therapist our company owner was fired for committing fraud. I do not know about the accuracy of that allegation. During the interview, the interviewing manager also told the therapist personal information about another family that I work with who used to receive services from the interviewing agency. The information was specific, identifying, and confidential. I am at a loss as to what to do about both of these situations. My gut tells me to: (1) contact the interviewing manager and, (2) tell the parent about the breach of confidentiality. I worry about potential fallout for the therapist who reported this all to me, and I worry that a hiring manager is spreading confidential information about a very vulnerable family as well as trying to tarnish the reputation of a brand new business."

• • • • • • • •

(b) If a client's legal rights are being violated, or if there is the potential for harm, behavior analysts must take the necessary action to protect the client, including, but not limited to, contacting relevant authorities, following organizational policies, and consulting with appropriate professionals, and documenting their efforts to address the matter.

This item constitutes the mandate for behavior analysts to take action, since under (a) they determined that there was potential for harm and that it fell under some identifiable regulatory authority. It is at this point that advanced professional skills are necessary to determine the action to be taken. If the nature of the harm is to a vulnerable client, then a mandatory-reporting call to the appropriate child or adult welfare agency is in order. Note that it is not the position of the reporter to determine how severe the harm is or what the consequences for reporting are; the behavior analyst simply makes the call and gives a full reporting of what is known firsthand. If this is a legal violation, the behavior analyst will need to contact the appropriate agency, such as the police or sheriff's department or possibly the FBI, depending on the nature of the violation. The following case illustrates a more direct course of action.

> **If the nature of the harm is to a vulnerable client, then a mandatory-reporting call to the appropriate child or adult welfare agency is in order.**

• • • • • • • •

CASE 7.02(B) BLATANTLY FALSE ASSUMPTION

"I was asked by the mother of a 9-year-old child with multiple disabilities to complete an independent evaluation of behaviors occurring at school. The school approved the independent evaluation and upon my initial meeting with the team, the child's mother reported that the student had recently seen several doctors and a neurologist due to indications of possible headaches. Given the information available, the doctor believed the child was having migraines. Upon reviewing the recent teacher data and through my initial observation, I was shocked to discover that the student was hitting her head up to 300 times per hour.

The teacher reported that, 'She just had to get it out of her system.' The behavior plan in place was to provide edibles as needed and to remove the child from the non-preferred activity only to return her once she stopped engaging in the behavior. The mother does not typically see these behaviors at home and the private occupational therapist has not seen the behaviors during her sessions. Appropriate treatment systems are not in place and I want to do the right thing, but considering I was referred to the case through an independent evaluation, I'm not quite sure what that is."

• • • • • • • •

(c) If an informal resolution appears appropriate, and would not violate any confidentiality rights, behavior analysts attempt to resolve the issue by bringing it to the attention of that individual and documenting their efforts to address the matter. If the matter is not resolved, behavior analysts report the matter to the appropriate authority (e.g., employer, supervisor, regulatory authority).

This step would be taken if there was no immediate harm to the client and if the individual who was in violation was available for a face-to-face meeting. Such encounters are obviously awkward and require a delicate touch and considerable finesse. Ideally, the behavior analyst begins the meeting with nonaccusatory questions to determine if the alleged information is confirmed by the accused. The most sought-after resolution is for the accused to admit to the accusations, recognize that a violation of the ethics Code has occurred, and agree to cease and desist.

> A behavior analyst who has an issue with a colleague has an obligation to meet with the person face-to-face and attempt to resolve the problem.

This would be appropriate if the accused was plagiarizing behavior programs or something of a similar nature. Another scenario might be that the accused denies the charges or claims that it is "no big deal," gives no indication that a Code violation has occurred, and has no plans to make any changes in behavior. In this case, it is necessary to report the individual to the BACB or other appropriate authority.

• • • • • • • •

CASE 7.02(C) ANONYMOUS ALLEGATIONS

"The email in question arrived in my electronic mailbox. It had a return address that I did not recognize and I soon realized why. The message was full of anger and specific allegations about a colleague who was easily identifiable from the details. It made reference to the colleague's children and her supervisor who was also easily identified. The particulars also alleged a dual-role conflict of interest resulting in favoritism in work assignments.

"The allegations were shocking and I immediately sent a return message to the sender saying, 'Please identify yourself.' There was no response and a second more strongly worded email followed a few days later. I waited three more days and then set up a meeting with each of the victims of the email and shared it with them. At the meeting, I indicated that in my opinion, the sending of an email such as this one amounted to unethical conduct. I outlined what I thought were the specific violations. A summary of those notes is presented below:

"Disguising one's true identity is a fundamentally dishonest act. It basically says, 'I want to lash out at you so that you will be hurt and can do nothing about it.' If we were to allow this type of conduct in our profession, we would soon lose all credibility in the community and devolve into a wild pack of vigilantes bent on vengeance for any infraction. A truthful and honest person who had a gripe about a colleague would seek the person out and discuss

the issues face to face. Handling a complaint with a colleague in a devious and underhanded way is most certainly unethical.

"Although sending anonymous email is not illegal, it is most certainly immoral; it is clearly contrary to the conscience of normal professionals and undermines the fundamental pact that we have with each other to respect each other and operate in a fair and evenhanded way with regard [to] our disagreements. An anonymous email is the equivalent of an attack in the night from the shadows on an unsuspecting victim, who was unaware and unable to defend herself.

"A behavior analyst who has a problem with a colleague has an obligation to meet with the person face-to-face and attempt to resolve the problem. The Code does not allow for any wiggle room on this issue and there is no excuse for handling a tough situation in some devious and backhanded way. It most certainly is uncomfortable to discuss a possible ethical violation with a colleague, but the concern has to be put on the table for discussion and grievances aired in a civil and calm manner. The accused individuals were able, with some electronic detective work, to track down the author of the email and demand a face-to-face meeting and an accounting for the person's anonymous actions."

• • • • • • • •

(d) If the matter meets the reporting requirements of the BACB, behavior analysts submit a formal complaint to the BACB. (See also, 10.01 Timely Responding, Reporting, and Updating of Information Provided to the BACB.)

It is no small matter to arrive at a point where a behavior analyst finds it necessary to report a colleague to the BACB for ethical violations and even more arduous when reporting a supervisor or CEO of the company where you work. Many will shrink from this responsibility, and yet it is this self-policing function that will keep our profession strong and protect our clients from harm. In this case, the victim in Case 7.02(c) decided she needed to report her anonymous accuser to the BACB. One of the victims of the anonymous attack sent a four page letter to the BACB; here is an excerpt of that letter listing the Professional Disciplinary Standards (Code 10.0) that she believed to have been violated:

• • • • • • • •

CASE 7.02(D) ANONYMOUS REPORTED TO THE BOARD

"Integrity: This behavior analyst has not been truthful and honest. She has not conformed to the legal and moral codes of the social and professional community, and she has refused to resolve this conflict in a responsible manner in accordance with law.

Maintaining confidentiality: This behavior analyst has failed to maintain confidentiality. She shared confidential information about me as well as my children.

Maintaining records: This behavior analyst failed to keep confidential information private. A third party was able to use her work computer, which contained very confidential information, including information about my two children and me.

Disclosures: This behavior analyst disclosed confidential information without my consent.

Ethical Violations by Behavioral and Nonbehavioral colleagues: This behavior analyst did not confront me with all of the issues stated in the email. She confronted me about one issue while we worked together, and it was resolved. Then almost 5 months after my employment ended, this email was deceptively and unlawfully sent to my former college professor without my knowledge or consent."

• • • • • • • •

RESPONSES TO QUESTIONS

CASE 7.01 ESTABLISHING AN ETHICAL CULTURE IN AN ABA BUSINESS

Statements such as this one represent an overt attempt by a behavior analyst-owner of an ABA company to make clear that ethical conduct is expected and respected and that all employees are not only to comply with the Code, but to encourage and support each other in that regard. This same agency is involved in starting a nationwide movement to encourage companies to support a Code of Ethics for Behavioral Organizations (COEBO). For further information, see Chapter 20 *and go to: http://www. coebo.com/the-code/.*

CASE 7.02(A) DOUBLE BREACH

The comments made to the therapist who was being interviewed about the owner of the company certainly represent a breach of confidentiality (unethical) and additionally possibly slander (illegal). Revealing personal information about a client to an unauthorized individual is an ethics infringement as well as a HIPAA violation (i.e., a breach of federal law), and this is serious business. However, since you were not present at the interview, the information is secondhand to you (i.e., hearsay). You may suggest to the therapist some actions that she can take, but you do not have standing in this case to take any action yourself. The therapist can certainly contact the parent, but another idea is to suggest that she contact the owners of the company where the interviewing manager works to report that they have an unethical person in their midst. The vulnerable family may wish to take action against the interviewing manager, but, again, they would have this information secondhand, which makes this difficult. To gain some perspective on the seriousness of this sort of gossip, "Failure to comply with HIPAA can result in civil and criminal penalties."[3] If the HIPAA violation is due to willful neglect and is not corrected, the minimum penalty is $50,000 per violation, with an annual maximum of $1.5 million.[4]

CASE 7.02(B) BLATANTLY FALSE ASSUMPTION

The behavior analyst in this case, after taking data at the school and showing it to the mother, advised her not to send her daughter back to the school, since it appeared to be a "toxic behavioral environment" that elicited and maintained self-injurious behavior. The mother decided to take this advice and requested an IEP meeting that her advocate attended. The behavior analyst presented her data from the school at the meeting and compared it with data from the home. The mother requested an immediate transfer of her child to another school she had selected. This request was granted with no resistance and no stipulations.

CASE 7.02(C) ANONYMOUS ALLEGATIONS

This is one of the most egregious acts of one behavior analyst against another that these authors have encountered. The victim found a computer program that tracked IP addresses as well as email accounts. The IP address matched the same IP address from the anonymous email. Therefore, the email was in fact sent from the "anonymous" work computer.

CASE 7.02(D) ANONYMOUS REPORTED TO THE BACB

We are not at liberty to disclose the outcome of the letter that was sent to the BACB. However, "Anonymous" quit her position shortly after the report was sent in and appears to have left the state entirely.

13

Public Statements (Code 8.0)

It is a common theme among behavior analysts, "We need to get the word out about ABA." This appears to be happening more frequently. Google News routinely has stories about new behavior analysis facilities opening up across the country. The judge in a major federal lawsuit in Miami in 2012 declared in a permanent injunction, "Plaintiffs have established through their expert witnesses that there exists in the medical and scientific literature a plethora of peer-reviewed meta analyses, studies, and articles that clearly establish ABA is an effective and significant treatment to prevent disability and restore developmental skills to children with autism and ASD. The State of Florida is hereby *ordered to provide, fund, and authorize Applied Behavioral Analysis treatment* to . . . all Medicaid-eligible persons under the age of 21 in Florida who have been diagnosed with autism or Autism Spectrum Disorder" (Lenard, 2012). There was a ripple effect

> The coincidental passage of insurance-mandated state laws supporting behavior analysis treatment has given professionals and practitioners a "voice" that they did not have previously.

of this order—behavior analysis services were made available to countless thousands of individuals across the country. Finally, from a legal standpoint, ABA is on the map. The coincidental passage of insurance mandated state laws supporting behavior analysis treatment has given professionals and practitioners a "voice" that they did not have previously. This public visibility must be restrained and responsible, as befits our science-based treatment methodology. The latest version of our Code reflects this concern and obligation.

8.0 PUBLIC STATEMENTS

Behavior analysts comply with this Code in public statements relating to their professional services, products, or publications, or to the profession of behavior analysis. Public statements include, but are not limited to, paid or unpaid advertising, brochures, printed matter, directory listings, personal resumes or curriculum vitae, interviews or comments for use in media, statements in legal proceedings, lectures and public presentations, social media, and published materials.

It is important to remember that this ethics Code is relevant any time you are communicating with the public about your products, services, or the field of behavior analysis. For example, you must uphold high standards of professional behavior (1.04), maintain confidentiality (2.06), not exaggerate your effectiveness (8.02), and acknowledge the contribution of others (8.03). Public statements are understood to include any form of advertising, listings in professional directories, publication of your vitae; any form of oral presentation, whether in a courtroom or public presentation; or in any form of print publication or on social media.

Here is an example of unethical conduct involving social media.

• • • • • • • •

CASE 8.0 TWO BEHAVIOR ANALYSTS GO ON A WEBSITE . . .

"Two behavior analysts provide practicum supervision within a BCBA course sequence. Together they posted disparaging

comments about the quality of the program and faculty on a popular social media site in response to a post having to do with congratulating a graduate of the program. They never used the department by name, but the institute of higher learning and program was identifiable from the post. The posts were discovered by a BCBA faculty member of the program."

• • • • • • • • •

If the two behavior analysts had concerns about the quality of the program, they should have taken this up with the faculty involved and attempted a resolution. Going public with their concerns was misdirected and unfair to the graduates of the program.

8.01 AVOIDING FALSE OR DECEPTIVE STATEMENTS (RBT)

(a) Behavior analysts do not make public statements that are false, deceptive, misleading, exaggerated, or fraudulent, either because of what they state, convey, or suggest or because of what they omit, concerning their research, practice, or other work activities or those of persons or organizations with which they are affiliated. Behavior analysts claim as credentials for their behavior-analytic work, only degrees that were primarily or exclusively behavior-analytic in content.

This item of the Code is designed to bring attention to a central tenant of our field, that behavior analysts always truthfully describe their background and training, their practice methods and outcomes, and the results of their research. Behavior analysts do not exaggerate or misrepresent behavior analysis in order to gain attention or build their reputations or their business. When behavior analysts are providing their credentials at a behavior analytic conference or on a website, they include only those that relate to ABA. For example, an individual who was initially trained as an occupational therapist, then earned her PhD in behavior analysis, would not refer to her OT credentials when describing her work in behavior analysis.

In the case here, the individual who is self-posting on a website may have a hard time separating her behavior analytic work from all the other training she has received.

• • • • • • • •

CASE 8.01(A) JILL OF ALL TRADES

"Jill is also trained and/or certified in the following areas: administering and interpreting Sensory Integration and Praxis Tests, Therapeutic Listening Program, is an Interactive Metronome Provider, has completed Auditory Integration Training, is a certified Irlen Syndrome Screener, and is certified in ABA."

• • • • • • • •

(b) Behavior analysts do not implement non-behavior-analytic interventions. Non-behavior-analytic services may only be provided within the context of non-behavior-analytic education, formal training, and credentialing. Such services must be clearly distinguished from their behavior-analytic practices and BACB certification by using the following disclaimer: "These interventions are not behavior-analytic in nature and are not covered by my BACB credential." The disclaimer should be placed alongside the names and descriptions of all non-behavior-analytic interventions.

The purpose of this code item is to avoid confusion in the marketplace between behavior analysis and all the other forms of treatment that are available. According to our standards, many of these are non-evidence-based. Behavior analysts see ABA as a singular approach to behavior that has its roots in the experimental analysis of behavior and which has now been extended to human applications with amazing, systematic, replicable results. To mix scientifically based treatments with fad therapies is simply unacceptable to the majority of behavior analysts in our field. The general public, untrained in the scientific method and susceptible to advertising consisting largely of glowing anecdotes, blushing testimonials, and glossy promises of recovery and cure, may put pressure on behavior analysts to use these fad procedures (Foxx & Mulick, 2016). However, the proper response is to not succumb to this pressure but rather to gently push back and educate. Mixing Floortime with ABA just because it brings in more money is clearly unethical. Consider this description on a behavior analyst's webpage:

• • • • • • • •

"Noreen has experience in DIR/Floortime, Verbal Behavior Therapy, Handwriting without Tears, Sensory Integration, Social Skills Training, Augmentative Communication, Anxiety Management, and much more . . ."

• • • • • • • •

Here is the proper way to educate the public that Noreen does not include these fad treatments with her behavior analysis work.

• • • • • • • •

"Noreen, a Board Certified Behavior Analyst, has worked with colleagues who use DIR/Floortime, Handwriting without Tears, Sensory Integration, Social Skills Training, Augmentative Communication, Anxiety Management and helps evaluate their effectiveness. Please note: these interventions are not behavior-analytic in nature and are not covered by my BACB credential."

• • • • • • • •

The case here is an example where the BCBA-D appears to have prior training and a longstanding commitment to DIR/Floortime and is prepared to recommend that non-evidence-based procedure over ABA.

• • • • • • • •

CASE 8.01(E) BCBA-D SUPPORTS FLOORTIME

"I have come across a BCBA-D whose written reports (on children for whom we provide behavioral consultation) suggest

Floortime as the treatment model over ABA based methods. In fact, she even states in one report that discrete trials should not be used and that Floortime is a better option. This person has been a proponent of Floortime for many years. She has provided Floortime services for a very long time. Her recommendations do not refer to any data, nor does she suggest we keep data. It has been quite difficult working with families and getting them to accept ABA methodology because they say that this clinician discouraged ABA more than once."

• • • • • • • •

(c) Behavior analysts do not advertise non-behavior-analytic services as being behavior-analytic.

(d) Behavior analysts do not identify non-behavior-analytic services as behavior-analytic services on bills, invoices, or requests for reimbursement.

(e) Behavior analysts do not implement non-behavior-analytic services under behavior-analytic service authorizations.

These sections of 8.01 make it clear that behavior analysts steer clear of any type of confounding of behavior analysis and non-behavior-analytic treatments, including facilitated communication, Floortime, sensory integration, gluten-free and casein-free diets, antifungal interventions, magnetic shoe inserts, weighted vests, and many more.[1] Additional "scary" treatments include Miracle Mineral Solution (which is actually bleach), chemical castration, chelation, hyperbaric oxygen therapy, and sheep stem cells.[2]

8.02 INTELLECTUAL PROPERTY (RBT)

(a) Behavior analysts obtain permission to use trademarked or copyrighted materials as required by law. This includes providing citations, including trademark or copyright symbols, on materials, that recognize the intellectual property of others.

(b) Behavior analysts give appropriate credit to authors when delivering lectures, workshops, or other presentations.

It is important when behavior analysts are giving presentations, writing, or being interviewed that they give appropriate credit to authors or researchers who were responsible for the material.

With regard to presentations, workshops and lectures, there is a natural tendency when "spreading the word" to use the first person ("I think the following . . . ") in order to appear more knowledgeable in front of an audience. This tendency should be resisted in favor of giving credit to those who actually conducted the research or made the conceptual breakthrough.

In print media, such as newspaper or magazine coverage, copy editors will often query authors to request original sources and make sure that copyrights and trademarks are protected.

Social media is another story altogether. Clearly, there are benefits related to reaching a wide audience and being able to get the word out quickly via social media. However, there are also problems related to this unmanaged, unsupervised and often out-of-control method of delivering information. While it is nearly impossible to rein in the massive amount of half-truths and distortions on social media, behavior analysts should make every attempt to not create the impression that material is theirs if it was developed by someone else.

8.03 STATEMENTS BY OTHERS (RBT)

(a) Behavior analysts who engage others to create or place public statements that promote their professional practice, products, or activities retain professional responsibility for such statements.

(b) Behavior analysts make reasonable efforts to prevent others whom they do not oversee (e.g., employers, publishers, sponsors, organizational clients, and representatives of the print or broadcast media) from making deceptive statements concerning behavior analysts' practices or professional or scientific activities.

(c) If behavior analysts learn of deceptive statements about their work made by others, behavior analysts correct such statements.

(d) A paid advertisement relating to behavior analysts' activities must be identified as such, unless it is apparent from the context.

This code item puts the responsibility for public statements squarely in the hands of behavior analysts who are originally responsible. When a behavior analyst hires others to write press releases, manage a webpage, or produce copy for Facebook, LinkedIn, Twitter, Instagram, Pinterest or other social networking sites, the behavior analyst is responsible for the content and postings.

8.04 MEDIA PRESENTATIONS AND MEDIA-BASED SERVICES

(a) Behavior analysts using electronic media (e.g., video, e-learning, social media, electronic transmission of information) obtain and maintain knowledge regarding the security and limitations of electronic media in order to adhere to this Code.

We appear to be living in The Age of the Hacker, and behavior analysis is not immune from the illegal and destructive use of material obtained through electronic media. Those who are on the cutting edge of digital media, e-commerce, teleconsulting, and online instruction to promote their business, train their clients, or educate their students must be aware that they are responsible for maintaining control over the data they create, receive, modify, and transmit. We certainly do not want to see a headline like this concerning behavior analysis: "US health insurance firm Premera Blue Cross has revealed its IT systems were breached, exposing the financial and medical records of 11 million customers."[3]

(b) Behavior analysts making public statements or delivering presentations using electronic media do not disclose personally identifiable information concerning their clients, supervisees, students, research participants, or other recipients of their services that they obtained during the course of their work, unless written consent has been obtained.

(c) Behavior analysts delivering presentations using electronic media disguise confidential information concerning participants, whenever possible, so that they are not individually identifiable to others and so that discussions do not cause harm to identifiable participants.

As a way of showing their human side, many behavior analysts will use photos of their clients on their web pages or in presentations. This is considered unethical, since it exposes people who are clients (and their families) and reveals to the world that they receive ASD, DD, or other behavioral services. We urge everyone to review their web pages, social media pages, and slide decks to correct this situation. If you are surfing the web or attending a talk and observe this, the proper procedure is to first call attention of this oversight to the creator or owner of the page or the speaker and ask him or her to make the necessary correction. Provide the rationale for the request, which is "our clients have a right to privacy and confidentiality." If this is not corrected in a reasonable time period, they should be reported to the BACB.

(d) When behavior analysts provide public statements, advice or comment by means of public lectures, demonstrations, radio or television programs, electronic media, articles, mailed material, or other media, they take reasonable precautions to ensure that (1) the statements are based on appropriate behavior-analytic literature and practice, (2) the statements are otherwise consistent with this Code, and (3) the advice or comment does not create an agreement for service with the recipient.

A good example of providing a quality public presentation on behavior analysis is a podcast interview of Conny Raaymakers, a BCBA.[4]

8.05 TESTIMONIALS AND ADVERTISING (RBT)

Behavior analysts do not solicit or use testimonials about behavior-analytic services from current clients for publication on their webpages or in any other electronic or print material. Testimonials from former clients must identify whether they were solicited or unsolicited, include an accurate statement of the relationship between the behavior analyst and the author of the testimonial, and comply with all applicable laws about claims made in the testimonial.

It is important to note at the outset that testimonials are simply another form of advertising and are fundamentally incompatible with behavior analysis. We are a data-based field, and testimonials are, at best, anecdotes. Furthermore, one of our core principles is that we provide individualized treatment to our clients based on their unique strengths and deficits, motivation, known reinforcers, and history of reinforcement. We do not expect identical outcomes for each client. A heart-rending testimonial from parents about how ABA "cured their child" no doubt makes the owner of the company feel great, but it can engender false hope in anyone who reads it and takes it seriously.

This section of the Code makes an important distinction between *current* clients and "former clients" for a good reason. Once a client has been discharged, presumably successfully, they cannot be involved in a dual-role conflict of interest. A totally different situation exists with current clients. Asking current clients to provide testimonials clearly puts the clients in an awkward position where they may feel the need to embellish their comments to impress the therapists or agency owners. Parents who are asked to give testimonials might be afraid that anything less than a glowing account might threaten the quality of the services their child receives. Current clients might think, and rightly so, that lavish praise may bring special services, privileges, or special attention to their child.

Using testimonials from former clients now requires the advertiser (most commonly in the form of a website of an ABA company) to meet strict guidelines for transparency and include a disclaimer.[5] A testimonial such as the one here would not be acceptable under 8.06 of the ethics Code, since it is clear that the child is *still* a client of the facility.

• • • • • • • •

"Brian has been with you guys for more than a year with some gaps in service, but he's not the same kid as he was when we started. He has come so far with your help and I couldn't be happier with the program and staff at Rocky Ridge. His language, behavior, social skills, academics and general attitude overall has improved drastically. RR has become such an important part of our lives and our family! I recommend them to everyone I talk to! – Brian's Mom"

• • • • • • • •

Once the treatment was complete and "Brian" was in regular school, the following testimonial *would* be acceptable.

• • • • • • • •

"Brian was with you guys for three years (with some gaps in service), but he's not the same kid as he was when we started. He is now enrolled in a regular kindergarten class and I couldn't be happier with the program and staff at Rocky Ridge. His language, behavior, social skills, academics and general attitude overall improved drastically. RR was an important part of our lives and our family! I recommend them to everyone I talk to! – Brian's Mom"

• • • • • • • •

Sometimes the ethical thing to do is provide a disclaimer for a testimonial. The following disclaimer for the testimonial from Brian's mother *would* be acceptable.

• • • • • • • •

"This testimonial was solicited from Brian's mother at discharge after three years of intensive therapy at Rocky Ridge. She was not paid for providing this testimonial, but she was invited to a special dinner for our graduates. This testimonial is based on the experiences of one family, and these dramatic results are not typical."

• • • • • • • •

Note the use of past tense indicating that Brian is no longer a client, that the testimonial was solicited, and that the mother received a form of compensation by way of a dinner. Also note that the disclaimer is required by the Federal Trade Commission (FTC).

For those who are still considering using testimonials, please note that the FTC has weighed in on this form of advertising and has specified strict guidelines.[6]

• • • • • • • •

Behavior analysts may advertise by describing the kinds and types of evidence-based services they provide, the qualifications of their staff, and objective outcome data they have accrued or published, in accordance with applicable laws.

• • • • • • • •

One good example of advertising without the use of testimonials is the website of Integrated Behavioral Solutions (https://ibs.cc). Here are some excerpts from the site.

• • • • • • • •

"Treatment programs are designed to deliver precision teaching of targeted skills in a variety of settings. IBS therapists provide direct therapy to children in home, in school, and in the community."

"Best-practices treatment programs for children with autism are supported by Board Certified Behavior Analysts, who monitor progress and adjust strategies when necessary."

"It is now very well established in the research literature that individuals with autism can make substantial progress in each of these areas when provided with appropriate services. For children, in particular, these should include early entry into a treatment program, intensive instructional programming (i.e., 25+ hrs/week, 12 months/year), many opportunities for one-to-one and very small group instruction, parent training, and mechanisms for ongoing program evaluation and adjustment."

"IBS provides these solutions to a variety of individuals (including children from 18 months to adults) in many different settings, which include intensive in-home programs, public school ABA classrooms, and community-based placements and facilities. Although our primary area of specialty is Autistic Spectrum Disorders, IBS also serves a variety of children and adults with other behavioral and developmental disorders."[7]

• • • • • • • •

8.06 IN-PERSON SOLICITATION (RBT)

Behavior analysts do not engage, directly or through agents, in uninvited in-person solicitation of business from actual or potential users of services who, because of their particular circumstances, are vulnerable to undue influence. Organizational behavior management or performance management services may be marketed to corporate entities regardless of their projected financial position.

• • • • • • • •

CASE 8.06 QUESTIONABLE SILENT AUCTION

"I have been asked to provide a donation to a silent auction on behalf of my practice. I have been specifically asked to donate an initial assessment (i.e.: VB-MAPPS), and a written summary of the results for the auction. I have been mulling over the ethical standards, and most of the issues that I can see arising can be clarified via the use of a signed contract in this situation. That said, the one issue that I see as still standing out is

really a grey area in my opinion is 8.07: 'In person solicitation.' My concern would be entering a family's home, with a child who has been newly diagnosed, and knowing they are vulnerable, and keeping the boundaries around the terms of the assessment explicitly clear. To me I see this as an issue of how you carry yourself professionally in this situation. Where one person could maintain the boundaries very clearly, and come in, do the job that they are contracted to do without leaving the person feeling like they 'owe' the BCBA anything, another professional may not be able to keep those boundaries as crystal clear. Given I am seeing this as a grey area, rather than a black and white response, I would really like any feedback in this situation."

• • • • • • • •

RESPONSES TO CASES

CASE 8.0 TWO BEHAVIOR ANALYSTS GO TO A WEBSITE . . .

The two BCBAs clearly violated Code 7.02(c): "If an informal resolution appears appropriate, and would not violate any confidentiality rights, behavior analysts attempt to resolve the issue by bringing it to the attention of that individual and documenting their efforts to address the matter." Since the "institute of higher learning and program" could be deduced from the posting, this would also be a violation of Code 8.0 pertaining to social media.

Depending on the nature of the posted comments on the media site, the graduate program may need to seek the advice of an attorney to see if slander or some similar charge might be appropriate as a basis for a lawsuit. Now that the violation has occurred, the BCBA who discovered the post has an obligation to confront the two BCBAs and ask for an explanation of their actions. If the response is not satisfactory, the situation should be reported to the BACB.

CASE 8.01(A) JILL OF ALL TRADES

Jill is a classic case of a person who appears to consider ABA as just another gizmo in her bag of tricks; her posting could mislead consumers into thinking that ABA is similar to the other training that she has had.

CASE 8.01(E) BCBA-D SUPPORTS FLOORTIME

The individual asking the question was advised to contact the BCBA-D directly and engage her in a discussion of the Code. When contacted several months later, she wrote, "The person is no longer a BCBA and did not renew her certification after our exchange."

CASE 8.06 QUESTIONABLE SILENT AUCTION

This is highly unusual. The family gets a free assessment, but then is more likely to sign up for behavioral services. This is an indirect form of solicitation but a solicitation, nonetheless. The best course of action is for you to decline the request to do the assessment and point out that you feel that this is an inappropriate form of solicitation.

Follow-up from the behavior analyst several months later: "I did not offer an assessment package as was requested. I did not want to provide a family who is already highly vulnerable with a new diagnosis. The situation could have been somewhat coercive as a result of such a donation. I did however decide to offer a training workshop for the auction, on a specific topic (on building cooperation and motivation to learn, or something similar), that could have been purchased by a school for example. I did not see the potential for harm with such a donation."

14

Behavior Analysts and Research (9.0)

M ost of the sections in the BACB ethics Code pertain to providing direct services to clients. However, there are a few
additional topics covered in the Code, and "Behavior Analysts and
Research" is one of those topics.

Even though they may be working primarily as consultants or
behavioral assistants, there will be times when practicing behavior analysts may find themselves in graduate programs or courses
where they will be involved in the design and carrying out of a
research project. Ethical considerations are of utmost importance
when conducting research, and, in most cases, the ethical issues
will be overseen by Institutional Review Boards (IRBs) that are in
place to approve, monitor, and review research. The underlying
role of IRBs is to protect the welfare of human research participants, and the BACB ethics Code provides an additional level of
specificity with regard to ethics.

Conducting research in behavior analysis involves the most
complex set of requirements that can be found in the Code. Some
of the requirements are quite broad and include the design and
reporting of your study, 9.01, as well as the admonition that whatever research you conduct must follow local and state laws and
regulations, including those requiring mandated reporting. The
characteristics of ethical and responsible research are spelled
out in a dozen detailed requirements in the Code, ranging from

gaining approval from a formal review board, 9.02(a) to protecting the "dignity and welfare" of those who participate to avoiding conflicts of interest. Section 9.03 includes the requirement to gain "informed" consent from participants or those who are their guardians, and 9.04 covers using confidential information gained from the research in teaching or other forms of instruction. For years, good practice for behavior analysts has included debriefing participants at the end of the study, and this is mentioned in 9.05. The new Code covers additional post-research topics such as the ethics of being involved in the grant and journal review process, 9.06, prohibitions against plagiarism, 9.07, and acknowledging in writing the contributions of others who have participated in the research. In a powerful concluding section, 9.09, the Code makes it very clear that behavior analysts do not falsify data, 9.09(a), do not leave out any findings that might change the implications of the work, 9.09(b), and do not republish data that has been published before, 9.09(c); and finally, behavior analysts share their original data with other professional researchers in order to advance the field, 9.09(d).

Behavior analysis research (as well as all other psychological research) is governed by the rules set out in the National Research Act of 1974,[1] which led to the establishment of university Institutional Review Boards (IRB), since almost all research is conducted in university settings. The goal is to review and approve of behavioral research with humans and to provide monitoring so that no harm is done to participants. In the process of reviewing proposals, the IRB members may conduct a risk-benefit analysis (See Risk-Benefit Analysis in the Glossary) to determine if the research should be conducted. If the IRB believes the risk is too great for the value that might be obtained, the research proposal may be rejected or sent back for revision. Because of the rigorous control over research, very few ethics complaints of violations come to the attention of the Behavior Analysis Certification Board. The majority of issues pertaining to research would be sent directly to the IRB, which is charged with responsibility for oversight.

9.0 BEHAVIOR ANALYSTS AND RESEARCH

Behavior analysts design, conduct, and report research in accordance with recognized standards of scientific competence and ethical research.

9.01 CONFORMING WITH LAWS AND REGULATIONS (RBT)

Behavior analysts plan and conduct research in a manner consistent with all applicable laws and regulations, as well as professional standards governing the conduct of research. Behavior analysts also comply with other applicable laws and regulations relating to mandated-reporting requirements.

This item makes clear that researchers must be aware of and abide by "applicable" state laws regarding the involvement of anyone participating in their research. *Applicable* would include those who are not able to give consent and thus are not aware of the implications of the agreement (including risks and time commitments).

9.02 CHARACTERISTICS OF RESPONSIBLE RESEARCH

(a) Behavior analysts conduct research only after approval by an independent, formal research review board.

Graduate students conducting research for the first time may find it daunting to jump through the many hoops necessary to pass the IRB's rigorous screening. More often than not, beginning researchers might have to submit revisions more than once in order to meet the high standards of an IRB. The purpose of this rigor is to make sure that research participants are not harmed in any way. Another purpose of the intensive review of research proposals is to protect the university from lawsuits, since the research is done with the university's permission, on university premises, and very likely is under the supervision of faculty.

To make the process of getting IRB approval more efficient, most IRBs will have a website through the university where all of the requirements will be listed and the necessary forms provided.

Taking baseline data is considered part of the experiment, so researchers should remember to gain IRB approval before taking even the first data point. It is considered unethical to do otherwise. A large part of the IRB review is a close examination of the consent forms that are used because it is considered unethical to take data on individuals without their permission.

(b) Behavior analysts conducting applied research conjointly with provision of clinical or human services must comply with requirements for both intervention and research involvement by client-participants. When research and clinical needs conflict, behavior analysts prioritize the welfare of the client.

A large percentage of applied behavioral studies are carried out in clinical or educational settings, and this element reminds us that behavior analysts respect the needs of those settings and clients' right to treatment in those settings. It is not appropriate, for example, to pull children out of class for extended periods of time to participate in an experiment that will not benefit them in any obvious way.

(c) Behavior analysts conduct research competently and with due concern for the dignity and welfare of the participants.

In a published study to test the effects of exercise on young children's academic behavior and performance, participants were required to engage in moderate running outside for 30 minutes. On rainy days, the experimenters decided to move the running to the hallways in the school, where the participants were accompanied by one of the researchers. Because of the presence of the researcher, it would be obvious to anyone at the school that these students were selected for some reason, and it is possible that they would receive teasing or questioning by their peers. This is a violation of their dignity and should not have been an option in the study.

(d) Behavior analysts plan their research so as to minimize the possibility that results will be misleading.

There are many ways to mislead readers about research, from using a vague but important sounding definition of behavior, e.g., "creativity" (when in actuality the participants are just assembling nuts and bolts), to employing an inter-observer reliability formula that makes scores appear higher than they are. Researchers have an ethical obligation to avoid any terminology, methods, or subject-selection procedures that would in any way misrepresent any aspect of their research to their audiences.

(e) Researchers and assistants are permitted to perform only those tasks for which they are appropriately trained and prepared. Behavior analysts are responsible for the ethical conduct of research conducted by assistants or by others under their supervision or oversight.

Poorly trained research assistants cannot only cause serious, even fatal, errors to creep into data collection (e.g., through behavior drift) but could, under some circumstances, put participants at risk. Researchers are ethically required to train assistants thoroughly. A part of thorough training includes direct observation and, perhaps, testing assistants regularly to assure their adherence to the methodology. Such a procedure will ensure that no harm comes to participants during implementation. This is especially the case for applied research done in the community. In a recent case, when a mother wanted to know if her child could be lured to a stranger's car, the therapist agreed to set up an experiment to test this possibility. The "experiment" was conducted in the parking lot of a well-known retail chain. The behavior analyst did not have the necessary safety precautions in place and had not thought through the possible outcomes. The mother ran screaming across the parking lot when her child followed an experimenter to his car, and she later called the police requesting they issue a warning to the child. Had this been submitted to the IRB in the form of a proposal, it is doubtful that it would have been approved.

(f) If an ethical issue is unclear, behavior analysts seek to resolve the issue through consultation with independent, formal research review boards, peer consultations, or other proper mechanisms.

Once a research project is approved and underway, there is an expectation that the behavior analyst will use the IRB as a resource in the case of any ethical issues that might arise. This may be one reason that few ethical research questions surface for our online ABAI (Association for Behavior Analysis International) Hotline.

(g) Behavior analysts only conduct research independently after they have successfully conducted research under a supervisor in a defined relationship (e.g., thesis, dissertation, specific research project).

"I want to do research" is a common refrain from undergraduates who become excited about ABA or some other area of psychology. They see published studies that appear to be rather simplistic (one recent study was conducted by a parent, with her child as the subject) and feel that they could do at least as well. Most published studies do not make a point of the fact that they were conducted under the auspices of a university IRB, since most journal editors understand this. Further, there is the somewhat nuanced relationship between behavior analysis practice and applied research; both take data, graph it, show it to others, and often present their results at conferences. This code item draws a fine line separating practice from research.

(h) Behavior analysts conducting research take necessary steps to maximize benefit and minimize risk to their clients, supervisees, research participants, students, and others with whom they work.

Historically, psychological research "used subjects" in their laboratories, where theories were tested and reputations made using college sophomores who were required to participate in experiments for their introduction to psychology courses. There was no mention of any benefit to participants as a result of their participation, and the risks were minimal, since the tasks were often trivial and contrived. When applied behavior analysis (ABA) came along (Baer, Wolf, & Risley, 1968), a new standard was set. Applied behavioral research began to address common problems in individual lives and in the culture, and studies were carried out in everyday settings such as neighborhoods, schools, and shopping malls or on city streets. There is a certain risk to working in the community, and it becomes the obligation of the researcher to mitigate those risks with procedures that usually involve assistants who are at the ready to prevent accident or injury. It is exciting to be working on an applied problem such as increasing carpooling, community recycling, or gun safety, but each has its own risks that must be anticipated. The IRB will insist on all possible protections for any possible threat to the safety of participants, and new applied researchers should be prepared to answer such questions in their proposals.

(i) Behavior analysts minimize the effect of personal, financial, social, organizational, or political factors that might lead to misuse of their research.

This ethical requirement for researchers is one of the most difficult to predict or monitor, since it is nearly impossible to determine how one's findings might be used or interpreted by others who may have an ax to grind or a political position to push. Nonetheless, it is the obligation of researchers to be vigilant against the misuse of their work. The place that this might occur in published research would be in the Discussion section of an article. Here, the author is able to generalize findings and make suggestions for future research as well as provide some caveats as to circumstances under which the methods might be applied. We encourage all budding researchers to take advantage of this opportunity.

(j) If behavior analysts learn of misuse or misrepresentation of their individual work products, they take appropriate steps to correct the misuse or misrepresentation.

The first author learned many years ago, quite by accident, that his work on time-out was being used to support the use of cardboard boxes used in classrooms as a punisher for elementary students. Fortunately, his connection with the principal prevented this from going very far, but, had it not been in his hometown, this type of misuse of information could easily have spread and possibly led to harm and negative publicity.

(k) Behavior analysts avoid conflicts of interest when conducting research.

As described in Code 1.06 (Multiple Relationships and Conflicts of Interest), conflicts of interest are to be avoided in all areas of practice, and this admonition applies to research as well. A conflict might occur if a researcher has a vested interest in the outcome of a study. An example of this would be if the research involves evaluating the effects of a certain medication on children's hyperactivity and the behavior analyst owns stock in the drug company that manufactures the drug. Or a therapist/researcher might have a special interest in demonstrating that a certain special treatment is superior to others, since it is named after his chain of clinics. Probably the most common conflict, in the form of a bias toward a certain outcome, has to do with grant funding and building one's vita. Grants are often written to test a certain theory and results that confirm that theory are more likely to be funded again in the future.

One of the most famous cases of research fraud involved Dr. Stephen E. Breuning,[2] who published "deliberately deceptive scientific papers" (NY Times, 1987) and was exposed by a colleague, Dr. Robert L. Sprague of the University of Illinois (Sprague, 1998). Bruening fabricated data to prove that antipsychotic medication could produce Tardive Dyskinesia. Breuning's interest and motive appeared to be the enhancement of his reputation as a researcher plus the resulting job advancement (he was promoted from a position at Coldwater Regional Center for Developmental Disabilities to professor at the Western Psychiatric Institute, University of Pittsburgh, where he would be more likely to receive large federal grants). Breuning later admitted guilt in "making false statements to a federal agency funding his research" (Scott, 1988), which resulted in his receiving $160,000 in grants from NIMH to study the effects of Ritalin and Dexadrine in controlling hyperactivity. Clearly, an excessive interest in getting ahead professionally powered by financial incentives can conflict with the search for truth.

(l) Behavior analysts minimize interference with the participants or environment in which research is conducted.

Ideally, behavioral research would be conducted without disturbing the routine of the participants (except to encourage more appropriate or less dangerous behavior). Some changes of schedule or routines may occur so that the behavior analyst may observe a phenomenon more closely or take more precise data, but in general, unless the IRB warrants the intrusion, the rule when conducting research is to not disturb the individual's environment. Circumstances that may justify interference would include dangerous aggressive, frequent disruptive, or self-injurious behavior or where clear improvements in health or education-related behaviors might result from treatment, training, or change of contingencies. Off limits would be any form of deprivation of food, rest, comfort, or friends, and any intrusion on the participant's right to privacy, movement, choice, etc. (Administration on Intellectual and Developmental Disabilities, 2000).[3]

9.03 INFORMED CONSENT

Behavior analysts inform participants or their guardian or surrogate in understandable language about the nature of the research; that they are free to participate, to decline to participate, or to withdraw from the research at any time without penalty; about significant factors that may influence their willingness to participate; and answer any other questions participants may have about the research.

This code item leaves nothing out and makes it quite clear that behavior analysis researchers have an obligation to go to whatever extent necessary to assure that the participants in their experiments understand the nature of their participation and any risks involved and that they can withdraw at any time. IRB committees will examine the consent forms closely to make sure that there are no loopholes, so that participants are safe from physical or emotional stress. The process of gaining informed consent has advantages to the researcher, as well. If there is some issue brought up by a participant, there will be documented evidence that the individual was informed of how the experiment would proceed and agreed in writing to participate.

9.04 USING CONFIDENTIAL INFORMATION FOR DIDACTIC OR INSTRUCTIVE PURPOSES

(a) Behavior analysts do not disclose personally identifiable information concerning their individual or organizational clients, research participants, or other recipients of their services that they obtained during the course of their work, unless the person or organization has consented in writing or unless there is other legal authorization for doing so.

(b) Behavior analysts disguise confidential information concerning participants, whenever possible, so that they are not individually identifiable to others and so that discussions do not cause harm to identifiable participants.

The purpose of this item is to protect participants from public exposure related to involvement in applied behavioral research. For example, parents would not like to see their child's name on a graph labeled "Cindy's Disruptive Behavior" or "Charles' Self-Injurious Behavior" as part of a lecture or presented at a conference. The normal solution is to assign numbers to the participants and simply present them, for example, as "Participant 14." Even initials of participants can be revealing in certain settings where everyone knows the others in the group, so that is discouraged. Using pseudonyms is acceptable as long as they are not stereotypic.

9.05 DEBRIEFING

Behavior analysts inform the participant that debriefing will occur at the conclusion of the participant's involvement in the research.

In many psychological studies, the true purpose of the research is kept from the participants so as not to bias their responses. Behavior analysts rarely conduct deceptive studies, but it must be established on the front end that there will be a debriefing at the conclusion of the experiment. Participants are given full knowledge of all facets of the study and may ask any questions they like.

9.06 GRANT AND JOURNAL REVIEWS

Behavior analysts who serve on grant review panels or as manuscript reviewers avoid conducting any research described in grant proposals or manuscripts that they reviewed, except as replications fully crediting the prior researchers.

Granting agencies organize review panels from a pool of researchers who serve as peers for one another. They must sign documents at the beginning of a review session, which could last a week or so, indicating that they will not reveal any information gained during the review nor act on any ideas or methodology they may discover in the process. It is understood also that they will be totally objective in their analysis of grants submitted. A very similar system operates with most journals, where the editor establishes a peer review process for each manuscript submitted and reviewers are sworn to keep all information secret and to not steal ideas for their own research. Any activity contrary to these values is considered unethical conduct.

9.07 PLAGIARISM

(a) Behavior analysts fully cite the work of others where appropriate.
(b) Behavior analysts do not present portions or elements of another's work or data as their own.

Plagiarism is a form of academic theft of using ideas, data, or actual written work and then taking credit for it. This can happen when a behavior analyst researcher is reading an article and finds an idea or passage that is then purloined and used without giving any credit to the original author. Such conduct is seriously frowned upon in academia and results in expulsion from the university or discharge from graduate school.

9.08 ACKNOWLEDGING CONTRIBUTIONS

Behavior analysts acknowledge the contributions of others to research by including them as co-authors or footnoting their contributions. Principal authorship and other publication credits accurately reflect the relative scientific or professional contributions of the individuals involved, regardless of their relative status. Minor contributions to the research or to the writing for publications are appropriately acknowledged, such as in a footnote or introductory statement.

In recent years, behavior analysis research has become a group affair, with sometimes as many as 10 authors contributing their knowledge and skills to produce a final product. It is standard practice for these cooperating professionals to establish at the beginning of the endeavor (which might last a year or two) what the ordering of the authors will be and how the secondary or minor contributions will be recognized. It is considered poor form to exclude someone who has worked diligently for months on end. This code item lists this type of exclusion as an unethical practice, since such lack of recognition would mean a rapid decrease in interest by all parties involved.

9.09 ACCURACY AND USE OF DATA (RBT)

(a) Behavior analysts do not fabricate data or falsify results in their publications. If behavior analysts discover errors in their published data, they take steps to correct such errors in a correction, retraction, erratum, or other appropriate publication means.

We have already discussed the Breuning case of falsifying data in 9.02(k). The hero in this incident was Dr. Robert L. Sprague. Dr. Sprague was one of Breuning's early colleagues and supporters who, despite their close relationship, determined that it was bad for the science (i.e., unethical) to allow this unscrupulous conduct to remain hidden. Training in the proper respect for scientific methodology begins in the undergraduate laboratory and continues through graduate school thesis and dissertation research. The role of the mentor cannot be understated in producing researchers who value truth and honesty above all else, even their own promotion. Faking data in academic circles rises to the level of sinful behavior. Everyone in a lab or research group has a vested interest in supporting the highest standards for trustworthiness, since any sign of data falsification will tarnish their reputations, too, and risk their employability. Researchers designing experiments must take special care to train students and technicians who collect data to adopt this reverence for exacting data. Student researchers and data collectors should immediately bring any errors to the attention of the lab director so that falsified data never appears in any publication. If errors are discovered, the researchers have a responsibility to make sure that they are corrected immediately, and all journals have methods for doing exactly that.

(b) Behavior analysts do not omit findings that might alter interpretations of their work.

In almost any study, including the best controlled, some of the data do not appear like the rest. These are often called "outliers," and such findings can skew the results in such a way as to decrease the likelihood of publication. There is a temptation to toss out these data, but that temptation must be resisted since the unusual, inconsistent, curious results are part of the *truth* of the phenomena being studied. To delete this data is to deceive colleagues who might wish to replicate the findings. Should researchers attempt this ruse and then have the deception uncovered by someone like Dr. Sprague, the wrath of the academic world would come crashing down upon the original researcher. So, in short, ethical behavior analysis researchers do not exclude data for any reason.

(c) Behavior analysts do not publish, as original data, data that have been previously published. This does not preclude republishing data when they are accompanied by proper acknowledgment.

A classic violation of this sacred rule of academia was originally cited in Bailey and Burch (2002, p. 203) in the case of Chhokar and Wallin (1984a, 1984b), where these researchers published two versions of the same study, including the same graphs, within the same year in the *Journal of Applied Psychology* and the *Journal of Safety Research*; for all practical purposes, only the titles were different.

(d) After research results are published, behavior analysts do not withhold the data on which their conclusions are based from other competent professionals who seek to verify the substantive claims through reanalysis and who intend to use such data only for that purpose, provided that the confidentiality of the participants can be protected and unless legal rights concerning proprietary data preclude their release.

It is important for behavior analysis researchers to share their data with colleagues who wish to replicate their findings; this is a significant element of the scientific process. It is how a field grows, gains credibility, and eventually becomes established as a discipline worthy of public support and long-term recognition. Secretive hoarding of data raises suspicions among colleagues as to the credibility of the methods and interpretation of the findings and, for these reasons, is considered unethical conduct.

Here are a series of scenarios that you may find useful to test your knowledge of ethics Code 9.0.[4]

• • • • • • • • • •

PART I

John is enrolled in a master's program at a local university and works at a private school for children with developmental disabilities. For a class, he developed a research proposal based on some readings that he completed for the class. He would like to extend the results of Mason and Iwata (1990) by examining the effects of sensory integration on non-injurious stereotypic behavior; he plans to examine the immediate and delayed effects of the therapy on stereotypy. He would like to expose the children to this therapy for 60 minutes each day. He will measure the level of stereotypy during the 60-minute session and during a 60-minute post-therapy session. Sensory integration is not typically used at the school, so John speaks with the school principal about the study. The children's schedule would have to be altered to include the 60-minute of sensory integration and the 60-minute post-therapy condition (no interaction from others). The school principal is excited by the idea and, after receiving additional details from John, gives him permission to conduct the study (the school does not have a human research committee.) John meets several times with his faculty advisor to discuss the experimental design in more detail. He then begins to collect baseline data on stereotypy for all of the children at the school.

    1) At this point, what has John done correctly and/or incorrectly?

PART II

John is quickly overwhelmed with all of this data collection, so he recruits some undergraduate students at the university to assist him with the study. When John begins to implement the sensory integration condition, he has several of the undergraduates observe a session so that they can also implement the therapy with some of the children. Shortly after the children begin the therapy, several of the teachers complain that the children are spending too much time in the therapy and post-therapy conditions. The teachers begin to arrange for some children to skip the therapy, making various excuses.

    1) At this point, what has John done correctly and/or incorrectly?
    2) What should John do now?

PART III

In a panic, John decides to cut the therapy sessions to 30 minutes and to remove the post-therapy sessions altogether. The teachers appear to be satisfied with this modification because the children begin to attend the therapy on a regular basis again. John finally finishes his data collection and begins to analyze the data. While closely inspecting his data, he notices that stereotypy consistently decreased during the first 15 minutes of each therapy session; however, these reductions were not maintained across the full 30 minutes. John believes that this is an important finding. Thus, he re-analyzes his data so that his graphs only include stereotypy that occurred during the first 15 minutes of each baseline and therapy session. The school principal is delighted when she views his graphs and immediately begins to tout the new therapy offered at her school. He overhears her telling the parents of prospective students that the therapy produces remarkable reductions in stereotypic behavior, which leads to improvements in attention and learning. John is a bit uncomfortable with this, but he is glad that the school principal is so pleased with his efforts. She has begun to talk about possible job opportunities for him at the school after he graduates, including a new position as director of research. She also tells him that she has never had her name on a research publication, so she is anxious to see the study on sensory integration in print. She encourages him to begin working on the manuscript and even gives him permission to work on it at the school.

   3) At this point, what has John done correctly and/or incorrectly?
   4) What should John do now?

• • • • • • • •

15

Behavior Analysts' Ethical Responsibility to the BACB (10.0)

This chapter, new to the 3rd Edition of *Ethics for Behavior Analysts*, completes the consolidation of the former *Professional Disciplinary and Ethical Standards* with the *Guidelines for Responsible Conduct for Behavior Analysts*. From this consolidation comes the BACB's new *Professional and Ethical Compliance Code for Behavior Analysts*. The first goal of this effort was to create "one enforceable document to (a) more clearly present the BACB's ethics code and (b) further expand the range of professional conduct from which disciplinary action might be taken. A second goal was to expand the capabilities of the BACB's disciplinary system in terms of timeliness, case volume, and corrective action." The new "Code will be enforceable in its own right and in its entirety." There remains an expectation that "minor violations of the Code will be handled when the matter is first addressed

> If the BACB legal department determines that a complaint should be acted upon, it will be assigned to either the Code Compliance Committee or to the Disciplinary Review Committee.

by the complainant with the certificant in question." (BACB newsletter, September 2014c, p. 2).

The BACB has created two "specialized committees" to handle ethics complaints. If the BACB legal department determines that a complaint should be acted upon, it will be assigned to either the Code Compliance Committee or to the Disciplinary Review Committee. The Code Compliance Committee will handle "less severe" complaints and will focus on feedback and remedial action. If a violation is deemed more severe, it will be assigned to the Disciplinary Review Committee, which may dispense "disciplinary sanctions" (BACB newsletter, September 2014c).

Under the new 10.0, there are several requirements that are spelled out in detail. Behavior analysts must provide "Truthful and Accurate Information" to the BACB, they must comply with all deadlines, and they must update all information provided to the BACB within 30 days. Certificants must not infringe on the BACB's "intellectual property rights" and must follow all the rules related to exam administration. Finally, behavior analysts must comply with all the BACB supervision and coursework standards, be familiar with the code, and report "non-certified practitioners" to relevant boards.

10.0 BEHAVIOR ANALYSTS' ETHICAL RESPONSIBILITY TO THE BACB

Behavior analysts must adhere to this Code and all rules and standards of the BACB.

10.01 TRUTHFUL AND ACCURATE INFORMATION PROVIDED TO THE BACB (RBT)

(a) Behavior analysts only provide truthful and accurate information in applications and documentation submitted to the BACB.

Certificants, candidates, and students applying for certification should be very careful in their preparation of documents presented to the BACB. They should be aware that BACB staff carefully check and often source the information on applications to verify that the details are valid. Registrars at accredited colleges and universities are able to back up claims made for degrees earned. When students are looking for a graduate program, it is their responsibility to vet programs under consideration carefully to ensure that they are legitimate. Sadly, there are scam artists on the Internet whose diploma mills may appear genuine. These businesses issue authentic-looking diplomas for a fee. Such "degrees" are not acceptable for certification.

(b) Behavior analysts ensure that inaccurate information submitted to the BACB is immediately corrected.

Once certified, behavior analysts need to stay in touch with the BACB to assure that any change from their original filing is updated immediately. This would include correcting misinformation, such as if a candidate reported their degree was from an accredited university but later discovered

> Once certified, behavior analysts need to stay in touch with the BACB to assure that any change from their original filing is updated immediately.

the university was not accredited. Similarly, if a certificant signed on a supervisee's verification form and later discovered the hours listed were incorrect, the certificant would be required to report the correction.

10.02 TIMELY RESPONDING, REPORTING, AND UPDATING OF INFORMATION PROVIDED TO THE BACB (RBT)

Behavior analysts must comply with all BACB deadlines including, but not limited to, ensuring that the BACB is notified within thirty (30) days of the date of any of the following grounds for sanctioning status:

(a) A violation of this Code, or disciplinary investigation, action or sanction, filing of charges, conviction or plea of guilty or nolo contendere by a governmental agency, health care organization, third-party payer or educational institution. Procedural note: Behavior analysts convicted of a felony directly related to behavior analysis practice and/or public health and safety shall be ineligible to apply for BACB registration, certification, or recertification for a period of three (3) years from the exhaustion of appeals, completion of parole or probation, or final release from confinement (if any), whichever is later; (*See also,* 1.04d *Integrity*)

If a behavior analyst is found in violation of this Code or is involved in a disciplinary investigation of any kind, this must be reported to the BACB within 30 days or suffer potential sanction from the BACB. This includes any disciplinary action by a university committee, state agency, licensing board, or other disciplinary action. In addition, any behavior analyst who is convicted of a felony related to behavior analysis or public health and safety may not apply for certification for a full three-year period, following the completion of the terms of the court.

> If a behavior analyst is found in violation of this Code or is involved in a disciplinary investigation of any kind, this must be reported to the BACB within 30 days or suffer potential sanction from the BACB.

(b) Any public health- and safety-related fines or tickets where the behavior analyst is named on the ticket;

This includes speeding tickets, DUI, reckless driving or any form of ticket where the person's name appears. Not included are traffic enforcement cameras that capture license plates but do not have the name of the person on the ticket.

(c) A physical or mental condition that would impair the behavior analysts' ability to competently practice; and

Any impaired certificant who is providing services has an obligation to make arrangements for providing coverage for all clients and immediately inform the BACB of this change in status. When the behavior analyst has completed drug, alcohol, or other rehab, the BACB may require verification of competency by an independent psychologist or psychiatrist who must confirm to the BACB that the behavior analyst is able to perform the tasks identified on the Job Task Analysis and can return to work with full functional abilities.

(d) A change of name, address or email contact.

Although this item may seem small, it is big in its implications. If you get married and change your name (or change it for any other reason), contact the BACB immediately. If your email address changes, you must notify the BACB. Email is the primary mode of communication from the BACB to you. If you move and change your address, inform the BACB immediately. This seemingly minor paperwork issue becomes important if for any reason an agency needs to check your status with the BACB. If you are having a background check for a new job or licensing board, for example, and the BACB does a search and reports you are not certified (because they could not find your name), you are out of luck. Similarly, if you are using a new name and have not notified the BACB of the name change, you may receive a cease and desist notice from the BACB.

10.03 CONFIDENTIALITY AND BACB INTELLECTUAL PROPERTY (RBT)

Behavior analysts do not infringe on the BACB's intellectual property rights, including, but not limited to, the BACB's rights to the following:

(a) BACB logo, ACS logo, ACE logo, certificates, credentials and designations, including, but not limited to, trademarks, service marks, registration marks and certification marks owned and claimed by the BACB (this includes confusingly similar marks intended to convey BACB affiliation, certification or registration, or misrepresentation of an educational ABA certificate status as constituting national certification);

The various logos, trademarks, service marks, etc. associated with the BACB are considered intellectual property of the BACB and may not be used by anyone under any circumstance unless approved by the BACB. If you have any questions about this, read the fine print on your BACB issued certificate and the terms of use section of the BACB webpage. While it might be tempting to screen grab a logo from the BACB webpage and put it on your own website, that is considered theft of this intellectual property, and consequences will ensue. Even well-intended uses such as piping a buttercream icing version of the BACB logo on a congratulatory cake are not permitted. Imprinting the logo on T-shirts or coffee mugs is also a violation of this ethics Code. The BACB prohibits such use in the interest of protecting the consumer who might assume that the wearer of the T-shirt or user of the mug is BACB certified. As the owner to those trademarks, the BACB would also rightfully be entitled to any and all profits from the sale of products bearing those marks.

(b) BACB copyrights to original and derivative works, including, but not limited to, BACB copyrights to standards, procedures, guidelines, codes, job task analysis, Workgroup reports, surveys; and

The claims in this code item to intellectual property extend to all other BACB-generated materials including exams, standards, and products that come from various BACB Workgroup reports. None of these materials can be used outside the BACB and, if their use is found, it should be immediately reported to the BACB.

(c) BACB copyrights to all BACB-developed examination questions, item banks, examination specifications, examination forms and examination scoring sheets, which are secure trade secrets of the BACB. Behavior analysts are expressly prohibited from disclosing the content of any BACB examination materials, regardless of how that content became known to them. Behavior analysts report suspected or known infringements and/or unauthorized access to examination content

> **Behavior analysts are expressly prohibited from disclosing the content of any BACB examination materials.**

and/or any other violation of BACB intellectual property rights immediately to the BACB. Efforts for informal resolution identified in Section 7.02 c) are waived due to the immediate reporting requirement of this Section.

Individuals (including behavior analysts) are not permitted to use memorized exam questions to create their own exams for distribution or to sell any such information to a company that creates facsimile exams. Try to be a good citizen/certificant and report any such violations to the BACB (note: you do not need to report this to the company who is using the BACB exam questions, as this requirement is waived). If you observe cheating during an exam, this should also be reported immediately to the exam proctor and the BACB.

10.04 EXAMINATION HONESTY AND IRREGULARITIES (RBT)

Behavior analysts adhere to all rules of the BACB, including the rules and procedures required by BACB approved testing centers and examination administrators and proctors. Behavior analysts must immediately report suspected cheaters and any other irregularities relating to the BACB examination administrations to the BACB. Examination irregularities include, but are not limited to, unauthorized access to BACB examinations or answer sheets, copying answers, permitting another to copy answers, disrupting the conduct of an examination, falsifying information, education or credentials, and providing and/or receiving unauthorized or illegal advice about or access to BACB examination content before, during, or following the examination. This prohibition includes, but is not limited to, use of or participation in any "exam dump" preparation site or blog that provides unauthorized access to BACB examination questions. If, at any time, it is discovered that an applicant or certificant has participated in or utilized an exam dump organization, immediate action may be taken to withdraw eligibility, cancel examination scores, or otherwise revoke certification gained through use of inappropriately obtained examination content.

As you can surmise from the length and detail of this code item, the BACB takes ANY activity that would compromise the integrity of the exams very seriously. All behavior analysts should help monitor and enforce this ban on revealing any aspect of exam administration. We have heard of agents standing in the parking lot outside testing centers asking for information about exam questions. These people should be reported immediately. If you are approached by a person or are sent information from someone claiming to have inside knowledge of exam preparations or administrations, report them immediately to the BACB.

10.05 COMPLIANCE WITH BACB SUPERVISION AND COURSEWORK STANDARDS (RBT)

Behavior analysts ensure that coursework (including continuing education events), supervised experience, RBT training and assessment, and BCaBA supervision are conducted in accordance with the BACB's standards if these activities are intended to comply with BACB standards. (*See also, 5.0 Behavior Analysts as Supervisors*)

Supervision and proper coursework are additional issues that are considered extremely important by the BACB. Again, it degrades the integrity of the certification process and poses a risk of harm to consumers if candidates are allowed to practice who have not been properly trained and supervised. These individuals could cause harm when faced with vulnerable clients presenting critical behavior problems. We have heard of BCBA supervisors, for example, who will sign supervision forms retroactively and candidates who have submitted falsified verification forms or have "miscounted" their hours. These are both violations of this code item. All supervisors must have a written contract with their supervisees that must be signed before completion of any experience hours. Likewise, the feedback forms must be signed during the supervisory period. The BACB may, at its discretion, request these documents independently from candidates and supervisors and compare them to assure that the dates match and that all information is correct. Supervisors may be sanctioned if they have been found to have retroactively dated forms or other documents. Similarly, candidates may not be able to count their experience hours. Other areas covered in this code item include continuing education units (CEUs) earned online or at conferences. Certificants must take care to report CEUs accurately and honestly. False reporting of CEUs is considered a violation of our ethics Code. Certificants may not count CEUs from ethics seminars or workshops that have not been approved by the BACB for ethics credit.

10.06 BEING FAMILIAR WITH THIS CODE

Behavior analysts have an obligation to be familiar with this Code, other applicable ethics codes, including, but not limited to, licensure requirements for ethical conduct, and their application to behavior analysts' work. Lack of awareness or misunderstanding of a conduct standard is not itself a defense to a charge of unethical conduct.

Familiarity with the ethics Code is essentially *required* of ALL candidates and certificants. "Ignorance will not set you free" is the motto to live by. Behavior analysts who try to use their lack of knowledge of the Code to excuse lapses of judgment in the daily execution of professional responsibilities should be reminded that this is not acceptable. Certificants who reside in states that license behavior analysts are similarly required to be aware of the code of ethics that governs their practice.

> "Ignorance will not set you free" is the motto to live by.

10.07 DISCOURAGING MISREPRESENTATION BY NON-CERTIFIED INDIVIDUALS (RBT)

Behavior analysts report non-certified (and, if applicable, non-registered) practitioners to the appropriate state licensing board and to the BACB if the practitioners are misrepresenting BACB certification or registration status.

"Infringers" are those individuals who practice behavior analysis without being licensed in a state that has mandated licensure. "Infringers" are also those individuals using the BACB's certification marks and cre-

> **Your help is requested to call out infringers on our profession by reporting them to the BACB.**

dentials when they have not been BACB certified or credentialed. Examples include confusingly similar marks or designations, such as "Board Certified in ABA," "Nationally Certified Behavior Analyst," "Behaviorist Certified in ABA," etc. Changing one or two words or letters does not make a certification mark appropriate for non-BACB authorized use. Your help is requested to call out infringers on our profession by reporting them to the BACB. Other licensed professionals (not certified in behavior analysis) may claim their license permits them to practice behavior analysis or represent that they are certified in behavior analysis. It may be necessary to check with other licensing boards in your state to determine if the state board includes behavior analysis in its scope of practice. If it is not included, yet the person is appearing to practice behavior analysis, the individual should be reported to that licensing board as well as to the behavior analyst licensing board in the state, if any. If the individual is also using a BACB certification or credential or a confusing similar designation, the individual should also be reported to the BACB.

Section

Three

Professional Skills for Ethical Behavior Analysts

In Section III, Chapters 16 through 20, we address three important skills for behavior analysts who want to improve their effectiveness in dealing with ethical issues. Chapter 16 presents a model for conducting a risk-benefit analysis that should be incorporated into professional practice. In Chapter 17, we outline some suggestions for delivering the ethics message effectively when the need arises. In Chapter 18, we present a valuable tool for BCBAs, the "Declaration of Professional Practices and Procedures for Behavior Analysts." This declaration can help to avoid misunderstandings about how behavior analysis services are delivered, and it should prevent ethics issues from consuming the time you could spend working with clients. Chapter 19 presents a dozen practical tips for your first job, and the new Chapter 20 is a description of *A Code of Ethics for Behavioral Organizations*, an exciting new strategy for strengthening the ethical relationship between individual behavior analysts and the company, school, clinic, or agency for which they work.

16

Conducting a Risk-Benefit Analysis

"*Behavior Analyst Indicted for Abusing Client*" is the worst nightmare of ABA professors and professionals everywhere. This shocking hypothetical headline means that someone we trained fell into a horrible situation where events spun out of control, fateful mistakes were made, a client was seriously injured, and now one of our own is going on trial with the possible outcome of a conviction and jail time. In this nightmare scenario, in addition to the unspeakable harm that has already come to the client, the damage to the reputation and professional life of the behavior analyst and to our field could be devastating. Ripple effects will be with the client's family forever, and the community will never forget that a child with disabilities was harmed in the name of behavioral treatment.

As upstanding, ethical behavior analysts, we want to prevent this tragedy at all costs, but how? The most straightforward way is by conducting a careful, thorough, risk-benefit analysis before treatment is implemented. Risk-benefit analysis is the comparison of the risk of a situation to its related benefits. Code (4.05) specifies: "To the extent possible, a risk-benefit analysis should be conducted on the procedures to be implemented to reach the objective."

A review of the current standard texts in ABA reveals little information about risk-benefit. One book, by Van Houten and Axelrod

221

(1993), contains a historically significant chapter that explains risk-benefit analysis in detail. In Chapter 8, "A Decision-Making Model for Selecting Optimal Treatment Procedure" (Axelrod, Spreat, Berry, & Moyer, 1993), the authors present a simple and elegant model for elucidating this rather obscure (for ABA) process. Spreat, the second author, originally presented his formulation as a mathematical model for treatment selection in which the various factors were weighted (Spreat, 1982). Spreat offered four elements to consider:

- Probability of treatment success
- The period of time it takes to eliminate a behavior
- The distress caused by the procedure
- The distress caused by the behavior

WHAT IS RISK?

Since 2008, when we discovered overnight that Wall Street bankers took great risks with our money using credit default swaps to make millions of dollars for themselves, *risk* has become an important new term for Americans.

While we are not able to generalize directly from this field of financial risk management (Crouhy, Galai, & Mark, 2006) to behavior analysis, there are some clear parallels to our profession. To prevent a catastrophe such as the hypothetical headline in the beginning of this chapter, we need to think of ourselves in part as risk analysts or risk managers who determine the factors that can cause "volatility" in our treatment processes. *Risk* is exposure to injury, loss, or danger. Most often, when we talk about risk in the behavioral setting, we are referring to the fact that a client could get hurt; however, for

> We need to think of ourselves in part as risk analysts who determine the factors that can cause "volatility" in our treatment process.

behavior analysts, the danger or loss can also be related to one's reputation or harm to the field. For the Board Certified Behavior Analyst, *volatility* is an unpredicted result of a treatment plan. An example of volatility occurs in a behavior plan when, rather than significantly reducing a self-stimulatory behavior such as hand flapping, the target behavior becomes far worse and morphs into face slapping and screaming tantrums. Identifying "risk factors" that would give us some clue as to the likelihood of this occurrence can prevent such unpredictable results.

RISK-BENEFIT ANALYSIS

In the area of public health, risk-benefit analysis is used to determine the risk of death. Risks of lung cancer due to smoking, tractor fatalities for farmers, police officers killed in the line of duty, and frequently flying professors (Wilson & Crouch, 2001) are all examples of health-related situations that are evaluated by public health agencies. Insurance companies calculate risk related to certain hobbies, such as skydiving or mountain climbing.

To calculate risk of death from certain occupations or activities, it is necessary to keep verifiable records over time. Since applied behavior analysis is not an activity for which there is a high probability of death, calculating risk using public health and insurance methods does not make sense. What does make sense is to conduct a risk-benefit analysis for the procedures we use on a regular basis. The goal is not to frighten people away from our effective technology of behavior change but to be upfront with them. We need to clarify for practitioners that some procedures can increase the probability of unintended behaviors; for example, time-out can produce "emotional responses" such as "crying, aggressiveness, and withdrawal" (Cooper, Heron, &

> Behavior analysts need to clarify for practitioners that some procedures can increase the probability of unintended behaviors.

Heward, 2007, p. 363). Doing nothing has its risks as well, and when the options are spelled out to consumers, they need to be aware of this choice and the possible consequences.

RISK FACTORS AND THE LACK OF RESEARCH

It is difficult to base our determination of risk factors on the research literature because studies or treatments with a great deal of risk indicate a failure of treatment and would not be published. The factors that can predict the failure of a behavioral program are imbedded in the memories of practicing behavior analysts who have learned about risk factors through experience. Some clues about risk factors can be gathered from journal articles where it is clear that the researchers have taken extra effort to ensure treatment protocols were followed to the letter. Further, in the research setting, interventions are often implemented by master's or PhD-level therapists who have years and years of training and experience. Finally, although experiments in behavior analysis are most often carried out in controlled settings that match experimental labs in their rigor, for the practicing behavior analyst who is working with low-income clients in a rural area, it is a different story altogether. To evaluate treatments, with only intermittent backup from the itinerant therapist, parents with less than a high school education might have to be trained on a short time frame to implement somewhat sophisticated procedures.

In this chapter, we propose a strategy that involves researching each behavioral procedure that is recommended and determining the risks and benefits (both from the literature and from professional experience). Presenting the risks and benefits to the consumer in this manner allows for frank and honest discussion so that no one is surprised if unexpected side effects of a treatment should occur partway through a session. Spreat's (1982) model was an important pioneering effort; however, considering the evolution of the practice of behavior analysis and risk analysis, we have developed a new four-step procedure for determining risks and benefits.

Four Steps for Assessing Risks and Benefits

1. Assess the *general risk* factors for behavioral treatment.
2. Assess the *benefits* of behavioral treatment.
3. Assess the *risk* factors for *each behavioral procedure.*
4. *Reconcile* the risks and benefits with the key parties involved.

GENERAL RISK FACTORS

In an attempt to understand how risk factors can affect the outcome of a treatment plan, we have identified eight risk factors that are very common (Figure 16.1). In all of these risk factors, there is the potential for harm to someone, which may include the client, mediator, a bystander, the BCBA, or, in a broader sense, the profession of behavior analysis.

The Nature of the Behavior Being Treated

As a general rule, the more severe or intense the problem behavior, the greater the risk of failure of the plan. Intense or severe behaviors do not become so overnight. Severe behavior problems almost always have a long incubation period during which they developed from some lesser form to the dangerous topographies that result in the client being referred to a behavior analyst. Most students in two-year master's programs will not have had an opportunity to learn from an expert how to handle all these dangerous behaviors. While they might have read several dozen studies and understand basic principles, the details and subtleties of such treatment are hard won by those who specialize in them. Moderately experienced behavior analysts could easily make a mistake in designing a program for severe aggression that could land them, the client, or other caregivers in the emergency room.

> As a general rule, the more severe or intense the problem behavior, the greater the risk of failure of the plan.

General Risk Factors for Behavioral Treatment

Instructions: After completing a Risk-Benefit Worksheet for each proposed procedure fill out this form and review with the relevant parties.

Risk Factors	Notes
1. Nature of the behavior to be treated--is it SIB or dangerous to others?	*Target behavior is non-compliance, running away, some threats of aggression against siblings.*
2. Are there sufficient personnel or mediators to administer the treatment?	*The Mom would be the primary mediator.*
3. Are they skilled and able to administer it correctly?	*This is her first time at trying to systematically implement a behavior program.*
4. Is the setting appropriate for the treatment? Safe, well lighted, clean, temp controlled?	*The home is clean and safe but there are two other siblings who can be a problem, they are younger and vulnerable and observations indicate that they reinforce some inappropriate behavior.*
5. Is the BA experienced in the treatment of this type of case?	*Yes, 3-yrs experience with in-home consultation.*
6. Is there any risk to others in the setting?	*Yes, some risk to the younger siblings if there should be any increase in aggression.*
7. Is there buy-in from the key people associated with this case?	*Mother is serious, grandma and mother-in-law could undermine the consistency of the program though.*
8. Is there any liability to the BA?	*BA is experienced, the program is standard, no unusual reinforcers, no restrictive procedures. Supervision is good.*

Summary of General Risks: *There are some risk factors that need to be considered before this project is undertaken. To be safe we should plan to have an in-home aide help the Mom with this intervention project and the BA needs to be available 24/7 for the first few days to make sure it goes well.*

Figure 16.1 A model general risk factors worksheet for behavioral treatment. These eight factors cover most behavioral applications, but others are included as necessary.

Sufficient Personnel to Administer the Program

As behavior analysts, we count on mediators in the client's natural environment to play a significant role in treatment. The BCBA's job is to do a functional assessment, to pinpoint the function correctly, and to then devise just the right program for a specific client such as a Prader–Willi, Angelman syndrome, or cerebral palsy client. Ordinarily, for a program to be effective, it needs to be in place for the better part of the client's waking hours. In a residential facility, this means at least two shifts per day. If a BCBA's behavior treatment plan is carried out only some of the time, it will be far less effective than if it is always in play.

Is the Mediator Well Trained?

Having sufficient numbers of staff members is no guarantee of success if they are not trained to a high degree of compliance with the program. Even positive reinforcement programs can fail if the mediator occasionally makes an error and reinforces an inappropriate behavior. In one facility, we found that evening shift personnel were afraid of a large, volatile, teenager with Prader–Willi Syndrome. Rather than follow the prescribed plan, they would bring in snacks and treats on their shift to bribe the client so he would cause them no trouble. One aide on the evening shift decided that he and the client (who had a history of elopement) would walk several blocks to a convenience store for the snacks. While the aide was distracted on a cell call to his girlfriend, the unsupervised teen jaywalked across a major highway

> Having sufficient numbers of staff is no guarantee of success if they are not trained to a high degree of compliance with the program.

into the path of an oncoming pickup truck. He died an hour later of severe head injuries. It turned out that these nightly trips were unauthorized and that no risk-benefit analysis had been conducted. The family was horrified at this unnecessary tragedy and sued the facility.

Is the Setting Appropriate for the Proposed Treatment?

It is established in our ethics Code that we work only in settings where behavioral procedures are likely to be effective (4.06, 4.07), because unsatisfactory settings put the procedures at risk for failure. In addition, the setting must not put the behavior analyst at risk.

In one case, a behavior analyst was asked to provide in-home behavioral services for a family in which the mother was an animal lover. Pets are fine, but in this case the mother had large tanks of turtles throughout the house, including in the kitchen. The tanks were full of scummy green water, and before long one of the children was diagnosed with salmonella. Recognizing that the behavior analyst was at risk for catching a contagious disease, the supervisor removed the behavior analyst from the home. In another case where in-home treatment was provided, a behavior analyst discovered that a single mother's boyfriend was using drugs in the home. The consultant was reluctant to terminate services because she felt that she should remain in the home to protect the child. Our advice was to contact the proper authorities and to get out of the home immediately.

Is the Behavior Analyst Experienced in the Treatment of This Type of Case?

This can be a hard question, especially for newly minted BCBAs or Board Certified assistant Behavior Analysts (BCaBAs), since they may not want to admit that they are in over their heads. Our Code specifically requires BCBAs to operate within the boundaries of their competence (1.02), but it is not specifically stated that to operate out of the boundaries of one's competence can present a risk to both the proper implementation of procedures and the safety of clients.

Is There Risk to Others in the Setting?

In-home and school applications as well as those that are implemented in sheltered work settings present subtle risks to the success of behavioral programs. These settings also present possible safety risks to nearby clients and staff when procedures are implemented. For example, one of the "considerations" in the use of time-out is that it can produce emotional responses and unexpected results. Clients who do not want to go to time-out might attempt to escape by hitting, kicking, slapping, or spitting on anyone who is in the area. The risks of behavioral procedures should never be downplayed to gain approval of the process. Instead, they should be discussed frankly with all parties so that everyone is aware of possible risks. Mitigation planning should also result from the awareness of risk, and extra staff members may need to be present during the first few days of treatment just to make sure everyone is safe.

Is There Buy-in From Key People Associated With This Case?

Buy-in means not only that others agree with your program proposal but also that they will do everything possible to ensure that it is implemented according to the plan. Buy-in will vary from setting to setting.

If you are operating in a school, it is obvious you need buy-in from the parent, teacher, and principal, but don't forget about the teacher's aide. Persons in this position can make or break a procedure by enthusiastically joining in or showing

> The risks of behavioral procedures should never be downplayed to gain approval of the process.

an "I could not care less" attitude. Buy-in should also be obtained from other key professionals such as the school psychologist, school counselor, and social worker to ensure program success. Any of these individuals can sabotage or sink a treatment by spreading rumors and using competing activities to undermine the program's effects. If there are any "anti-ABA" people in the building, the behavior analyst should work to bring them around before the treatment begins.

Personal Liability: Risk to the Board Certified Behavior Analyst

This risk factor is related to Code 1.02 and 1.03, the question of the competence of the BACB to handle this case. Is there any possible liability directly to the behavior analyst? If a time-out is to be employed and the BCBA demonstrates the procedure, there is some chance that the young client could accidentally get hurt in the process. Will the parents want to hold the BCBA liable? Is there some way to mitigate this by doing the demonstration with the teacher or aide the day before so that there is no direct physical contact? If so, this would be preferable and would reduce liability.

BENEFITS OF BEHAVIORAL TREATMENT

In conducting a balanced risk–benefit analysis, it is necessary to review the benefits of treatment as well as the risks. We recommend developing a form such as the one shown in Figure 16.2, where the benefits are in writing for discussion with all of the relevant parties.

Benefits of Behavioral Treatment

Instructions: After completing a Risk-Benefit Worksheet for each proposed procedure fill out this form and review with the relevant parties.

Benefits	Notes
1. Client behavior is greatly improved, comes into contact with many new reinforcers and more choices	Client becomes compliant with requests, running away eliminated, no aggressive threats.
2. Client environment is greatly improved because of change in behavior—less stress for caregiver, peers	There is a calmer environment for the child and everyone else, low stress
3. Caregivers feel more in charge, improved morale, eagerness to move forward with the client	Mom can return to her preferred role of loving, nurturing, and guiding her child.
4. Peers in the setting may change their behavior toward the client, providing more opportunities for social reinforcers	Peers are no longer afraid of client, now willing to spend play time with him
5. Liability to the setting is greatly reduced	Mom feels responsible and in charge

Summary of Benefits: The benefits are great for this client in this setting, this procedure, if effective, could turn him around and greatly improve his quality of life.

Figure 16.2 Benefits of behavioral treatment. These five factors cover many behavioral situations, but others may be included as necessary.

Client Direct Benefit

As behavior analysts, our profession is primarily concerned that the client benefit directly from proposed interventions. However, in many cases, we are not explicit about what is expected. Spelling this out in terms of change of rates of behavior and the time frame for success are important here. You should discuss each target behavior in this section, as shown in the notes.

Indirect Benefits to the Setting

Often overlooked in an assessment of benefits are those related to the "climate" of the treatment setting. A formerly noncompliant, aggressive child who is now able to listen to requests and follow them quickly and with a smile can totally change the atmosphere in a home or classroom, and gains such as these should be considered possible indirect benefits.

Benefits to Mediators and Caregivers

Other often-neglected benefits of behavioral treatment are those that are provided to the mediator of successful treatments and for other caregivers in the environment. If you properly prepare mediators and caregivers for the interventions they are about to carry out and they are successful, this can produce a sense of confidence and pride in their accomplishments.

> If you properly prepare mediators and caregivers for the interventions they are about to carry out and they are successful, this can produce a sense of confidence and pride in their accomplishments.

Benefits to Peers in the Setting

While we spend most of our time focusing on the client, other individuals in the setting should not be overlooked as indirect beneficiaries of a successful treatment. In the case of a client's peers, especially if they have been targets of aggression or have been ignored, they will appreciate the reduction in fear and anxiety as well as possible additional attention from parents and teachers.

General Liability to the Setting Is Decreased

If a client is being treated in a rehabilitation or educational setting and exhibits dangerous behaviors, there is some liability to the overseeing organization. Parents or surrogates of students or other clients in the setting can sue for damages and can hold the owners or administrators responsible for any harm that might come to their family member. A client who ceases running away, threatening, or harming other clients or staff means one less headache for administrators and fewer calls to the attorneys who have to prepare for possible litigation.

RISK-BENEFITS FOR EACH BEHAVIORAL PROCEDURE

All behavioral procedures, including those that are benign (such as positive reinforcement), have risk factors associated with them. In some texts these are referred to as "considerations" (Cooper et al., 2007, p. 370). Of course, they have benefits as well. To help behavior analysts look at the risks and benefits of specific behavioral procedures, we have developed a series of worksheets. As shown in Figure 16.3, the sample worksheet for time-out, the *considerations* (i.e., risks) include increased aggression, avoidance, and reductions in desirable behavior. The benefits for time-out, as shown in the worksheet, include moderate-to-rapid decrease in behavior, convenience, and the fact that time-out can be combined with other behavioral procedures. The responsible BCBA will want to research each behavioral procedure that is proposed and prepare a procedures worksheet. Care should be taken to ensure that the summary at the bottom of the page is balanced and objective.

Risk-Benefit Worksheet

ABA Procedure: Time-Out

Special Methods: 1) Non-exclusion time-out (planned ignoring, withdrawal of positive reinforcer, contingent observation, time-out ribbon) 2) Exclusion time-out (time-out room, partition time-out, hallway time-out)

Risks	Notes
1. Can produce unexpected results	This could be a problem but the BA can be in the room for the first few days.
2. Can produce emotional responses	Mom is worried about this.
3. Can stigmatize the client in the setting where it is used	This has not been a problem with this teacher in the past.
4. The mediator using time-out may try it on others	The BA will need to monitor the aide, teacher will also watch for unsanctioned uses.

Benefits	Notes
1. Ease of application	This is a plus since we are working with classroom aides
2. Time-out is widely accepted as an appropriate treatment	The school administration is okay with time-out as long as it is approved by the parents, they have a time-out room, it is approved safe.
3. Rapid suppression of behavior	The teacher would appreciate a quick reduction in the target behavior
4. Can be combined with other procedures	We will use teacher administered token economy for appropriate behavior

Summary Risks vs Benefits: Overall it would appear that the benefits outweigh the risks for time-out in this setting. It will be necessary for the BA to be present the first week to make sure all goes well. The mother has approved the use of time-out for at least one month to see how it works.

Figure 16.3 A model risk-benefit worksheet for one specific procedure, time-out. One worksheet is filled out for each ABA procedure after reviewing research on the risks and benefits. The summary at the bottom represents a balanced, honest representation to the client of the risks vs. the benefits.

RECONCILE THE RISKS AND BENEFITS WITH THE KEY PARTIES INVOLVED

Including risk-benefit analysis in our standard operating procedures essentially adds one more important step to the process of providing ethical treatment. After the intake, a functional assessment is performed. Then a review of the literature reveals a list of likely treatments ranked from most to least restrictive.

At this point, a risk-benefit analysis of the proposed procedures is carried out by filling out forms similar to those previously shown, and a meeting is held with the consumer (or surrogate) to review the notes (see Figure 16.4). There may be some give and take with the person if there are questions about certain side effects or possible unpredictable behavioral effects. These should be noted and revisions made as necessary. If, after the discussion, the consumer does not feel comfortable with a procedure, it may be necessary to withdraw one method in favor of another. It is important to note that it is far better to have this discussion on the front end rather than have some sort of blow-up partway

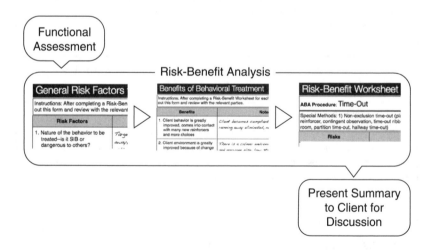

Figure 16.4 Reconciling the risks and benefits with the key parties involved. The procedure starts with a functional analysis, and after considering the risks and benefits, a summary is presented to the client for discussion.

through a course of treatment. At the conclusion of the meeting, all parties should reach consensus on the course of action to be taken. The necessary paperwork will be signed and filed, and treatment can begin with assurance that the risks have been identified and minimized to everyone's satisfaction.

THREE ADDITIONAL BENEFITS FOR THE BCBA AND THE PROFESSION

While they will probably not appear on a risk-benefit form or enter into the discussion with clients, three additional benefits deserve consideration. First, the BCBA or BCaBA who is able to make significant improvements in target behaviors as well as to improve the quality of life for the client and others will have not only a sense of relief that everything worked according to plan but also increased confidence in his ability to

> Being able to show positive effects builds confidence, improves morale, and encourages future participation in the profession.

take on similar cases in the future. Being able to show positive effects builds confidence, improves morale, and encourages future participation in the profession. A second benefit is the reduction of liability to the designer of the behavior plan. Getting through a case successfully means the dark cloud of uncertainty has disappeared, at least for the present.

One last benefit is the possible contribution to the body of knowledge of ABA and good public relations for the field. While we cannot solicit testimonials from clients, clients often tell others that they were satisfied or even overjoyed with the behavior analysis services that improved their lives.

17

Delivering the Ethics Message Effectively

Behavior analysts are becoming increasingly sophisticated when it comes to knowing and understanding the content of the Professional and Ethical Compliance Code for Behavior Analysts. In-service training, written materials, continuing education opportunities, and conferences throughout the country are providing behavior analysts with high quality professional training related to the Code.

However, while they may know the code items, many behavior analysts have a difficult time with knowing what to say to another person or exactly how to handle a situation when an ethics problem has been identified. Telling others "No" or giving direct, honest feedback that what they are doing is not appropriate are tasks that fall into the range of awkward and uncomfortable for many people, behavior analysts included. Knowing exactly what to say and what to do when faced with an ethics issue is often far more difficult than identifying the actual issue and specific code item.

> What behavior analysts are having a hard time with is what to say to another person or exactly how to handle a situation when an ethics problem has been identified.

THE IMPORTANCE OF COMMUNICATIONS SKILLS

Topping off the list of skills for the behavior analyst who wants to make a difference is the ability to be a good communicator. In *25 Essential Skills and Strategies for the Professional Behavior Analyst: Expert Tips for Maximizing Consulting Effectiveness* (Bailey & Burch, 2010), we presented three chapters on interpersonal communications with colleagues, supervisors, and direct reports. We also described how effective communication or a lack of communication skills affects one's ability to persuade and influence others. When it comes to delivering a message about ethics, you will need to be as much a communicator as you are a behavior analyst.

There will be times when you will need to address an ethics question immediately. This means thinking on your feet and knowing the ethics Code. You might need to refer to the Code for the exact section number and wording, but it is the responsibility of every behavior analyst to know and understand the content that is covered in the Code.

Know the Ethics Code

Immediate Response Required

A Board Certified Behavior Analyst (BCBA) was working with Ami, a 5-year-old girl whose parents were divorced. The child's father was a wealthy businessman who owned a nationally recognized chain of electronics stores. Because he traveled constantly, he saw his little girl only periodically. Ami was basically mute, but, over a short period of time, the behavior analyst had her saying words and short phrases. Shortly after Ami began speaking in three-word sentences, the dad, on one of his infrequent visits home, observed a session. Tears rolled down his cheeks, and as he was leaving, he said, "You have done such wonderful things for Ami . . . I know you are just getting started, and money is probably tight. I would like to give you a little token of appreciation. Maybe you and your roommates could use a new flat-screen TV and a Blu-Ray disc player. Does that sound good?" The behavior analyst had to respond immediately, or a *delivery truck would be dropping off a $2,000 high-definition TV to her apartment. Because she attended an ethics workshop at her state association meeting, she knew behavior analysts should not accept gifts. Even though she could not cite the Code number, she had the perfect instant response: "Thank you so much for appreciating the work I've done with your daughter. We behavior analysts have an ethics Code, and I am not allowed to accept gifts. I am delighted you are so pleased with Ami's progress."*

Buy Some Time

Unlike the situation where you need to respond immediately, there will be other times when confronted with an ethical issue that you need to buy some time by saying, "Let me get back to you on that. I will call you later this afternoon" or "I need to check on this; I'll have an answer for you at Tuesday's meeting." Buying time is a good strategy if the ethical issue seems to be in a gray area and you feel the need to review the ethics Code, talk to your supervisor, or consult with a trusted colleague.

A behavior analyst who was enrolled in a master's degree program was consulting in the homes of several children. At one visit, a mother said, "You know, there are times when we are busy during the week, and it is hard to fit in these therapy sessions. You don't have classes on the weekends, so I was thinking maybe we could change some of our sessions to Saturday

> **Buying time is a good strategy if the ethical issue seems to be in a gray area.**

mornings. What do you think?" This was a gray area for the young behavior analyst. She needed to recuperate on the weekends, to meet with her study group, and to prepare for exams. Something about this request just didn't feel right. The behavior analyst was acquainted with the Code and was certain there was not one that said, "It is unethical for you to give up your weekends." "I'll have to check with my supervisor and get back to you," was the perfect response. Later that day, the supervisor took her call and said a request like this was a mixed professional/ethical issue. The firm had a policy that therapy sessions are run when supervisors are available to handle emergencies (i.e., no weekends).

On the ethical side, the parent agreed at the onset to certain conditions for the therapy (i.e., weekdays only). If the parent was now acting as though she could move sessions around depending on her changing mood or social opportunities, there was a good chance the child's verbal behavior training was not a high priority. The feedback to the mother was straightforward: "I checked with my supervisor about changing our sessions to Saturdays. She says this is against our company policy, which permits us to work only during hours that supervisors are available to handle emergencies. I'm sorry, but we'll have to stick with our regular weekday sched-ule. If you really want to switch to another day, my supervisor said to just give her a call. Do you need her number?"

There may be times when feedback about an ethical issue needs to be given to a client, parent or family member, another behavior analyst, a nonbehavioral professional, a supervisor, or a supervisee. In each case, the behavior analyst should think about whether delivering the message is enough. Does a supervisor need to be contacted? Do staff members need to be informed about some-thing a client did? Should an agency be notified about something that has been witnessed?

DELIVERING THE ETHICS MESSAGE TO A CLIENT

The ethics Code identifies the client as the individual person along with the family and agency (Code 2.01). In the following case, we are referring to the client as the individual with the target behaviors. In most cases, clients are children, and they won't be involved with ethical misconduct. However, there are situations where behavior analysts work with high-functioning adult clients, and they can present some ethical challenges.

Shari was a BCaBA who was assigned to work to a group home for high-functioning male clients. When Dan, one of the clients, started flirting with her, she put his inappropriate comments on extinction. Then he asked, "Shari, why don't you and I go out on Friday night? You can come and pick me up, and we can go to a movie and out to eat." Clients in the group home had many opportunities for community outings, and this was clearly a request for a "date." Shari knew instantly that dating a client would be a violation of the ethics Code. What should she say?

Here are some things she should *not* say:

> "Well, okay, Dan, and we can work on your social skills. Let me
>   think about it."
> "I'm busy on Friday night."
> "Umm, no, Dan, I've got a boyfriend."
> "Sorry, I'm just not that into you."

These excuses imply that if she was not busy and did not have a boyfriend, Shari would be open to going out with Dan. Accepting the invitation with a plan of training social skills along the way will send a mixed message to Dan. He will think he's just scored a date. Remember the fundamentals of good communication: don't send mixed messages, and don't lie. Shari could say, "Dan, I like you as a friend, but I work here, and it is not appropriate for me to go out with a client. Staff members go on outings with the group and some take clients out for training, but we can't go on dates with clients. In my job, I have something called an ethics Code—it is a set of rules that says I cannot go out with clients. It just would not be appropriate."

> **Remember the fundamentals of good communication: don't send mixed messages, and don't lie.**

When Shari was telling us her story, we knew what was coming before she said it. She did a good job giving Dan the message as previously presented, and then he said, "I'm getting my very own

Table 17.1 Breakdown of Shari's Initial Response to the Date Request

What You Do	What You Say
Use of an autoclitic	"Dan, I like you as a friend ..."
State the facts/situation	"But I work here, and it is not appropriate for someone who works here to go out with a client ..."
Refer to the Code	"I have something called a Code of Ethics ..."
Tell what the Code says	"It says I can't go out with clients ..."
Summarize	"It would not be appropriate."

place in a few weeks. I won't be a client anymore, and I have a job lined up at Goodwill. Then can we go out?"

When clients and family members transition to the status of "no longer a client," it brings up a special ethical dilemma. Is there any likelihood that they will come back into the system? Does your company have a policy about dating former clients (or their parents)? Shari replied with, "Dan, I like you as a friend, but I'm sorry, I'm not interested." Table 17.1 provides some guidelines for knowing what to say when someone asks you to do something unethical.

DELIVERING THE ETHICS MESSAGE TO PARENTS AND FAMILY MEMBERS

As much as parents love their children and family members and want to help them, it is astounding how many ethical challenges they can present for behavior analysts. Not taking data, making up stories, not carrying out the program, and crossing the line so their attempts of discipline constitute abuse are just some of the issues reported by behavior analysts.

Erica M. was the mother of Cooper, a 10-year-old boy who was diagnosed with autism. Cooper had very basic expressive language (one to two word sentences such as "Want milk," and "Go outside"). He had frequent tantrums that were set off by noises and not getting what he wanted. He also had a self-stimulatory behavior of licking the area under his bottom lip frequently enough to cause calloused skin the full length of his lower lip. There were two other children in the busy home. The BCBA, Melvin, was becoming increasingly frustrated because Cooper's behaviors were getting worse both at school and home, Mrs. M. was not taking the data needed, and the other children revealed that when Cooper was having a tantrum, she gave him a cookie "to get him to calm down."

Melvin went to the home and met with Mrs. M. He told her how the data were important "so we can help Cooper's behavior get better." It seemed as though the heart-to-heart talk worked magic, and Mrs. M. had the data sheets ready when Melvin arrived for the next few visits. Before long, Melvin began to notice that something was strange about the data. One day's data was scored for a time period when Melvin knew Cooper was attending an after-school event. Further, the data showed that Cooper was engaging in no self-stimulatory face licking, yet his face was so inflamed there was bleeding at the edges of the calluses. Melvin knew that Mrs. M. was busy making up the data as he pulled into the driveway.

Here's what Melvin should *not* do or say:

> *He should not storm into the house and say, "Mrs. M., you have been making up the data. I have been truthful with you, and if you are going to lie to me, I quit. I know when the data are not real."*

Here's what Melvin *should* say: (He found a better way to handle this situation so he could get the necessary data. He talked to Mrs. M. at the beginning of the next session):

> *"Hi, Mrs. M. I noticed your new rose bushes. They look so nice. My mom always had a rose garden when I was growing up." (Mrs. M. talked about her gardening.) Without asking for the data sheet, Melvin said, "Let's talk about Cooper. So, how has it been going?" (Mrs. M. simply said, "Okay.") "Would you say he was having more tantrums or less or about the same?" (Mrs. M. said that some days were worse than others). Melvin said, "This has got to be tough for you. You really have your hands full, and I know a 10-year-old with tantrums can be a real challenge." At this point Mrs. M. began to talk about how she was tired and some days she wasn't sure she could do it all. "You're a great mom," he said. "I know your kids mean the world to you. Can*

we take a look at the data for the last few days?" He reviewed the data sheet and asked, "With all you've got going, how are you feeling about taking data?" Mrs. M. said, "Okay." Then Melvin told her, "You know, these data don't make sense. When I look at the boxes you've checked off—see here and here—it looks like Cooper is never having a tantrum or licking his face. But his lips are dried and chapped. Can you talk to me about that?" Mrs. M. said she had noticed Cooper licking his lips when he watched television and worked on the computer at night. This was the "screen time" he earned as a reinforcer, and data weren't collected then. This made sense, and Melvin was able to modify the data collection procedure. Melvin then asked about the data for tantrums. Mrs. M. admitted she was too busy to fill out the forms. She usually did it right before Melvin arrived, and sometimes she forgot what happened a few days earlier. Melvin felt that he'd simply caught Mrs. M. making up data, so he said, "I really need your help getting the data taken properly. In my field, we have a Code of ethics, and it actually says I am required to have accurate data to provide behavioral treatment for Cooper. If I believed the data were not accurate and we couldn't get it right, Cooper could lose his behavioral services. I would not be able to work with him anymore. Anytime you have questions, just let me know."

Table 17.2 summarizes what Melvin should do and say in this situation.

Table 17.2 Breakdown of Melvin's Response to Mrs. M. Regarding Falsifying Data

What You Do	What You Say
Establish rapport	"Hi, Mrs. M. I noticed your roses . . . "
Ask questions/listen	" . . . how has it been going?"
	" . . . how are you feeling about taking the data?"
Be respectful/understanding of others	"This has gotta be tough for you . . ."
State the facts/situation	"This data doesn't make sense."
Refer to the ethics Code	"In my field, we have a Code of ethics . . ."
Summarize—describe what could happen if the ethics Code is not followed	"Cooper could lose his behavioral services."

DELIVERING THE ETHICS MESSAGE TO AGENCIES, SUPERVISORS, OR ADMINISTRATORS

Unfortunately, we've had a number of behavior analysts in our workshops describing situations where an administrator has asked the behavior analyst to do something unethical. Asking the behavior analyst to make up data or assessment results or to say that services for a client were needed when they were not (or vice versa) or asking the consultant to work with a friend's child who was not an official client are some of the administrator-related ethics issues our workshop participants have encountered.

In some cases, the behavior analyst ends the story with, "and so I no longer work there. I could not sleep at night. I found another job." In other cases, the behavior analyst said, "I didn't know what to do. I love the clients, and I love the actual job. I was afraid if I told anyone or refused to do what was asked, I would get fired. I need my job. I've got two mouths to feed at home."

Wendy was the new BCBA at a residential facility. She had the job of her dreams in her favorite city. After she had been on the job a few months, the administrator called her into the office. "Rumor has it that we are having a review team visit sometime toward the end of the week. I need your help with some behavior programs." She went on to explain that the review team would be checking for assessments and data that were missing for several clients from the last review. She then slid a list across the desk to Wendy. The administrator was asking Wendy to make up assessment results for four clients who had not yet been seen by behavioral services.

Here's what Wendy should not say (we always urge restraint in dealing with supervisors; think before you speak—there is often a lot on the line):

> *Don't ever say, "Are you kidding me?" or "Are you out of your freaking mind? No way am I lying for you," or "Wait until the board hears this."*

Here's what Wendy *should* say:

> *"So, what is it you want me to do?" The administrator tells her, "Just fill in the forms" (i.e., essentially make up the assessment results). In a respectful tone, Wendy tells the administrator, "I know you really want the facility to pass the review, but I haven't even seen these clients and this would not be right." The administrator's jaw is getting tense. She reminds Wendy that the facility could be in trouble with the state or even lose funding. "Ms. Schultz, I really love working here. I love the program, and I appreciate how much you care about the clients. But I am a Board Certified Behavior Analyst, and I have a code of ethics to uphold. You know I cannot fabricate assessment results. We could get in a lot more trouble for making up data than for not having it. How about this? I will schedule assessment dates for the clients and document those. I can do an initial visit with each client, and I will have notes on my visits when the assessment team comes. How would you feel about this?"*

Table 17.3 shows the analysis of Wendy's response.

Table 17.3 Breakdown of Wendy's Response to Administrator Request

What You Do	What You Say
Ask questions	"So what is it you want me to do?"
Be respectful and understanding of others	"I know you want the facility to do well on the review . . ."
Present your point of view	"but I have never assessed the clients and this would not be right."
	"I really love working here, I love the program . . ."
Reinforce what others are doing right	"and I appreciate how much you care about the clients"
Refer to the ethics Code	"but I have a Code of ethics to uphold and I can't fabricate assessment results . . ."
Present a solution	"How about this? I can schedule assessment dates . . ."

DELIVERING THE MESSAGE TO NONBEHAVIORAL PROFESSIONALS

One of the most frequently asked ethical questions is: What do I say when other professionals aren't following the ethics Code? The problem is that other professionals do not have to adhere to our Code. They can spend every one of their professional days doing alternative fad treatments that are not scientifically validated. The problem comes when a behavior analyst and these professionals overlap on a case and are treating the same client.

Ian was the BCaBA on a treatment team for Cassie, a kindergarten client with autism. The child was ambulatory, but she had motor problems that resulted in an unusual gait, tripping easily, and dropping things. Although she was approaching 6 years of age, Cassie's expressive language was very limited, with only a few words to identify objects. When upset, the little girl would shriek, drop to the floor, curl into a ball, and refuse to get up. The occupational therapist (OT), Debbie, believed that sensory integration therapy was the best course of treatment. "She needs a day full of sensory activities so she can learn to make sense of her environment," the OT said at the treatment team meeting. "You can see she gets on the floor in the fetal position because we are not properly challenging her senses. Rolling on the exercise ball, playing with toys, and jumping on the mini-trampoline are all exercises that will help Cassie's brain develop and her behavior improve."

Here's what Ian *should not* say at the treatment team meeting (In meetings, we also urge restraint and firmly believe the advice "Think before you speak" applies here too.):

> Ian should *not* say, "And just exactly how would this help her brain improve?" or "Are you a big expert on brain functioning now?" or "No offense, but your field is not scientifically validated."

Here's what *should* be said to the nonbehavioral professional. Ian has completed his assessment of the child and felt, as a behavior analyst, he needed to address the tantrums and refusal to work. He also wanted to get Cassie moving along with language, and his plan was to talk to the speech therapist about discrete trial training. Ian understood that embarrassing other professionals in front of their colleagues is not a good way to win friends. Ideally, Ian would have seen what was coming and been able to meet with the OT before the meeting. He didn't, so the conversation in the treatment team went like this:

> *After Debbie, the OT, gave her spiel, Ian said in a calm, friendly voice, "I agree with Debbie that Cassie has some motor problems. She does fall down, and Debbie is right—it looks like she does not have good trunk control. I agree that Cassie could benefit from some exercise to strengthen her core and improve her balance. But I want to talk about the behavioral issues. When Cassie screams and drops to the floor, she is having a tantrum. I don't know what sets this off yet, but I would like to have tantrums added to the plan as a target behavior."*
>
> *The OT said, "If Cassie doesn't have to sit at the table like she is in college and she gets the exercise and play she needs, I am sure she'll be fine." Maintaining a calm and friendly demeanor, Ian told the team, "Tantrums are a behavioral issue.*

Table 17.4 Breakdown of Ian's Response to the Nonbehavioral Professional

What You Do	What You Say
Listen to others	Ian was polite while Debbie (OT) gave her report.
Be respectful of others	"I agree with Debbie that Cassie has motor problems . . ." etc.
Present your point of view	"I want to talk about the behavioral issues . . ."
State what you would like to happen	"I would like to have tantrums on the plan as a target behavior . . ."
Refer to the Ethics Code	"I'm bound by a Code of ethics that says the next step is a functional analysis."
Present a solution	"We need to put the FA and behavior program with data collection on her plan."

Table 17.4 shows the analysis of Ian's verbal reply to the nonbehavioral professional.

In Cassie's case, we do not know what sets off the tantrums. As a behavior analyst, I'm bound by a Code of ethics that says the next step is to do a functional analysis. This will involve taking data throughout the school day. If I am going to work with Cassie, we need to put the FA and behavior program with data collection on her plan."

DELIVERING THE MESSAGE TO ANOTHER BEHAVIOR ANALYST

In some ways, dealing with another behavior analyst who is violating the ethics Code is easier than dealing with others, because the behavior analyst should know the Code. In other ways, it can be more difficult and awkward to give feedback to a behavioral colleague, especially if that colleague is working for a competing program or consulting firm.

Matt was a BCBA whose students (BCaBAs) told him about another behavior analyst (Dr. X) who was billing for clients she never saw. It seems the BA would talk to staff, then would write a program or send a data sheet and would bill for the services. Matt felt very uneasy about this, but he decided he should intervene. He called Dr. X and asked if she had a few minutes to talk. Matt began the conversation like this: "We've known each other for a long time, and we're both professional behavior analysts. I've been hearing about a situation that I wanted to ask you about. Is there any chance you consult via phone and don't see the clients?"

Matt's response is shown in the breakdown of Table 17.5.

If Dr. X had said no, this was a misunderstanding, she did this only once when she was sick but immediately got out to see the client when he was well, the conversation could have ended.

Unfortunately, Dr. X said that business was booming and that she was just trying to cover all the bases. When she knows the staff members are reliable, she will consult by phone and email; she can help more clients and meet the demand and improve her cash flow. "I've got boat payments too, you know," was her parting

Table 17.5 Breakdown of Matt's Response to the Virtual Behavior Analyst

What You Do	What You Say
Be respectful of others	"I know you care about people . . ."
Ask questions	"Is there any chance you consult via phone?"
Present your point of view	"I don't want to see you get in trouble . . ."
Refer to the ethics Code	"Have you looked at the ethics Code lately?"
Present a solution	"You could hire BCBAs to work for you."

shot. Matt's response was, "I know you care about people and you have always been a responsible professional. I don't want to see you get in trouble or your reputation get trashed. Have you looked at the Code lately? You could hire BCBAs to work for you; then they would sign the assessments and be responsible. My reading of the Code is that you can't sign an assessment for a client you have never seen. I just wanted to let you know I'm concerned as a fellow professional."

SUMMARY

Knowing the ethics Code forward and backward does not guarantee that you will be effective in helping others understand it. You will probably have several opportunities each week to educate someone about our ethics Code and to indicate why it is important as we strive to deliver effective treatment.

The first part of being effective is identifying something that is not quite right. The second part is knowing what to say and how to say it. This can be difficult, especially for new, younger BCBAs who may have to bring the ethics message to someone older with a lot more experience. They should know and should follow

> Knowing the ethics Code forward and backward does not guarantee that you will be effective in helping others understand it.

18

Using a Declaration of Professional Services

When it comes to ethics, prevention is a far better strategy than having to solve the awkward or difficult problems that arise because someone didn't know the difference between right and wrong. Ethical challenges confront the BCBA on almost a daily basis. Most are not crisis sized but rather are more like the daily meteor showers that our Earth experiences from outer space. Tiny pings on the radar of decision making can irritate, confuse, and confound the behavior analyst who is try-

> Tiny pings on the radar of decision making can irritate, confuse, and confound the behavior analyst who is trying to do the right thing.

ing to do the right thing. These small challenges can sneak up on you just when you least expect them. They are camouflaged in normal conversations in the form of requests for small favors or tiny slivers of gossip. Wouldn't it be great if everyone would just follow the rules? Or, in our terms, why can't we bring some stimulus control to this aggravating situation? Well, there is good news. It is possible to put up something similar to a video gamer's *deflector shield*. To prevent many ethics problems from occurring in the first place, the solution we are proposing is the use of a Declaration of Professional Practice and Procedures for Behavior Analysts. First suggested in one of our ethics workshops by Kathy Chovanec of Louisiana, this document is widely used in other professions to clarify rules and boundaries with clients at the initiation of services, before the meteor shower of ethical issues comes raining down.

> **Ethical challenges confront the Board Certified Behavior Analyst (BCBA) almost on a daily basis.**

Figure 18.1 shows a version of the full document that you can adapt to suit your particular situation. You might want to have more than one version for different types of clients. For example, a declaration for in-home services will vary considerably from residential group home consultation procedures.

AREAS OF EXPERTISE

The declaration starts by informing your client, or better yet your prospective client, about who you are and your credentials. The client should know some basic academic information about you, where you got your degree, the field in which you earned the degree, and the specific degree (e.g., BA, MA, PhD). Some consultants might be uncomfortable about providing this information, particularly if the degree is in experimental psychology or pastoral coun-

> **Clients have a right to know up front if you are practicing within the boundaries of your training and expertise.**

seling or was earned through a series of online courses from an unaccredited college. In any event, clients have a right to know about the education and training of their consultants. They should also know how many years you have been practicing and, most importantly, what you consider your specialty. Disclosing your specialty area is very important, because clients have a right to know up front if you are practicing within the boundaries of

Declaration of
Professional Practices and Procedures
for Behavior Analysts[1]

[YOUR NAME, Degree]
Board Certified Behavior Analyst™ (or other title)

[Your mailing address & telephone number & email]

For My Prospective Client/Client's Family

This document is designed to inform you about my background and ensure that you understand our professional relationship.

1. AREAS OF EXPERTISE

[Basically, in this section you explain your area of expertise. This can be as long or as short as you want as long as the client is fully informed of your area(s) of competence.]

I have been practicing as a behavior analyst for _____ years. I obtained my degree in *(field of study)* in *(year)*. My specialty is _____ (e.g., working with preschool children, parent training, etc.).

2. PROFESSIONAL RELATIONSHIP, LIMITATIONS, AND RISKS

What I Do

Behavior analysis is a unique method of treatment based on the idea that most important human behavior is learned over time and that it is currently maintained by consequences in the environment. My job as a behavior analyst is to work with behavior you would like to change. With your input, I can help you discover what is maintaining a behavior, discover more appropriate replacement behaviors, and then set up a plan to teach those behaviors. I can also develop a plan to help you acquire a new behavior or improve your skill level. Some of the time I will be treating you directly, and at other times I may be training significant others as well.

How I Work

As a behavior analyst, I do not make judgments about behavior. I try to understand behavior as an adaptive response (a way of coping) and suggest ways of adjusting and modifying behaviors to reduce pain and suffering and increase personal happiness and effectiveness.

You will be consulted at each step in the process. I will ask you about your goals; I will explain my assessment and the results of my assessment in plain English. I will describe my plan for intervention or treatment and ask for your approval of that plan. If at any point you want to terminate our relationship, I will cooperate fully.

Please know that it is impossible to guarantee any specific results regarding your goals. However, together we will work to achieve the best possible results. If I believe that my consultation has become nonproductive, I will discuss terminating therapy and providing referral information to you for a smooth transition.

---

[1] For clients/family members who would have a difficult time reading this document as written, you will need to explain each section in easy-to-understand language.

Figure 18.1 Declaration of professional practices and procedures for behavior analysts.

3. CLIENT RESPONSIBILITIES

I can only work with clients who fully inform me of any and all of their concerns. I will need your full cooperation as I try to understand the various behaviors that are problematic for you. I will be asking a lot of questions and making a few suggestions, and I need your total honesty with me at all times. I will be showing you data as part of my ongoing evaluation of treatment and expect that you will attend to the data and give me your true appraisal of conditions.

One of the most unique aspects of behavior analysis as a form of treatment is that decisions are made based on objective data that are collected on a regular basis. I will need to take baseline data to first determine the nature and extent of the behavior problem that we are dealing with; then I will devise an intervention or treatment and continue to take data to determine if it is effective. I will show you this data and will make changes in treatment based on this data.

Under my code of ethical conduct, I am not allowed to work with you in any other capacity except as your behavior therapist or consultant. If I am working in your home with your child, it is not appropriate for you to leave the premises at any time or to ask me to take your child to some other location that is not directly related to my services.

I will need a list of any prescribed or over-the-counter medications and/or supplements in addition to any medical or mental health conditions; this information is kept confidential.

Behavior analysis therapy does not mix well with non-evidence-based treatments. If you are currently involved with other therapies, please tell me now. If, during the course of our treatment, you should contemplate starting other therapies, please let me know immediately so we can discuss the implications.

I expect that if you need to cancel or reschedule your appointment that you call as soon as you are aware of the change. If I do not receive 24-hour notification of your cancellation or you fail to show for an appointment, then you may be charged for the appointment.

4. CONDUCT CODE

I assure that my services will be rendered in a professional and ethical manner consistent with accepted ethical standards. I am required to adhere to the *Professional and Ethical Compliance Code for Behavior Analysts* issued by the Behavior Analyst Certification Board*. A copy of this Compliance Code is available upon request.

Although our relationship involves very personal interactions and discussions, I need you to realize that we have a professional relationship rather than a social one. According to my professional code of ethics, it is not appropriate for me to accept gifts or meals and it is not appropriate for me to be involved with your personal activities, such as birthday parties or family outings. [Modify this to suit your situation.]

Figure 18.1 (continued)

your training and expertise. In a recent case, for example, a Board Certified Behavior Analyst with two years' experience in autism and developmental disabilities was asked by a parent to help with a suicidal and possibly homicidal teen on the autism spectrum. When she reminded the frantic mom that this was not her area of expertise, she was scolded for not being sensitive to the mother's

If at any time and for any reason you are dissatisfied with our professional relationship, please let me know. If I am not able to resolve your concerns, you may report these to the following: Behavior Analyst Certification Board, Inc. 8051 Shaffer Parkway, Littleton, CO 80127, USA

1-720-438-4321, info@bacb.com, http://bacb.com

5. CONFIDENTIALITY

In [your state], clients and their therapists have a confidential and privileged relationship. I do not disclose anything that is observed, discussed or related to clients. In addition, I limit the information that is recorded in your file to protect your privacy. I need you to be aware that the confidentiality has limitations, as stipulated by law, including the following:

- I have your written consent to release information.
- I am verbally directed by you to tell someone else about a particular situation.
- I determine that you are a danger to yourself or others.
- I have reasonable grounds to suspect abuse or neglect of a child, disabled adult, or an elder adult.
- I am ordered by a judge to disclose information.

6. APPOINTMENTS, FEES, AND EMERGENCIES

[In this section you will describe how appointments are set and how fees are charged. It may also be necessary to indicate who to contact in case of emergencies.]

The current fee for my services is_____. Billing will be handled as follows:_____. [Modify this to suit your situation.]

7. This document is for your records. Please sign the attached form indicating that you have read and understand the information in this declaration.

WITNESS	CLIENT

BEHAVIOR ANALYST	DATE

Figure 18.1 (continued)

needs: "I'm desperate here, can't you see that? I'm afraid he's going to hurt himself or someone else, and I don't know who else to turn to. You've got to help me." When the BCBA told the mother that a referral to a suicide counselor was needed, the mother replied, "I don't want anyone else to know about this; I've got enough trouble as it is. Please don't tell anyone. Just tell me what to do."

Because behavior analysts have an obligation to keep current with new developments, this section of your declaration should be updated every year. If you lose clients because they do not feel comfortable with your expertise, consider this a blessing in disguise. Surely you do not want to find yourself partway down the therapy road, have something go terribly wrong, and then have it revealed that you were not qualified to take the case.

PROFESSIONAL RELATIONSHIP, LIMITATIONS, AND RISKS

What I Do

This section begins the dialogue in which you explain the basis for behavior analysis services. This can be a challenge to explain in plain English, or Spanish, or H'mong, but it is here that you express your understanding of human behavior. In the sample declaration (item 2), we say that behavior analysis is "Based on the idea that most important human behavior is learned over time and is maintained by consequences in the environment." It is critical to put this philosophy on the table to make sure your client understands your position. We also stress the notion that, as behavior analysts, we work with input from clients and that we develop a plan to acquire new behaviors. It is also important to let clients know that you work with significant others, so family members will play a key role in the therapy if this is part of the treatment design.

How I Work

It is important to spell out for clients that we do not make judgments about behavior and that it is part of our belief system that "psychological" pain and suffering come from behaviors that do not adapt well to the current environment. We do consult with parents, teachers, and other individuals significant in the life of our client (with permission). This should be clearly spelled out at the initial meeting where the declaration is presented. This concept is not likely to be something parents or family members might understand otherwise. Most people would expect you to come in and work only with the individual child or adult, much like the individual session a psychiatrist would have.

It is a strong selling point of behavior analysis that we are not interested in changing only behavior per se, but rather we work toward achieving important life goals for the client. We refer to this as

> **Behavior analysts work toward achieving important life goals for the client.**

"increasing personal happiness and effectiveness," but you can explain this in your own terms in the declarations you develop.

Finally, in the last part of this section, we urge BCBAs to make clear to clients that we are not in the "cure" business and that we do not guarantee results. If clients don't understand from the beginning that results aren't guaranteed, they will surely become disenchanted when expected outcomes are not forthcoming.

CLIENT RESPONSIBILITIES

Up to this point, the declaration has been a clarification of your qualifications and how you operate. In this section of the declaration, you'll cover the possibly touchy subject of what your expectations are for clients. We need and expect their full cooperation and their total honesty in dealing with us. In a recent case, it was discovered that the mother-in-law did not approve of applied behavior analysis services for the child. In most circumstances this might not matter, but in this matriarchal family, it did. Her position was that the tantrums, aggression, and noncompliance of the 7-year-old client were the result of poor discipline, and she blamed her son for not using his belt often enough. "He's just spoiled; he does not need psychologists poking around in his life. My son is to blame for treating a 7-year-old like a baby." The mother-in-law managed to cause so much trouble that the case was terminated, following standard protocols and necessary referrals.

If you can accomplish buy-in to the behavior analysis approach, you will probably be asking parents or family members to take data. The success of the treatment depends on those who take the data being absolutely honest about it. There may be considerable pressure to make the behavior analyst happy by presenting data that show the problem is solved. Fake data are a behavior analyst's worst nightmare. Essentially the mediators—whether parents, teachers, or night shift supervisors—is saying they do not value data collection; it means nothing to them. The importance of accurate data should be brought up not only prior to the onset of services but also occasionally during the entire treatment process.

> A total of 40% of adult Americans think astrology is scientific and 92% of college graduates accept alternative medicine.

Behavior analysts need to know more about the client than what the data related to the target behavior show. Many people are surprised that we are interested in medications that the client might be taking. Of course, it is critical to know about drugs and medications because they could affect the client's behavior. A particular concern these days is the contamination of our evidence-based methodology with popular but confounding and potentially dangerous treatments, or "cures," as they are sometimes called. It is best to find out when services begin if there are any procedures or substances in use such as strange or exotic vitamins, diets, or even "natural" products such as bee pollen as treatments. Data from the National Science Foundation biennial report (Shermer, 2002) shows what we're up against when it comes to dealing with nonscientists. The Shermer report (2002, p. 1) states that "30 percent of adult Americans believe that UFOs are space vehicles from other civilizations, 60 percent believe in ESP, 40 percent think astrology is scientific, 70 percent accept magnetic therapy as scientific, and 92 percent of college grads accept alternative medicine." In a broader sense, there is a more fundamental problem, which is that "70 percent of Americans still do not understand the scientific process, defined in the study as comprehending probability, the experimental method and hypothesis testing" (Shermer, p. 1).

Finally, to prevent annoying requests for last-minute schedule changes, it is a good idea to include your personal, or your company's official, policy on appointments. Note that we indicate a 24-hour notification policy, but your company may prefer some other time frame. If your policy is that missed weekday appointments cannot be moved to weekend days, this should be stated in the declaration.

Ethics Code

Behavior analysts should be proud of their strict Professional and Ethical Compliance Code and should make sure that all clients are aware of these standards. We recommend making a copy of the Code and presenting it to new clients, possibly with key sections highlighted. As a behavior analyst, you should also inform clients that if they have any questions about your conduct, they may contact the BACB directly.

One very important element we always recommend including in the declaration is a clear statement on gifts and invitations to dinners, parties, and celebrations. These small tokens of appreciation can start the unwary behavior analyst down the slippery slope to compromise of professional judgment and create dual relationships.

CONFIDENTIALITY

Breaches of confidentiality are among the most frequently occurring problems for BCBAs. Consultants are often asked to give out information that is confidential. Professionals who should know better also sometimes reveal confidential information. We recommend telling clients directly that you will keep any information given to you as strictly confidential and that you cannot give out information about any other clients. It is also wise to inform clients of the limits to confidentiality; that is, if you feel that the individual is a danger to himself or herself or others, you can share this information (Koocher & Keith-Spiegel, 1998, p. 121).

Be sure to check your local laws regarding reporting of abuse or neglect and include this information in your declaration. At our ethics workshops, we've had at least two cases reported to us in the past year where a BCBA saw abuse or evidence of abuse, reported it, and then was quickly fired by the family. Abuse notification is supposed to be confidential, but often there are leaks or the family figures out who reported the incident. Avoiding possible loss of revenue from a dropped case is no reason to look the other way when it comes to abuse and neglect; to do so is not only unethical but is also a violation of the law.

APPOINTMENTS, FEES, AND EMERGENCIES

In this final section of the declaration, you'll need to spell out the details of how appointments are made, your fees, how billing is handled, and the method for dealing with emergencies. At a recent conference on ethics for itinerant teachers who work in the homes of DD clients, there was considerable discussion as to whether clients should be given the cell phone numbers of their therapists. Most of the teachers who gave out their cell numbers regretted the decision. However, after giving some thought about the implications in your particular situation, you should specify the rule for phone calls from your clients. As a final item in this section, billing is a topic that most behavior analysts would not discuss with clients. At a minimum, you must describe how this is done and who should be contacted if there are complications. Other than turning in their hours, under normal circumstances, BCBAs are not involved in billing and will refer questions to a bookkeeper or the client's case manager.

DISCUSSION, AGREEMENT, SIGNATURES, DATE, AND DISTRIBUTE

At the end of the declaration information session, which could take 30 minutes or so, the client and the behavior analyst should sign the declaration. A witness should also be present to ensure that signatures are authentic. Date the document, provide a copy to the family, and keep one for your files.

19

A Dozen Practical Tips for Ethical Conduct on Your First Job

As a student, thoughts about ethical problems in your chosen profession probably seem far, far away and much more theoretical than practical at this point. However, in the not-too-distant future, perhaps just a few months from now, you will be taking your first job, and you will almost immediately begin to confront very real ethical dilemmas, some of which could affect the rest of your professional life. The purpose of this chapter is to outline some common issues that you are likely to encounter early on and to provide you with some practical tips for handling these issues.

CHOOSING A SETTING OR COMPANY

Your first big decision will involve choosing your first professional position. You might think that the primary considerations involve salary, location, potential for advancement, and matching your professional interests and behavioral skills. All of these are clearly important factors, but one additional choice involves consideration of the ethics and values of the company or organization itself. Currently, behavior analysts are a hot commodity in many cities across the country. For some agencies, hiring a Board Certified Behavior Analyst is essential for funding or to get relief from a federal lawsuit. In such cases, the agency may offer very high starting salaries and extensive benefit packages just to get you on board. Be wary and ask lots of questions about these positions that appear too good to be true. There is some chance that you will be asked to sign off on programs that you have not written, to approve procedures with which you are not familiar, or to support agency strategies that are more public relations smoke and mirrors than behavioral methodology. It is appropriate to ask about the history of the agency, company, or organization. Who founded it? What is the overall purpose or mission? How does behavior analysis fit into this mission? Are there any political issues connected with the organization? For example, is this company currently the target of a lawsuit? Are there any "citations" from a recent state or federal survey? How many other behavior analysts are currently employed there? What does the turnover in behavior analysts look like? What is the funding stream? Who are the clients? Who will you be supervising? Are they Board Certified Assistant Behavior Analysts (BCaBAs)? Will you be expected to attract and hire BCBAs?

You should be able to discern from the answers and the way the interviewer handles your questions whether there might be some ethical problems with the way that the company is run. A recent case, for example, involved a small private school for children with autism that had been started by parents. The school, initially headed by a BCBA-D, came under some scrutiny by parents and former employees when it was learned that the BCBA-D quit and was not replaced by another BCBA. Furthermore, two of the BCaBAs also left the organization and were not replaced by qualified professionals. The school, which originally attracted parents with its claim of a behavioral approach led by a certified person, still advertised itself as "behaviorally based" and still charged top dollar. It seems clear that going into this organization after more than two years without any behavior analysts could be a very challenging situation where it is likely that your keen awareness of ethical problems will be required. In another case, a rehabilitation facility that was part of a national chain billed itself as behavioral but hired a nonbehavioral person as the administrator. This is quite common, but in this case the individual was subtly anti-behavioral in her manner in dealing with the BCBAs and in her mode of operation. BCBAs were told that functional assessments did not need to be done on every client because it was obvious in some cases what the problem was, that data did not need to be taken—it took up too much time—and that she "trusted her staff's impressions" of client progress. In this case, the BCBA did not ask enough questions in the initial interview, she did not actually meet the administrator who held these views, and she was just a little too eager to start bringing home a paycheck.

WORKING WITH YOUR SUPERVISOR

In your job interview with the company or organization, it is a good idea to ask to meet your supervisor (this is rarely offered, but an ethical agency will comply if you make the request). Usually you will meet with the administrator, go on a brief tour, perhaps have lunch with some of the professional staff members, and then sit down with someone from the personnel office to negotiate your salary and benefits. However, meeting with the actual person by whom you will be supervised and report to is essential if you want to start your first job on a strong ethical foundation. There are many things you want to learn from potential new supervisors, including their style—are they a reinforcing kind of person or somewhat negative or withdrawn? Are they interested in working with you, or do they want you do to their work? Is there any chance they are somewhat jealous of you (you might have a degree from a prestigious graduate school) and you might be somewhat threatening? You should feel certain that you will not be asked to do anything unethical: (1) you will be able to do your work responsibly; (2) you will have the time and resources to do a great, ethical job; and (3) your supervisor will be there to guide you through troubled waters should the occasion arise. Your supervisor sets the tone for your work: "Just get it done; I don't care how" is far different from, "Be thorough, get it right, we want what is best for the clients." So, in meeting with new supervisors, you might ask about their philosophy of management and about the most difficult ethical issue they have encountered in the last year and how they handled it. Or

> In your first three months on any job, you have a grace period where you can ask questions without appearing to be dumb.

you might ask about any ethical issues you might encounter in your work. Just an open-ended question here should start the conversation going, and you can carry it from there with follow-up questions. When you're finished with this interview, you should have a secure, optimistic feeling about working for this person. If you feel apprehensive, think twice about taking the position, even if it is more money than you ever thought you'd see in a first job.

LEARN JOB EXPECTATIONS UP FRONT

If you have followed our suggestions up to this point, you will be happy and excited about your new position as a professional behavior analyst, making a good living, and helping people. Before you get too carried away, it would be a good idea to clarify exactly what you are supposed to do on a day-to-day basis. In your first three months on any job, you have a grace period where you can ask questions without appearing to be dumb. If you are going to be analyzing behavior, doing functional assessments, writing programs, and training staff, you should be well prepared from your graduate work. However, each agency and organization has its own method for doing each of these tasks. Your first assignment is to find out how administrators want it done. So, ask for copies of "exemplary" intake interviews, case work-ups, functional assessments, and behavioral programs. You can avoid embarrassing and potentially ethically challenging situations if you know how your new consulting firm routinely handles complaints from consumers, inquiries from review committees, and issues with state agencies. You can make sure that your ethical standards match the other professionals if you review minutes of habilitation team meetings and take a look at behavior programs written by previous behavior analysts. You might also want to know in advance if you are expected to chair the weekly case review meetings or to simply attend and whether, in these meetings, there is open discussion of ethical issues. One of the most important job-related ethical issues involves whether you will be working within your level of competence or whether you will be asked to take on cases or tasks for which you are not fully qualified.

One freshly graduated BCBA joined some others in a mental health facility, where she was assigned to the retarded-defendant program for which she was highly qualified. After a few weeks, she was asked to do some IQ testing on some mental health patients on short notice and under the pressure of a short deadline. She avoided taking intelligence-testing classes in graduate school and pointed this skill deficiency out to her supervisor, along with a question about why this requirement was not mentioned in the job interview. Then she pointed out how the BACB Code discourages behavior analysts from working out of their area. In some cases, this can brand a person as "not a team player," but really it is an ethical issue. Even if she did do the testing, it wouldn't be valid, and what if someone made a decision based on the test scores? This would surely be unethical. So, to avoid situations like this one, make sure that you ask plenty of questions early on, in the job interview and

> Most people just starting out on their first job are excited to be doing what they've dreamed about for years: practicing behavior analysis as a professional and making a difference in people's lives.

once you've started work, about what is expected, and establish the ethical boundaries necessary to protect yourself from engaging in unethical behavior.

DON'T GET IN OVER YOUR HEAD

Most people just starting out on their first job are excited to be doing what they've dreamed about for years: practicing behavior analysis as a professional and making a difference in people's lives. Early on, you are likely to be so grateful to have a job that you will do nearly anything to please your supervisor and upper-level management. Your enthusiasm could actually cause some harm, however, if it turns out that you take on more than you can handle or take on cases without some recognition of their difficulty. Your most important goal is to do a first-class job on every case that you are assigned. If you put your heart and soul into your work and watch out for conflicts of interest and "do no harm," you will be fine. But if you take on too many cases, then the next thing that will happen is that something falls through the cracks and clients start complaining, or your supervisor notices that your reports are sloppy, or the peer review committee starts making negative comments about your programs. In behavior analysis, doing more is not always associated with doing better. Quality counts. This is especially the case because you are affecting the life of a person with your work. You owe it to your clients as well as yourself to take only the number of cases that you can do well.

This same philosophy holds for taking on cases for which you have no expertise. In your training, you may not have worked at all with clients who are sex offenders or who are mentally ill or who are profoundly physically disabled. You do not do yourself or the client any favors by taking these cases. You will no doubt be under a lot of pressure to do so from parents, teachers, or program administrators, but if you just think of the harm that could be done by taking a case and then handling it badly, you will think twice about this decision. The easiest and most ethical stance to take is to always work within your range of competence. If you want to increase your range, the proper thing to do is to find another professional to serve as your mentor, someone who can give you proper training. You may also want to consider taking additional graduate course-work in a certain specialty area in addition to doing a practicum with supervision from an expert in that area.

USING DATA FOR DECISION MAKING

One of the distinguishing characteristics of the profession of behavior analysis is the reliance on data collection and data analysis. For us, data count. The Florida Association for Behavior Analysis has a motto: "Got data?" This logo is available on T-shirts, coffee mugs, and key chains as a takeoff on the "Got milk?" campaign. If there is anything that distinguishes us from other human services professionals, it is that we have a strong ethic in favor of objective data (not anecdotal, not self-report, not survey, not questionnaire) on *individual* behavior and the use of these data to evaluate the effects of treatments we devise and implement. Technically speaking, it is unethical to start an intervention without baseline data and an FA. And it is unethical to continue a treatment without taking additional data to see if it was effective. Most behavior analysts agree to this, and, although it is procedural, it is written into our Code of ethics (Code 3.01). So, as long as you are taking data and using them to evaluate a procedure, you are ethically in the clear, right? Well, not exactly. It is actually a little more complicated than this. First of all, as you know, there are data, and then there are *data*. The latter is reliable (meaning reliability checks that are carried out under specified conditions with a second, independent, observer, and reach a certain standard) and socially validated (meaning that standards of social validity have been met, again under specified conditions). It can be argued that a practicing behavior analyst not only has to take data to be ethical but that the data have to be reliable and valid; after all, there is a lot riding on the data: treatment decisions, medication decisions, retain or discharge decisions. As an ethical behavior analyst, you would not want to use data that were tainted by observer bias or that had a reliability of, for example, 50%. Furthermore, you wouldn't want to make treatment decisions if you thought the data had no social validity. So, what do you do as an ethical behavior analyst? You carry a burden to not only be data-based in your decision making but also to assure the client, client-surrogates, and your peers that you have quality data (again, not self-report, not anecdotal, not questionnaire).

One final issue about the use of data in decision making: this has to do with whether your treatment was in fact responsible for any behavior change. Again, to be ethical, it would appear that it is your responsibility to know in a functional sense that it was your treatment that worked and not some outside or coincidental variable. This suggests that as a practical, ethical matter you should be looking for ways of demonstrating experimental control either with a reversal, multi-element, or multiple-baseline design. If you put in a treatment and the behavior changes, you cannot in all honesty say it was your intervention, because you don't really know this for sure. Right about the time you instituted your treatment plan, the physician could have made a medication change, or the client may have developed an illness, or gotten some bad news, or perhaps someone else put in an intervention about the same time without your knowledge (e.g., the dietician cut back the person's calories, the client's roommate kept him up most of the night, etc.). In summary, as an ethical behavior analyst, you are obligated to be data-based in your decision making and to develop a high-quality data collection system that allows you to address issues of reliability, validity, and demonstrations of experimental control. You will find that professionals in many areas don't take all of these issues into consideration, and you should be proud to be part of a profession that takes data so seriously.

TRAINING AND SUPERVISING OTHERS

As a behavior analyst, you are probably already aware that others—usually paraprofessionals, who are trained by you—do much of the actual behavior treatment. Your job as the behavior analyst is to take the referral, qualify it to make sure it falls into the behavioral problem area (as opposed to, e.g., being a nursing problem or education issue), and then perform an appropriate functional assessment to determine likely causes of the behavior. Once this is determined, you will draw up a behavior program based on empirically tested, published interventions and then train someone to carry out the interventions. The ethical burden here is that you have to not only do the functional assessment according to accepted protocols but also to properly train the parents, teachers, residential staff, aides, or others. You are ultimately responsible for the program's effectiveness. This means that the program is carried out to your specifications. We know from the research literature that some methods of training work and that some don't. The most reliable form of training is not to simply give the parent a written program and then ask, "Are there any questions?" It is also not acceptable to explain the program and then leave a written copy. It is far more effective, and ethical, if you demonstrate the procedure, then have the parents practice, then provide feedback, have them try again, and so on until they do it right. Then you give them a written copy and maybe a videotape just to make sure, and then you may leave, but only for a short time, because you need to make a spot check a few days later to observe to see if they are doing it right. If not, you will need to do some correction, some more role play, and some more feedback, and then another visit a few days later. This is ethical training. Anything less is unethical.

Probably within six months of taking your first job, you will be supervising others (in some positions it may be immediate). As a behavior analyst, you again have a high standard to meet in terms of the quality of your supervision. Because we have such an extensive literature on ways of changing behavior in the workplace (in fact, there is a whole subspecialty called performance management; see Daniels & Bailey, 2014 for details), you now have an ethical obligation to be an effective supervisor. It's not all that difficult for a person steeped in basic behavior analysis procedures.

First, make sure you use the most effective antecedents. Don't lecture; demonstrate. After the demonstration, ask your supervisees to show you what they've learned. Then give immediate positive feedback. If you are training on written materials—for example, how to prepare a behavior program—show your trainee a sample of the best program that you can find. If necessary, break the task into smaller "bites" of material. And consider using backward chaining if necessary. Practice giving positive reinforcement for work you see and receive every day, many times a day. You will soon discover that your supervisees and trainees seek you out for advice and assistance; they will want to show you their work and get your approval. If you are working in a large organization, you could easily become the most reinforcing person without even trying hard.

The time will come when you do have to give negative feedback or show disapproval. If you've worked hard to give out contingent reinforcers, the person who receives this punisher will initially be somewhat shocked. He or she might have gotten the initial impression that you were just a "goody-two-shoes." Remember, the purpose of this correction is to change behavior, not punish the person, so you will also want to keep reinforcing the appropriate behavior. And don't forget your autoclitics (Skinner's [1957] *Verbal Behavior*, Ch. 12), those little comments that mean so much when you have to give someone negative feedback. "You know that I value what you do and that your work here has been excellent; now let me just point out something that is not quite right in this behavior program." One of the best books that can be used as a basic primer for business and professional skills is Dale Carnegie's (1981) *How to Win Friends and Influence People*. You should review this little gem as a supplement to what you have learned about behavioral supervision.

TIME KEEPING FOR BILLING

An essential part of professional ethics is accountability. One of the most important aspects of accountability is that you keep track of how you spend your time. Time is your primary commodity. For your first position, you may find that you are working on a "billable hour" model of compensation. In this system, the agency or consulting firm you are working for has contracted for your services at a certain rate per hour, and every documented hour that you work can be billed. You then receive a biweekly or monthly check based on your total number of billable hours. Although it may seem like a small matter, keep consistent, precise records of each and every billable unit—usually a quarter hour. Do not rely on your memory at the end of the day to reconstruct your activities, and do not average them out over a week. You will probably be able to find an app for your phone that will allow you to keep track of your date, time, and duration of contact as well as a brief note of your activity. At the end of the billing cycle, all you then need to do is perform a few simple calculations to determine your billing to the agency or consulting firm. One important feature of this accounting is that you understand how critical it is to your firm that you actually match your hours of service to the contracted hours. If your agency or consulting firm has contracted with a facility for you to spend 20 hours per week onsite, it is inappropriate for you to provide only 16 hours of service. First, the determination was made by the facility and your consulting firm that 20 hours was needed. The facility has set aside a certain amount of money for your services, and they have mutually agreed that they need 20 hours of consulting or therapy. For you to decide on your own to take a day off is inappropriate and constitutes a violation of the Code 1.04(c).

Needless to say, accurate and honest time accountability is essential to protect you from any allegation that you have been overbilling or that you have attempted to defraud a client or the government. This is especially urgent because there are cases being prosecuted at a high rate of physicians who are billing for clients they do not see or for services that are never rendered.

WATCH FOR CONFLICTS OF INTEREST
One of the subtlest unethical problems that can develop for any professional is that of a conflict of interest. Much is made in the

clinical literature of the problem of the psychotherapist having sex with clients either during or after therapy as a prime example of a conflict of interest and exploitation of a vulnerable person (the client) by a more powerful person (the therapist). Another example is the therapist developing some sort of business or social relationship with a client or former client, such as hiring that person to do work around the house or garden. In these cases, it is easy to see that such a relationship in our field could "impair the behavior analyst's objectivity" and affect his or her decision making. It would be a bad idea, for example, to take as a client someone you know, such as a friend, neighbor, or relative.

In behavior analysis, other relationships could be problematic that appear to be unique to our field. Behavior analysts are not restricted to the role of therapist. They are also supervisors, consultants, teachers, and researchers. Behavior analysts may sit on local or statewide human rights or peer-review committees. They may own a consulting firm or be an elected member of a professional association. The role of behavior therapist is also complicated by the fact that some therapy may be done in the home of the client, as in discrete-trial therapy with autistic children. In this case, the family of the child client may develop a stronger bond with the behavior analyst than would be the case if the sessions were conducted in a clinic or at school. It has been reported often that parents under these circumstances begin to see the therapist as part of the family and will want to include them on outings or invite them to birthday parties or other family events. Surely participating in such events would begin to "impair the behavior analyst's objectivity" and would serve as a prime example of a conflict of interest when the time came to give an objective account of the child's progress or for a recommendation to terminate the case. Serving on a peer-review committee where you are supposed to render an impartial judgment about the quality of a treatment program could present an objectivity problem if a friend or former student developed the case being reviewed. An owner of a consulting firm has a built-in conflict of interest when evaluating a new client; the potential income from the case may cloud the judgment of the owner from determining that it would be in the client's best interest to refer to another behavior analyst who has more expertise with a special behavior problem. Of course, the same conflict exists at the individual therapist level when he or she must decide to take a client who has been referred. Decisions in all these cases revolve around the question of what is in the client's best interest (Code 2.0: "The behavior analyst has a responsibility to operate in the best interest of clients") rather than what would benefit the therapist, the consulting firm, or the agency.

FIND A "TRUSTED COLLEAGUE" RIGHT AWAY

It is difficult to make ethical decisions in isolation. Without a sounding board, what appears to you to be an easy call may in fact be quite a complex dilemma. It is not always easy to determine whether some harm might come from a particular intervention. The effects could be delayed or subtle, and someone else with more experience than you could be a big help in making such a decision. Over time, you will feel more confident about your behavioral decisions, but in the beginning, to help build your confidence, we strongly recommend that you find a "trusted colleague" as soon as possible. Ideally, this would be another behavior analyst who is easily accessible and who is not your supervisor or your employer. For political and other reasons, the colleague probably should not work for "the competition" in your geographical area. Your trusted colleague is someone that you will entrust some rather deep thoughts of yours such as (1) "Am I really prepared to take this case?" or (2) "My supervisor is telling me do to X, but it seems unethical to me. What should I do?" or, even more importantly, (3) "I think I've made a big mistake; what do I do now?" With luck, you won't encounter any of these dilemmas in your first three months on the job, and you can use this time to try to find a person who is knowledgeable and whom you can trust. In your off-hours, your first three months on the job should be spent interacting with other professionals from your workplace and in your general locale. It's a good idea to get to know social workers, nurses, physicians, case managers, psychologists, and client advocates as well as any other behavior analysts in your area. This networking will serve other purposes, also, such as making referrals; in this process of getting to know your colleagues you should make the acquaintance of someone who can be more than a casual business associate and become a confidant. You will want to size up this person's approach to ethics and make sure that his or her approach to dealing with complex issues appears to be sound, thoughtful, and deliberate, not glib or cavalier. A BCBA with five or more years of experience who is careful in what she does, has a good solid reputation, and who seems friendly and approachable would be a good candidate. You want to find your trusted colleague well before anything "hits the fan," because you will want to have a well-established rapport with the person and feel confident that you can in fact trust him or her with your urgent ethical situation.

TOUCHING PEOPLE

Unlike ordinary office-based psychotherapy, behavior analysis often involves getting up close and personal with your clients. Especially for those behavior analysts working with the developmentally disabled, the physically challenged, and the behavior-disordered client, our treatments may involve touching or holding the person. Innocuous procedures like graduated guidance involve putting your hands on the client to help him or her learn how to do some task like self-feeding or dressing. Toilet training can involve helping the person remove his or her clothes, and tooth brushing requires the behavior analyst to stand behind the client and help manipulate the brush. Many behavior analysts routinely give "hugs" or brief shoulder massages as reinforcers without thinking of the possible adverse consequences. In all of these cases, even the most benign and well-intentioned action on your part could be misconstrued or misinterpreted as "inappropriate touching."

This accusation could come from the client, the client's parents, a nearby caregiver, or even a visitor who just happened to be on the scene. Other more intrusive behavioral procedures are even more problematic: time-out almost always involves holding the client while taking him or her to the time-out room. Manual restraint, or attempting to apply mechanical restraints, can also present issues of potential misinterpretation or misperception (from "You hurt me" to "You hurt him deliberately" to "Were you groping her? I think you were, you pervert; I'm going to call the police!").

The ethical behavior analyst will always abide by the dictum "Do no harm" and will avoid, at all costs, doing anything to in any way physically or emotionally harm a client. But the cautious, ethical behavior analyst will also make sure that he or she is never the target of a mistaken or malicious accusation of physically inappropriate behavior toward a client. To this end, we make the following recommendations:

1. To avoid a false client allegation of inappropriate touching, always make sure to have another person (often called a "witness") present.
2. Make sure the witness knows what you are doing and why you are doing it.
3. If you are involved in any sort of physical restraint use, make sure that you have been properly trained and certified to do so.
4. If you know of a client who has a history of false reports of inappropriate touching, be wary of close contact with that person unless you have done (1) and (2).
5. Avoid cross-sex therapeutic interactions (male therapist–female client) unless there is absolutely no alternative (you will still want to follow rules (1) and (2), however).

The purpose of these recommendations is not to encourage you to become cold and impersonal in your interactions with clients but rather to promote some thinking about how your warm and affectionate behavior might backfire on you.

DEALING WITH NONBEHAVIORAL COLLEAGUES

Most of your professional time will be spent with colleagues who are not behavior analysts. Depending on the setting and the history of the agency or organization, this could present you with some serious ethical dilemmas. For example, if as part of a habilitation team you find that the consensus of the group is that your client should receive "counseling," you have an ethical obligation to propose a behavioral alternative, Code 2.09(b), and to raise questions about whether there are any data on treatment efficacy, Code 2.09(a), for "counseling." This could make you somewhat unpopular on the team. Furthermore, if this treatment is actually implemented, you have an obligation to request that data be taken to evaluate it (Code 2.09(d)).

To make matters worse, if you are ethical in following this ethics Code, you are likely to be in the spotlight when it comes time to evaluate your proposed interventions. You should be ready with copies of published studies to justify your treatments and be scrupulous about taking objective and accurate data to determine if the interventions in fact worked with this client.

You may soon discover that the other professionals with whom you deal are not very aware of the ethics code for their field or pay it little heed. Or worse, you may discover that their code of ethics is not very clear on issues regarding client's rights, use of empirically based procedures, or the evaluation of treatments using data. New students working in the field for the first time are often shocked at the cavalier way meetings are conducted and decisions are made regarding clients. It is not unusual for one person to dominate the meetings, with a clear motive of getting it over with as soon as possible. Often no data are presented, and weak or no rationales are given for pushing certain treatment approaches. Convenience, a "just go along" attitude, and disregard for ethics in general are often the mode for these meetings, which appear to be held more for show than for function.

Initially, as a new and probably junior member of the treatment team, you will probably want to sit quietly and observe; try to determine who is in charge and what the custom is for handling decision making. You may need to consult with your supervisor about how to best handle these situations and to consult the Code for key foundation points. Before you accuse anyone in public of engaging in unethical conduct, it would be wise to again check with your supervisor and then possibly meet with the person in question outside of the meetings to discuss your concerns. This may also be a time for you to consult with your trusted colleague. In extreme cases, where you and your supervisor feel that you have done everything possible to have some impact but have been unsuccessful, it may be necessary to terminate your involvement. Code 2.15 addresses the circumstances for such a dramatic move and describe how this should be done.

So, to end on a positive note, it is important to point out that the vast majority of nonbehavioral colleagues are kind and caring, mean well, and will tolerate you if you accept them. Most have never heard of behavior analysis, so you will have a chance to be an ambassador for the field and to educate them about current developments and how we are, in the utmost, concerned about the ethical, effective, and humane treatment of clients. Be patient, and give them a chance to educate you about their field. Be a good listener and a positive supportive person, and you will grow immeasurably as a professional yourself. Be honest about your own shortcomings (e.g., you may know very little about medications and how they work with certain behaviors) and open to other points of view. Over time, you will gain some perspective on how others view behavior and understand how you can nudge them toward a more behavioral perspective.

> **Be a good listener and a positive supportive person, and you will grow immeasurably as a professional yourself.**

SEXUAL HARASSMENT

Sexual harassment is one of those awkward, ugly topics that few people want to discuss unless pressed to do so. Despite years of education, legal rulings, and company fines, it still exists (U.S. EEOC, 2004). As a behavior analyst, you might think that you will never be subject to this kind of treatment by others. Although you would never intentionally treat another person in this degrading way, nonetheless, a few behavioral aspects of sexual harassment should be discussed for the new behavior analyst.

First, we need to address unwanted sexual advances. If you have some special work circumstances, you might be more likely to encounter this problem. BCBAs who work in the client's home may find that there are occasions when they are alone with a single parent of the opposite sex. Young female therapists seem most vulnerable if there is a divorced or single male in the house. The problem can start innocently enough with the person acting very interested in your work, perhaps sitting close, making strong eye contact, or smiling a lot. You might take this as just a very interested person who thinks that you and your work are fascinating. An extra-warm greeting, a hug that lasts just a little too long, or a touch to the arm or shoulder are the first clues that there may be something else afoot. Behavior analysts are trained to be superb observers of behavior, and this is the skill that you want to bring to bear at this time. Behavior analysts also know how to use differential reinforcement of other behaviors (DRO), punish behaviors, put them on extinction, or bring them under stimulus control to reduce their rate of occurrence. So, if you detect the early stages of unusually "familiar" behaviors, it is time to swing into action. Step one is to monitor your own behavior closely to make sure that you are not sending out any improper signals that advances might be welcome. This can be very difficult for a behavior analyst, because another aspect of your training no doubt involved becoming a big reinforcer for those around you, particularly your clients. This can easily be misconstrued as having a personal interest in the individual. Having determined that you are not in any way encouraging the person, you need to begin working on ways of decreasing the behavior. You might use DRO by reinforcing the person for sitting a little farther away from you; for any "romantic" eye-contact responses, look at the floor or at your paperwork, appear distracted, or abruptly conclude the meeting. Inappropriate touching can be handled with a "cold hard stare," with no smiling and possibly a no-nonsense, "That's really not appropriate, Mr. Robinson." If you catch this in the early stages and punish these tentative behaviors, your problem may be solved. If it has gone further than this and the person is very inappropriate (e.g., calling you at home, leaving personal email messages, or making any attempt to touch you), you need to discuss this immediately with your supervisor to determine if it is appropriate to inform authorities. If you believe you are being stalked, contact the authorities; your safety is of utmost importance.

The second major concern regarding sexual harassment is the possibility that someone else will accuse you of this behavior. We specifically train behavior analysts to be effective interpersonally, and this includes using head nodding, smiling, warm handshakes, and strong, effective verbal reinforcers. We encourage new consultants to "become a reinforcer" for those around you if you want to be effective. Different reinforcing behaviors are appropriate in different settings. In business and organizational settings, smiling, handshakes, and positive comments are all appropriate; on the shop floor, a pat on the back or shoulder hug might be acceptable. But you need to be careful that those you are "reinforcing" don't get the wrong idea and think that you are attracted to them. You might be working with a withdrawn child, for example, and trying to get her to stay on task or complete an assignment. At the first sign of success, you break into a smile, give "high fives," and then a hug. Over time, this will probably work to increase the on-task behavior; however, you may begin to also increase your rate of hugs, or they may become a little more enthusiastic. The next thing you know you get called into the principal's office, and she says, "I've just gotten off the phone with little Lucy's mother. Lucy has complained that you touched her in her private areas. Is this true?"

The best advice to new behavior analysts is to be courteous, polite, and friendly, but in all cases be professional. Do not let your enthusiasm for the progress of your client overwhelm you or the excitement of meeting a goal prompt you to get overly emotional and all "touchy-feely" with a client. Watch what you do with your hands at all times. As a check on your performance, ask yourself, "What if Channel Six Eyewitness News was here taping this? Would I still engage in this behavior?" If the answer is "No," then you need to modify your own behavior to prevent any misunderstanding or false accusations.

> The world would surely be a better place if everyone adopted the behavior analyst's ethical principles and put them to practical use every day.

A FINAL NOTE

Most behavior analysts get so caught up in the intense minute-to-minute practice of their profession that it is difficult to stop and ask, "Is there an ethical problem here?" For example, you might be caught off guard at the grocery store by an individual who wants to know about another client. It starts off innocently enough, but then the inappropriate question slips out: "I saw you working with Jimmy C., Marge's little boy. Why are you working with him?" Or, you are working hard to please your new supervisor and are right at your limit when she asks you to "drop everything and take charge of this now." Your tendency is to do what you are told, to try to be a compliant worker. But the task might be out of your range of competence or it might be unethical ("Bring your bottle of Wite-Out;[1] we've got to fix some records. The review team is due here tomorrow").

It is hoped that this book will help you think about ethics not in a theoretical or purely moral sense but rather in the practical sense of doing the right thing; doing no harm; being just, truthful, fair, and responsible; affording dignity to your clients; promoting their independence; and in general treating others the way that you would like to be treated. The world would surely be a better place if everyone adopted the behavior analyst's ethical principles and put them to practical use every day.

20

A Code of Ethics for Behavioral Organizations[1]

Adam Ventura
World Evolve, Inc.
and
Jon S. Bailey
Florida State University

THE ORIGIN OF A CODE OF ETHICS FOR BEHAVIORAL ORGANIZATIONS

The foundation for the first organization to create a code of ethics for behavioral organizations was established in 2005. It was then that Dr. Jon Bailey began receiving ethics questions from former students, participants in ethics workshops, and from individuals using the Association for Behavior Analysis International Hotline. In case after case, it appeared that professional behavior analysts who were sincerely attempting to adhere to the Guidelines for Responsible Conduct were being hindered by their own companies. Obstacles to ethical conduct were thrown at these behavior analysts from every direction. There were too many cases to manage, cost-cutting procedures such as prepackaged "cut-and-paste" behavior programs, restrictions on the use of functional analysis prior to treatment, and even pressure to bill for more hours than actually worked. It seemed impossible for these honest, hardworking professionals to meet both their employment requirements and their ethics Code obligations. And then a solution appeared in the form of a new idea. Why not create a code of ethics for organizations, one that would require administrators, CEOs, and boards of directors to commit in writing to support the BACB Guidelines (which are now the Professional and Ethical Compliance Code for Behavior Analysts)? Knowing that Adam Ventura had both a strong interest in ethics at the organizational level and the ability to implement change, Jon Bailey approached him in 2014 and proposed a joint (nonprofit) venture to take the concept to an actual working model.

COEBO

COEBO is an acronym from a paper, "The *C*ode *o*f *E*thics for *B*ehavioral *O*rganizations,"[2] which began as a seven-item proposal that organizations providing behavior analytic services would sign and agree to uphold within their respective companies. The original concept was that COEBO would be analogous to a national Better Business Bureau® specifically tailored for ethics for organizations delivering behavior analysis services. An ethical organization would supplement the BACB Code and "wrap around" the behavior analysts that work there to eliminate any subtle forces to act unethically.

Through many discussions with behavior analysts and providers in the community, it became clear that the code needed to be expanded. In approximately one year of vetting by over 50 representative agencies from around the world who strongly support ethics, that confirmation grew into a comprehensive code of ethics with 10 comprehensive categories. The COEBO began as an idea to improve organizational behavior and grew into an assembly of behavior analysts, business owners, academics, and consumers of behavior analytic services collaborating to advance their shared goal of improving the ethical conduct of organizations that provide behavior analytic services into one succinct set of guidelines. Over time, our work together on this very vital matter became affectionately known as the "COEBO Movement."

COEBO OPERATIONAL DEFINITIONS

Throughout the process of creating this organizational code of ethics, we identified the importance of operationally defining what an organization that provided behavior analytic services was so that interested parties could easily classify their entity as being behavioral or not. For that purpose, we established the following definition of a *behavioral organization*:

> *A behavioral organization is an entity registered as a corporation (Type C or S) or as a limited liability company (LLC) that employs or contracts with professionals who are certified or registered with the Behavior Analyst Certification Board (BACB) to conduct applied behavior analysis services, as defined by the BACB, within the community. A behavioral organization employs at least one full time certified practitioner in good standing with the BACB and employs or contracts at least one Board Certified Behavior Analyst (BCBA) in good standing with the BACB.*
>
> (http://bacb.com/maintain)

While deliberating over who would or could be held accountable for implementing this new code of ethics, it seemed necessary to identify different types of workers within a given organization and the parts of the code for which they should be responsible. The following operational definition for a behavioral worker emerged:

> *A worker is: Any employee, contractor, student, or intern that has a current work agreement with the behavioral organization and is assigned by the behavioral organization to provide applied behavior analysis services to consumers or other organizations within the community.*

A need grew organically out of this movement for providers to publicly declare that their organization's behavior was ethical.

COEBO CREDENTIALING

As vetting continued, there was some expansion of the guidelines and a determination to develop a code for providers so they could publicly declare that their organization's conduct was ethical. We then began working toward a way of confirming that an agency or business that was interested would meet our standards.

WHY WE CREATED THE COEBO

With a focus on how the COEBO could help to improve the behavior analysis work environment, participants pinpointed three areas where it was felt that the COEBO could have the biggest impact. These were: (1) screening and recruitment of new employees, (2) consumer protection, and (3) COEBO provider relations.

Screening and Recruitment of New Employees

Every year, hundreds of students finish master's and doctoral programs in behavior analysis and leave their cohorts of friends and trusted mentors to enter the workforce. After spending two or more years running the intense and rigorous gauntlet of conceptual behavior analysis, arduous data collection sessions, and detailed analysis of hundreds of journal articles, these champions of study embark triumphantly on a journey to identify an organization to put their well-honed and mastered skills to use.

Upon graduation, the bright-eyed, newly minted BCBAs are showered with emails offering what appear to be glamorous jobs around the world helping children with special needs and disseminating the gospel of behavior analysis. This propaganda comes complete with offers of substantial remuneration (high five figures), hedonistic benefits ("Ski in the morning and surf in the afternoon"), and flexible schedules a part-time retiree would envy. Interviews are replete with rhetoric on how prospective employers and their companies make a difference in the community and how employment with their institution would allow the naive behavior analysts to make a difference in the world every day they come to work. Once hired, these freshman behavior analysts quickly develop an acute sense of regret when they realize that the companies are not what they seemed.

As discussed previously, recruitment, much like sales, can involve bait and switch scenarios resulting in ill-informed decision making by behavior analysts looking for jobs. This practice ultimately produces disillusioned employees with serious morale problems. However, with the advent of an organizational authentication process for the COEBO, job seekers can quickly and easily

> Job seekers can quickly and easily identify organizations that behave ethically and have company policies and standards that mirror their own goals and values.

identify organizations that behave ethically and have company policies and standards that mirror their own goals and values.

Unfortunate scenarios like the one just described were one of the topics discussed when the utility of the code was debated and whether or not to move forward with the project. Although the topic of recruitment was discussed at length, two other areas of concern were discussed as well: consumers and other providers.

Consumer Protection

In an effort to protect not only the employee but the consumer as well, the COEBO takes into account the well-being of consumers and the delivery of ABA services within the provider community. Every day, parents of children recently diagnosed with a developmental disability walk out of a doctor's office with a diagnosis report in one hand, a prescription for ABA therapy in the other, and a determined look in their eyes. Saddled with bad news, these warrior parents return home with a renewed sense of resolve, determined to help their children. As they frantically search the

Internet for the meaning of ABA and someone to provide them with this mysterious service, their search becomes peppered with advertisements claiming that ABA services provided by this or that company can cure autism. They are bombarded with manufactured testimonials from what appear to be fake consumers claiming that a company is "the best" and that they would "recommend it to everyone!"

Eventually, the family locates a provider and manages to speak with someone. Their discussion is brief. Each question the guardian asks about ABA is met swiftly with a rebuttal involving insurance and the cost of the service. Later, on the first day of services, a therapist knocks on the door of the family's home without notice and explains that he is there to begin ABA therapy. The parents graciously invite the therapist into their home and ask him about his education and experience in ABA. The therapist reveals that this is his first job in ABA and that he is not really sure what to do, but he was told that a supervisor would be coming by once per month for an hour to check on them.

This type of horror story is the wellspring from which the COEBO was born. Consumer information is of paramount importance when making a decision on a service that could have a profound impact on the health and well-being of a child. The COEBO provides consumers and their families with a safeguard against such inappropriate business behavior and allows consumers to more comfortably peruse the ABA therapy marketplace without fear of obtaining an ABA "therapy lemon."

COEBO Provider Relations

As the number of clients requesting ABA services increases, the number of organizations providing these services increases as well, creating an expanding community of providers. Within this community, small- to medium-size businesses arise, and the mixture of behavior analysis and entrepreneurialism begins. When this cocktail of science and business is created and two otherwise disparate fields are unwillingly thrust together, a slow-burning reaction occurs, resulting in the weaker of the two forces being diluted by the influence of the stronger force.

From an economic standpoint, there is currently a supply and demand problem: the need is great and the demand for services is high, thus creating a void in the supply of trained professionals to service these consumers. Despite the supply problem, the COEBO was created in part to help establish an equal playing field where all behavioral organizations would play by the same set of rules describing how to ethically treat each other within the marketplace.

CONSTITUTION OF THE COEBO ORGANIZATION

A Mission-based Organization. Throughout the evolution of COEBO, we understood the logic of utilizing behavior analytic principles and technologies. So, in an effort to evoke quality behavior from the COEBO provider community, we decided to incorporate behavior analytic technologies into the COEBO development. In essence, we felt that a behavioral organization should use behavior analysis to accomplish its goals. To begin this process, we thought it was important to explain to the behavior analysis community why COEBO existed, articulate those thoughts into a condensed, easily measureable statement, and then create contingencies that help us achieve that purpose; in short, we decided to create a mission-based organization.

Our Mission and Vision. Our hope was that one day, the majority of behavioral organizations around the world would strive to obtain and maintain credentials from the COEBO organization. These two simple, but powerful, statements became our mission and vision and served to develop subsequent measures and pinpoints that would eventually become the foundation of our organization.

Structure of the Organization. To bring COEBO to life, a network of professionals in behavior analysis was created to help achieve this purpose. From this network, a declaration of business ethics was enacted, and a doctrine was established to create a community of ethically behaving organizations.

Initially, an email listserv of behavior analysts from around the country was created as a working group to help gather suggestions for updates to the code. Later, this listserv was used to petition professionals from within the behavioral community to join together as a panel to decide on issues on which the community could not agree. Once this board was created, a constitution was needed to help ratify the inner workings of this entity and establish the working organization.

> A federation was devised whereby a union of self-governing organizations all agreed to behave in accordance with a code of ethics designed by a central organization created from the community of providers later referred to as the COEBO Community.

In an effort to avoid a top-down organizational structure, it was decided that a separation of powers was best to help emphasize the doctrine of community and collaboration. Two separate but equal divisions were established to help manage the workflow of operations within this new organization. The first division was designed as an executive committee that would create, update, and interpret the code. This committee is made up of both the COEBO Board and the COEBO Community and structured as a bicameral body so that everyone will have a say in what items are added, changed, or removed from the code. The second division was created as an administrative committee designed to take care of logistical operations for the organization. With these branches in place and an organization created, what was left was to open the doors to providers of behavioral services. Thus, an association was created whereby a union of organizations, the COEBO Community, all agreed to behave in accordance with a code of ethics designed by a central organization.

THE CODE OF ETHICS FOR BEHAVIORAL ORGANIZATIONS

Here is a working version of the COEBO as of September 1, 2015. To retrieve an up-to-date copy, please go to COEBO.com.[3]

1. COEBO Compliance

a. Behavioral organizations only provide truthful and accurate information in documentation submitted to COEBO and correct inaccurate information immediately.

b. Behavioral organizations hold all workers accountable to COEBO and require them to take and pass a competency-based examination on the COEBO as well as annual follow-up trainings.

2. BACB Compliance

a. Behavioral organizations in COEBO must uphold the BACB® *Professional and Ethical Compliance Code for Behavior Analysts.*

b. For COEBO members, the Code applies to all behavioral and nonbehavioral workers across all departments in their organization.

3. Responsible Conduct of a Behavioral Organization

a. *Integrity:* Behavioral organizations follow through on their professional obligations, commitments, and contractual agreements and refrain from making professional commitments or agreements that they cannot keep with their workers and consumers of their services.

b. *Coercive Contingencies:* Behavioral organizations do not advance any social or economic contingencies (e.g., bonus, raise, promotion, etc.) that might unduly influence the behavior of any board-certified professional in their organization to violate the BACB Guidelines.

c. *Accepting Gifts:* Behavioral organizations do not allow any behavioral or nonbehavioral worker to accept gifts, money, in-kind services, or goods in any amount or value that was not originally outlined in their agreement for services.

d. *Reporting:* Behavioral organizations do not ask any behavioral or nonbehavioral professional to modify timesheets, reports, or clinical recommendations to satisfy organizational needs and follow all applicable rules and guidelines communicated by funding sources.

e. *Whistle Blowing:* Behavioral organizations support any workers who come forward with any claim of undue pressure to violate the BACB® *Professional and Ethical Compliance Code for Behavior Analysts* or COEBO.

f. *Ethics Officer/Committee:* Behavioral organizations appoint an internal ethics officer and/or ethics committee to address internal ethical issues.

4. **The Behavioral Organization's Responsibility to the Consumer**

a. *Consumer Rights:* Behavioral organizations obtain any relevant consent from consumers of their services and inform the consumers of their services, before the commencement of service delivery, where they can file complaints about any service provided by their organization.

b. *Terms & Financial Arrangements:* Prior to the implementation of services, behavioral organizations provide, in writing, the terms of consultation, requirements for providing services, financial agreements, and responsibilities of all parties. If terms change, behavioral organizations will notify consumers.

5. **The Behavioral Organization's Responsibility to the Worker**

a. *Continuing Education:* Behavioral organizations support all of their credentialed workers in fulfilling their continuing education requirements. They provide workers with flexibility in scheduling as long as the event does not interfere with ethical treatment of their clients or create undue hardship on the organization.

   b. *Materials:* Behavioral organizations provide their *behavioral* workers with materials that they require to complete their job ethically provided that the materials requested are reasonable and do not create undue hardship on the organization.
   c. *Supervision:* Behavioral organizations provide adequate supervision by a qualified supervisor for all behavioral workers requiring supervision. Behavioral organizations do not ask supervisors to supervise more individuals than one person can competently manage.
6. **The Behavioral Organization's Responsibility to Behavior Analysis**
   a. Behavioral organizations make every effort to have their workers participate in behavior analytic events and promote behavior analysis to the public.
   b. Behavioral organizations make every effort to have their workers participate in behavior analytic events and promote COEBO to the public.
7. **Behavioral Organizations Responsibility to Other Behavioral Organizations**
   a. *Hiring and Recruitment:* Behavioral organizations will not advance any social or economic contingencies (e.g., bonus, raise, promotion, etc.) that might unduly influence any behavioral or nonbehavioral worker to solicit another behavioral organization's workers to leave their organization or make disparaging remarks about other organizations.
   b. *Collaboration and Cooperation:* Behavioral organizations make any and all reasonable efforts to work in concert with other behavioral organizations.
8. **Behavioral Organization and Service Delivery**
   a. *Caretaker Training:* Behavioral organizations provide stakeholder training to consumers of their services.
   b. *Evidenced Based Services:* Behavioral organizations only provide behavioral services that are evidence based and true to the BACB Task List and/or Seven Dimensions of

Applied Behavior Analysis and will abstain from offering or promoting "alternative treatments" that are not
evidence based.

c. *Competence:* Behavioral organizations do not ask behavioral workers to work out of their area of competence.

d. *Transferring Services:* Behavioral organizations will
make reasonable efforts to locate and contact another
suitable provider within the vicinity of the consumer
unless the consumer requests otherwise and will ensure
that all consumer files, materials, data, or information
required for continuity of care is transferred to the new
provider within a reasonable time frame.

9. Behavioral Organization and Media

a. *Marketing:* Behavioral organizations accurately represent the services they provide and do not engage in
misleading, false, or deceptive statements. Behavioral
organizations do not exploit consumers of their services
for marketing purposes or solicit testimonials and/or
post testimonials in any format.

10. Behavioral Organization and Compliance with the Law

a. *Laws and Regulations:* Behavioral organizations conform
to the legal and moral codes of the social and professional community of which the behavioral organization
is a member.

b. *Confidentiality:* Behavioral organizations will take any
and all reasonable precautions to respect the confidentiality of those with whom they work and consult.

SUMMARY

When creating the code, its utility was discussed in great detail,
as well as how this type of organizational declaration of ethical
behavior could be helpful in the field of behavior analysis.

If an organization could identify itself as a reputable, ethical company, many benefits would arise from such an endeavor. Recruitment of new students and employees, consumer information, and

interprovider relations would all benefit. A community of providers would be established, all of who would agree to comply with the same ethical code. ABA providers who could identify themselves as behaving ethically would be able to compete on an equal playing field. Thus, adoption of the code attests not only to the ethical behavior of each individual organization but also the ethical behavior of the ABA community as a whole.

Section

Four

The BACB Code, Glossary, Scenarios, and Further Reading

In Section IV, we present the latest version of the Professional and Ethical Compliance Code for Behavior Analysts (8–11–15) in Appendix A, followed by the glossary to accompany it, developed by the BACB, in Appendix B. Appendix C contains 50 ethics scenarios, which now include "Hints" about how to approach solutions to these ethical dilemmas, and Appendix D contains our list of suggested further reading in ethics. This section also includes the references and the subject index.

Appendix A: Professional and Ethical Compliance Code for Behavior Analysts

The Behavior Analyst Certification Board's (BACB's) Professional and Ethical Compliance Code for Behavior Analysts (the "Code") consolidates, updates, and replaces the BACB's Professional Disciplinary and Ethical Standards and Guidelines for Responsible Conduct for Behavior Analysts. The Code includes 10 sections relevant to professional and ethical behavior of behavior analysts, along with a glossary of terms. Effective January 1, 2016, all BACB applicants, certificants, and registrants will be required to adhere to the Code.

PROFESSIONAL AND ETHICAL COMPLIANCE CODE FOR BEHAVIOR ANALYSTS

CONTENTS

3.0 Assessing Behavior
3.01 Behavior-Analytic Assessment [RBT]
3.02 Medical Consultation
3.03 Behavior-Analytic Assessment Consent
3.04 Explaining Assessment Results
3.05 Consent-Client Records

4.0 Behavior Analysts and the Behavior-Change Program
4.01 Conceptual Consistency
4.02 Involving Clients in Planning and Consent
4.03 Individualized Behavior-Change Programs
4.04 Approving Behavior-Change Programs
4.05 Describing Behavior-Change Program Objectives
4.06 Describing Conditions for Behavior-Change Program Success
4.07 Environmental Conditions that Interfere with Implementation
4.08 Considerations Regarding Punishment Procedures
4.09 Least Restrictive Procedures
4.10 Avoiding Harmful Reinforcers [RBT]
4.11 Discontinuing Behavior-Change Programs and Behavior-Analytic Services

5.0 Behavior Analysts as Supervisors
5.01 Supervisory Competence
5.02 Supervisory Volume
5.03 Supervisory Delegation
5.04 Designing Effective Supervision and Training
5.05 Communication of Supervision Conditions
5.06 Providing Feedback to Supervisees
5.07 Evaluating the Effects of Supervision

6.0 Behavior Analysts' Ethical Responsibility to the Profession of Behavior Analysts
6.01 Affirming Principles ^{RBT}
6.02 Disseminating Behavior Analysis ^{RBT}

7.0 Behavior Analysts' Ethical Responsibility to Colleagues
7.01 Promoting an Ethical Culture ^{RBT}
7.02 Ethical Violations by Others and Risk of Harm ^{RBT}

8.0 Public Statements
8.01 Avoiding False or Deceptive Statements ^{RBT}
8.02 Intellectual Property ^{RBT}
8.03 Statements by Others ^{RBT}
8.04 Media Presentations and Media-Based Services
8.05 Testimonials and Advertising ^{RBT}
8.06 In-Person Solicitation ^{RBT}

9.0 Behavior Analysts and Research
9.01 Conforming with Laws and Regulations ^{RBT}
9.02 Characteristics of Responsible Research
9.03 Informed Consent
9.04 Using Confidential Information for Didactic or Instructive Purposes
9.05 Debriefing
9.06 Grant and Journal Reviews
9.07 Plagiarism
9.08 Acknowledging Contributions
9.09 Accuracy and Use of Data ^{RBT}

10.0 Behavior Analysts' Ethical Responsibility to the BACB
10.01 Truthful and Accurate Information Provided to the BACB ^{RBT}
10.02 Timely Responding, Reporting, and Updating of Information Provided to the BACB ^{RBT}
10.03 Confidentiality and BACB Intellectual Property ^{RBT}

10.04 Examination Honesty and Irregularities [RBT]

10.05 Compliance with BACB Supervision and Coursework Standards [RBT]

10.06 Being Familiar with This Code

10.07 Discouraging Misrepresentation by Non-Certified Individuals [RBT]

PROFESSIONAL AND ETHICAL COMPLIANCE CODE FOR BEHAVIOR ANALYSTS

RBT=The Code element is relevant to Registered Behavior Technicians™

@2015 Behavior Analyst Certification Board®, Inc. All rights reserved. Reprinted by permission. The most current version of this document is available at www.BACB.com. Contact ip@bacb .com for permission to reprint this material.

1.0 RESPONSIBLE CONDUCT OF BEHAVIOR ANALYSTS

Behavior analysts maintain the high standards of behavior of the profession.

1.01 Reliance on Scientific Knowledge (RBT)

Behavior analysts rely on professionally derived knowledge based on science and behavior analysis when making scientific or professional judgments in human service provision, or when engaging in scholarly or professional endeavors.

1.02 Boundaries of Competence (RBT)

(a) All behavior analysts provide services, teach, and conduct research only within the boundaries of their competence, defined as being commensurate with their education, training, and supervised experience.

(b) Behavior analysts provide services, teach, or conduct research in new areas (e.g., populations, techniques, behaviors) only after first undertaking appropriate study, training, supervision, and/or consultation from persons who are competent in those areas.

1.03 Maintaining Competence through Professional Development (RBT)

Behavior analysts maintain knowledge of current scientific and professional information in their areas of practice and undertake ongoing efforts to maintain competence in the skills they use by reading the appropriate literature, attending conferences and conventions, participating in workshops, obtaining additional coursework, and/or obtaining and maintaining appropriate professional credentials.

1.04 Integrity (RBT)

(a) Behavior analysts are truthful and honest and arrange the environment to promote truthful and honest behavior in others.

(b) Behavior analysts do not implement contingencies that would cause others to engage in fraudulent, illegal, or unethical conduct.

(c) Behavior analysts follow through on obligations, and contractual and professional commitments with high quality work and refrain from making professional commitments they cannot keep.

(d) Behavior analysts' behavior conforms to the legal and ethical codes of the social and professional community of which they are members.

(e) If behavior analysts' ethical responsibilities conflict with law or any policy of an organization with which they are affiliated, behavior analysts make known their commitment to this Code and take steps to resolve the conflict in a responsible manner in accordance with law. (See also, 10.02(a) Timely Responding, Reporting, and Updating of Information Provided to the BACB)

1.05 Professional and Scientific Relationships (RBT)

(a) Behavior analysts provide behavior-analytic services only in the context of a defined, professional, or scientific relationship or role.

(b) When behavior analysts provide behavior-analytic services, they use language that is fully understandable to the recipient of those services while remaining conceptually systematic with the profession of behavior analysis. They provide appropriate information prior to service delivery about the nature of such services and appropriate information later about results and conclusions.

(c) Where differences of age, gender, race, culture, ethnicity, national origin, religion, sexual orientation, disability, language, or socioeconomic status significantly affect behavior analysts' work concerning particular individuals or groups, behavior analysts obtain the training, experience, consultation, and/or supervision necessary to ensure the competence of their services, or they make appropriate referrals.

(d) In their work-related activities, behavior analysts do not engage in discrimination against individuals or groups based on age, gender, race, culture, ethnicity, national origin, religion, sexual orientation, disability, language, socioeconomic status, or any basis proscribed by law.

(e) Behavior analysts do not knowingly engage in behavior that is harassing or demeaning to persons with whom they interact in their work based on factors such as those persons' age, gender, race, culture, ethnicity, national origin, religion, sexual orientation, disability, language, or socioeconomic status, in accordance with law.

(f) Behavior analysts recognize that their personal problems and conflicts may interfere with their effectiveness. Behavior analysts refrain from providing services when their personal circumstances may compromise delivering services to the best of their abilities.

1.06 Multiple Relationships and Conflicts of Interest (RBT)

(a) Due to the potentially harmful effects of multiple relationships, behavior analysts avoid multiple relationships.

(b) Behavior analysts must always be sensitive to the potentially harmful effects of multiple relationships. If behavior analysts find that, due to unforeseen factors, a multiple relationship has arisen, they seek to resolve it.

(c) Behavior analysts recognize and inform clients and supervisees about the potential harmful effects of multiple relationships.

(d) Behavior analysts do not accept any gifts from or give any gifts to clients because this constitutes a multiple relationship.

1.07 Exploitative Relationships (RBT)

(a) Behavior analysts do not exploit persons over whom they have supervisory, evaluative, or other authority such as students, supervisees, employees, research participants, and clients.

(b) Behavior analysts do not engage in sexual relationships with clients, students, or supervisees, because such relationships easily impair judgment or become exploitative.

(c) Behavior analysts refrain from any sexual relationships with clients, students, or supervisees, for at least two years after the date the professional relationship has formally ended.

(d) Behavior analysts do not barter for services, unless a written agreement is in place for the barter that is (1) requested by the client or supervisee; (2) customary to the area where services are provided; and (3) fair and commensurate with the value of behavior-analytic services provided.

2.0 BEHAVIOR ANALYST'S RESPONSIBILITY TO CLIENTS

Behavior analysts have a responsibility to operate in the best interest of clients. The term client as used here is broadly applicable to whomever behavior analysts provide services, whether an individual person (service recipient), a parent or guardian of a service recipient, an organizational representative, a public or private organization, a firm, or a corporation.

2.01 Accepting Clients

Behavior analysts accept as clients only those individuals or entities whose requested services are commensurate with the behavior analysts' education, training, experience, available resources, and organizational policies. In lieu of these conditions, behavior analysts must function under the supervision of or in consultation with a behavior analyst whose credentials permit performing such services.

2.02 Responsibility (RBT)

Behavior analysts' responsibility is to all parties affected by behavior-analytic services. When multiple parties are involved and could be defined as a client, a hierarchy of parties must be established and communicated from the outset of the defined relationship. Behavior analysts identify and communicate who the primary ultimate beneficiary of services is in any given situation and advocate for his or her best interests.

2.03 Consultation

(a) Behavior analysts arrange for appropriate consultations and referrals based principally on the best interests of their clients, with appropriate consent, and subject to other relevant considerations, including applicable law and contractual obligations.

(b) When indicated and professionally appropriate, behavior analysts cooperate with other professionals, in a manner that is consistent with the philosophical assumptions and principles of behavior analysis, in order to effectively and appropriately serve their clients.

2.04 Third-Party Involvement in Services

(a) When behavior analysts agree to provide services to a person or entity at the request of a third party, behavior analysts clarify, to the extent feasible and at the outset of the service, the nature of the relationship with each party and any potential conflicts. This clarification includes the role of the behavior analyst (such as therapist, organizational consultant, or expert witness), the probable uses of the services provided or the information obtained, and the fact that there may be limits to confidentiality.

(b) If there is a foreseeable risk of behavior analysts being called upon to perform conflicting roles because of the involvement of a third party, behavior analysts clarify the nature and direction of their responsibilities, keep all parties appropriately informed as matters develop, and resolve the situation in accordance with this Code.

(c) When providing services to a minor or individual who is a member of a protected population at the request of a third party, behavior analysts ensure that the parent or client-surrogate of the ultimate recipient of services is informed of the nature and scope of services to be provided, as well as their right to all service records and data.

(d) Behavior analysts put the client's care above all others and, should the third party make requirements for services that are contraindicated by the behavior analyst's recommendations, behavior analysts are obligated to resolve such conflicts in the best interest of the client. If said conflict cannot be resolved, that behavior analyst's services to the client may be discontinued following appropriate transition.

2.05 Rights and Prerogatives of Clients (RBT)

(a) The rights of the client are paramount and behavior analysts support clients' legal rights and prerogatives.

(b) Clients and supervisees must be provided, on request, an accurate and current set of the behavior analyst's credentials.

(c) Permission for electronic recording of interviews and service delivery sessions is secured from clients and relevant staff in all relevant settings. Consent for different uses must be obtained specifically and separately.

(d) Clients and supervisees must be informed of their rights and about procedures to lodge complaints about professional practices of behavior analysts with the employer, appropriate authorities, and the BACB.

(e) Behavior analysts comply with any requirements for criminal background checks.

2.06 Maintaining Confidentiality (RBT)

(a) Behavior analysts have a primary obligation and take reasonable precautions to protect the confidentiality of those with whom they work or consult, recognizing that confidentiality may be established by law, organizational rules, or professional or scientific relationships.

(b) Behavior analysts discuss confidentiality at the outset of the relationship and thereafter as new circumstances may warrant.

(c) In order to minimize intrusions on privacy, behavior analysts include only information germane to the purpose for which the communication is made in written, oral, and electronic reports, consultations, and other avenues.

(d) Behavior analysts discuss confidential information obtained in clinical or consulting relationships, or evaluative data concerning clients, students, research participants, supervisees, and employees, only for appropriate scientific or professional purposes and only with persons clearly concerned with such matters.

2.07 Maintaining Records (RBT)

(a) Behavior analysts maintain appropriate confidentiality in creating, storing, accessing, transferring, and disposing of records under their control, whether these are written, automated, electronic, or in any other medium.

(b) Behavior analysts maintain and dispose of records in accordance with applicable laws, regulations, corporate policies, and organizational policies and in a manner that permits compliance with the requirements of this Code.

2.08 Disclosures (RBT)

Behavior analysts never disclose confidential information without the consent of the client, except as mandated by law, or where permitted by law for a valid purpose, such as (1) to provide needed professional services to the client, (2) to obtain appropriate professional consultations, (3) to protect the client or others from harm, or (4) to obtain payment for services, in which instance disclosure is limited to the minimum that is necessary to achieve the purpose. Behavior analysts recognize that parameters of consent for disclosure should be acquired at the outset of any defined relationship and is an ongoing procedure throughout the duration of the professional relationship.

2.09 Treatment/Intervention Efficacy

(a) Clients have a right to effective treatment (i.e., based on the research literature and adapted to the individual client). Behavior analysts always have the obligation to advocate for and educate the client about scientifically supported, most-effective treatment procedures. Effective treatment procedures have been validated as having both long-term and short-term benefits to clients and society.

(b) Behavior analysts have the responsibility to advocate for the appropriate amount and level of service provision and oversight required to meet the defined behavior-change program goals.

(c) In those instances where more than one scientifically supported treatment has been established, additional factors may be considered in selecting interventions, including, but not limited to, efficiency and cost-effectiveness, risks and side-effects of the interventions, client preference, and practitioner experience and training.

(d) Behavior analysts review and appraise the effects of any treatments about which they are aware that might impact the goals of the behavior-change program, and their possible impact on the behavior-change program, to the extent possible.

2.10 Documenting Professional Work and Research (RBT)

(a) Behavior analysts appropriately document their professional work in order to facilitate provision of services later by them or by other professionals, to ensure accountability, and to meet other requirements of organizations or the law.

(b) Behavior analysts have a responsibility to create and maintain documentation in the kind of detail and quality that would be consistent with best practices and the law.

2.11 Records and Data (RBT)

(a) Behavior analysts create, maintain, disseminate, store, retain, and dispose of records and data relating to their research, practice, and other work in accordance with applicable laws, regulations, and policies; in a manner that permits compliance with the requirements of this Code; and in a manner that allows for appropriate transition of service oversight at any moment in time.

(b) Behavior analysts must retain records and data for at least seven (7) years and as otherwise required by law.

2.12 Contracts, Fees, and Financial Arrangements

(a) Prior to the implementation of services, behavior analysts ensure that there is in place a signed contract outlining the responsibilities of all parties, the scope of behavior-analytic services to be provided, and behavior analysts' obligations under this Code.

(b) As early as is feasible in a professional or scientific relationship, behavior analysts reach an agreement with their clients specifying compensation and billing arrangements.

(c) Behavior analysts' fee practices are consistent with law and behavior analysts do not misrepresent their fees. If limitations to services can be anticipated because of limitations in funding, this is discussed with the client as early as is feasible.

(d) When funding circumstances change, the financial responsibilities and limits must be revisited with the client.

2.13 Accuracy in Billing Reports

Behavior analysts accurately state the nature of the services provided, the fees or charges, the identity of the provider, relevant outcomes, and other required descriptive data.

2.14 Referrals and Fees

Behavior analysts must not receive or provide money, gifts, or other enticements for any professional referrals. Referrals should include multiple options and be made based on objective determination of the client need and subsequent alignment with the repertoire of the referee. When providing or receiving a referral, the extent of any relationship between the two parties is disclosed to the client.

2.15 Interrupting or Discontinuing Services

(a) Behavior analysts act in the best interests of the client and supervisee to avoid interruption or disruption of service.

(b) Behavior analysts make reasonable and timely efforts for facilitating the continuation of behavior-analytic services in the event of unplanned interruptions (e.g., due to illness, impairment, unavailability, relocation, disruption of funding, disaster).

(c) When entering into employment or contractual relationships, behavior analysts provide for orderly and appropriate resolution of responsibility for services in the event that the employment or contractual relationship ends, with paramount consideration given to the welfare of the ultimate beneficiary of services.

(d) Discontinuation only occurs after efforts to transition have been made. Behavior analysts discontinue a professional relationship in a timely manner when the client: (1) no longer needs the service, (2) is not benefiting from the service, (3) is being harmed by continued service, or (4) when the client requests discontinuation. (See also, 4.11 Discontinuing Behavior-Change Programs and Behavior-Analytic Services)

(e) Behavior analysts do not abandon clients and supervisees. Prior to discontinuation, for whatever reason, behavior analysts: discuss service needs, provide appropriate pre-termination services, suggest alternative service providers as appropriate, and, upon consent, take other reasonable steps to facilitate timely transfer of responsibility to another provider.

3.0 ASSESSING BEHAVIOR

Behavior analysts using behavior-analytic assessment techniques do so for purposes that are appropriate given current research.

3.01 Behavior-Analytic Assessment (RBT)

(a) Behavior analysts conduct current assessments prior to making recommendations or developing behavior-change programs. The type of assessment used is determined by client's needs and consent, environmental parameters, and other contextual variables. When behavior analysts are developing a behavior-reduction program, they must first conduct a functional assessment.

(b) Behavior analysts have an obligation to collect and graphically display data, using behavior-analytic conventions, in a manner that allows for decisions and recommendations for behavior-change program development.

3.02 Medical Consultation

Behavior analysts recommend seeking a medical consultation if there is any reasonable possibility that a referred behavior is influenced by medical or biological variables.

3.03 Behavior-Analytic Assessment Consent

(a) Prior to conducting an assessment, behavior analysts must explain to the client the procedure(s) to be used, who will participate, and how the resulting information will be used.

(b) Behavior analysts must obtain the client's written approval of the assessment procedures before implementing them.

3.04 Explaining Assessment Results

Behavior analysts explain assessment results using language and graphic displays of data that are reasonably understandable to the client.

3.05 Consent-Client Records

Behavior analysts obtain the written consent of the client before obtaining or disclosing client records from or to other sources, for assessment purposes.

4.0 BEHAVIOR ANALYSTS AND THE BEHAVIOR-CHANGE PROGRAM

Behavior analysts are responsible for all aspects of the behavior-change program from conceptualization to implementation and ultimately to discontinuation.

4.01 Conceptual Consistency

Behavior analysts design behavior-change programs that are conceptually consistent with behavior-analytic principles.

4.02 Involving Clients in Planning and Consent

Behavior analysts involve the client in the planning of and consent for behavior-change programs.

4.03 Individualized Behavior-Change Programs

(a) Behavior analysts must tailor behavior-change programs to the unique behaviors, environmental variables, assessment results, and goals of each client.
(b) Behavior analysts do not plagiarize other professionals' behavior-change programs.

4.04 Approving Behavior-Change Programs

Behavior analysts must obtain the client's written approval of the behavior-change program before implementation or making significant modifications (e.g., change in goals, use of new procedures).

4.05 Describing Behavior-Change Program Objectives

Behavior analysts describe, in writing, the objectives of the behavior-change program to the client before attempting to implement the program. To the extent possible, a risk-benefit analysis should be conducted on the procedures to be implemented to reach the objective. The description of program objectives and the means by which they will be accomplished is an ongoing process throughout the duration of the client-practitioner relationship.

4.06 Describing Conditions for Behavior-Change Program Success

Behavior analysts describe to the client the environmental conditions that are necessary for the behavior-change program to be effective.

4.07 Environmental Conditions that Interfere with Implementation

(a) If environmental conditions prevent implementation of a behavior-change program, behavior analysts recommend that other professional assistance (e.g., assessment, consultation or therapeutic intervention by other professionals) be sought.

(b) If environmental conditions hinder implementation of the behavior-change program, behavior analysts seek to eliminate the environmental constraints, or identify in writing the obstacles to doing so.

4.08 Considerations Regarding Punishment Procedures

(a) Behavior analysts recommend reinforcement rather than punishment whenever possible.

(b) If punishment procedures are necessary, behavior analysts always include reinforcement procedures for alternative behavior in the behavior-change program.

(c) Before implementing punishment-based procedures, behavior analysts ensure that appropriate steps have been taken to implement reinforcement-based procedures unless the severity or dangerousness of the behavior necessitates immediate use of aversive procedures.

(d) Behavior analysts ensure that aversive procedures are accompanied by an increased level of training, supervision, and oversight. Behavior analysts must evaluate the effectiveness of aversive procedures in a timely manner and modify the behavior-change program if it is ineffective. Behavior analysts always include a plan to discontinue the use of aversive procedures when no longer needed.

4.09 Least Restrictive Procedures

Behavior analysts review and appraise the restrictiveness of procedures and always recommend the least restrictive procedures likely to be effective.

4.10 Avoiding Harmful Reinforcers (RBT)

Behavior analysts minimize the use of items as potential reinforcers that may be harmful to the health and development of the client, or that may require excessive motivating operations to be effective.

4.11 Discontinuing Behavior-Change Programs and Behavior-Analytic Services.

(a) Behavior analysts establish understandable and objective (i.e., measurable) criteria for the discontinuation of the behavior change program and describe them to the client. (See also, 2.15d Interrupting or Discontinuing Services)

(b) Behavior analysts discontinue services with the client when the established criteria for discontinuation are attained, as in when a series of agreed-upon goals have been met. (See also, 2.15d Interrupting or Discontinuing Services)

5.0 BEHAVIOR ANALYSTS AS SUPERVISORS

When behavior analysts are functioning as supervisors, they must take full responsibility for all facets of this undertaking. (See also, 1.06 Multiple Relationships and Conflict of Interest, 1.07 Exploitative Relationships, 2.05 Rights and Prerogatives of Clients, 2.06 Maintaining Confidentiality, 2.15 Interrupting or Discontinuing Services, 8.04 Media Presentations and Media-Based Services, 9.02 Characteristics of Responsible Research, 10.05 Compliance with BACB Supervision and Coursework Standards)

5.01 Supervisory Competence

Behavior analysts supervise only within their areas of defined competence.

5.02 Supervisory Volume

Behavior analysts take on only a volume of supervisory activity that is commensurate with their ability to be effective.

5.03 Supervisory Delegation

(a) Behavior analysts delegate to their supervisees only those responsibilities that such persons can reasonably be expected to perform competently, ethically, and safely.
(b) If the supervisee does not have the skills necessary to perform competently, ethically, and safely, behavior analysts provide conditions for the acquisition of those skills.

5.04 Designing Effective Supervision and Training

Behavior analysts ensure that supervision and trainings are behavior-analytic in content, effectively and ethically designed, and meet the requirements for licensure, certification, or other defined goals.

5.05 Communication of Supervision Conditions

Behavior analysts provide a clear written description of the purpose, requirements, evaluation criteria, conditions, and terms of supervision prior to the onset of the supervision.

5.06 Providing Feedback to Supervisees

a) Behavior analysts design feedback and reinforcement systems in a way that improves supervisee performance.
b) Behavior analysts provide documented, timely feedback regarding the performance of a supervisee on an ongoing basis. (See also, 10.05 Compliance with BACB Supervision and Coursework Standards)

5.07 Evaluating the Effects of Supervision

Behavior analysts design systems for obtaining ongoing evaluation of their own supervision activities.

6.0 BEHAVIOR ANALYSTS' ETHICAL RESPONSIBILITY TO THE PROFESSION OF BEHAVIOR ANALYSIS

Behavior analysts have an obligation to the science of behavior and profession of behavior analysis.

6.01 Affirming Principles (RBT)

a) Above all other professional training, behavior analysts uphold and advance the values, ethics, and principles of the profession of behavior analysis.
b) Behavior analysts have an obligation to participate in behavior-analytic professional and scientific organizations or activities.

6.02 Disseminating Behavior Analysis (RBT)

Behavior analysts promote behavior analysis by making information about it available to the public through presentations, discussions, and other media.

7.0 BEHAVIOR ANALYSTS' ETHICAL RESPONSIBILITY TO COLLEAGUES

Behavior analysts work with colleagues within the profession of behavior analysis and from other professions and must be aware of these ethical obligations in all situations. (See also, 10.0 Behavior Analysts' Ethical Responsibility to the BACB)

7.01 Promoting an Ethical Culture (RBT)

Behavior analysts promote an ethical culture in their work environments and make others aware of this Code.

7.02 Ethical Violations by Others and Risk of Harm (RBT)

(a) If behavior analysts believe there may be a legal or ethical violation, they first determine whether there is potential for harm, a possible legal violation, a mandatory-reporting condition, or an agency, organization, or regulatory requirement addressing the violation.

(b) If a client's legal rights are being violated, or if there is the potential for harm, behavior analysts must take the necessary action to protect the client, including, but not limited to, contacting relevant authorities, following organizational policies, and consulting with appropriate professionals, and documenting their efforts to address the matter.

(c) If an informal resolution appears appropriate, and would not violate any confidentiality rights, behavior analysts attempt to resolve the issue by bringing it to the attention of that individual and documenting their efforts to address the matter. If the matter is not resolved, behavior analysts report the matter to the appropriate authority (e.g., employer, supervisor, regulatory authority).

(d) If the matter meets the reporting requirements of the BACB, behavior analysts submit a formal complaint to the BACB. (See also, 10.02 Timely Responding, Reporting, and Updating of Information Provided to the BACB)

8.0 PUBLIC STATEMENTS

Behavior analysts comply with this Code in public statements relating to their professional services, products, or publications, or to the profession of behavior analysis. Public statements include, but are not limited to, paid or unpaid advertising, brochures, printed matter, directory listings, personal resumes or curriculum vitae, interviews or comments for use in media, statements in legal proceedings, lectures and public presentations, social media, and published materials.

8.01 Avoiding False or Deceptive Statements (RBT)

(a) Behavior analysts do not make public statements that are false, deceptive, misleading, exaggerated, or fraudulent, either because of what they state, convey, or suggest or because of what they omit, concerning their research, practice, or other work activities or those of persons or organizations with which they are affiliated. Behavior analysts claim as credentials for their behavior-analytic work, only degrees that were primarily or exclusively behavior-analytic in content.

(b) Behavior analysts do not implement non-behavior-analytic interventions. Non-behavior-analytic services may only be provided within the context of non-behavior-analytic education, formal training, and credentialing. Such services must be clearly distinguished from their behavior-analytic practices and BACB certification by using the following disclaimer: "These interventions are not behavior-analytic in nature and are not covered by my BACB credential." The disclaimer should be placed alongside the names and descriptions of all non-behavior-analytic interventions.

(c) Behavior analysts do not advertise non-behavior-analytic services as being behavior-analytic.

(d) Behavior analysts do not identify non-behavior-analytic services as behavior-analytic services on bills, invoices, or requests for reimbursement.

(e) Behavior analysts do not implement non-behavior-analytic services under behavior-analytic service authorizations.

8.02 Intellectual Property (RBT)

(a) Behavior analysts obtain permission to use trademarked or copyrighted materials as required by law. This includes providing citations, including trademark or copyright symbols on materials, that recognize the intellectual property of others.

(b) Behavior analysts give appropriate credit to authors when delivering lectures, workshops, or other presentations.

8.03 Statements by Others (RBT)

(a) Behavior analysts who engage others to create or place public statements that promote their professional practice, products, or activities retain professional responsibility for such statements.

(b) Behavior analysts make reasonable efforts to prevent others whom they do not oversee (e.g., employers, publishers, sponsors, organizational clients, and representatives of the print or broadcast media) from making deceptive statements concerning behavior analysts' practices or professional or scientific activities.

(c) If behavior analysts learn of deceptive statements about their work made by others, behavior analysts correct such statements.

(d) A paid advertisement relating to behavior analysts' activities must be identified as such, unless it is apparent from the context.

8.04 Media Presentations and Media-Based Services

(a) Behavior analysts using electronic media (e.g., video, e-learning, social media, electronic transmission of information) obtain and maintain knowledge regarding the security and limitations of electronic media in order to adhere to this Code.

(b) Behavior analysts making public statements or delivering presentations using electronic media do not disclose personally identifiable information concerning their clients, supervisees, students, research participants, or other recipients of their services that they obtained during the course of their work, unless written consent has been obtained.

(c) Behavior analysts delivering presentations using electronic media disguise confidential information concerning participants, whenever possible, so that they are not individually identifiable to others and so that discussions do not cause harm to identifiable participants.

(d) When behavior analysts provide public statements, advice, or comments by means of public lectures, demonstrations, radio or television programs, electronic media, articles, mailed material, or other media, they take reasonable precautions to ensure that (1) the statements are based on appropriate behavior-analytic literature and practice, (2) the statements are otherwise consistent with this Code, and (3) the advice or comment does not create an agreement for service with the recipient.

8.05 Testimonials and Advertising (RBT)

Behavior analysts do not solicit or use testimonials about behavior-analytic services from current clients for publication on their webpages or in any other electronic or print material. Testimonials from former clients must identify whether they were solicited or unsolicited, include an accurate statement of the relationship between the behavior analyst and the author of the testimonial, and comply with all applicable laws about claims made in the testimonial.

Behavior analysts may advertise by describing the kinds and types of evidence-based services they provide, the qualifications of their staff, and objective outcome data they have accrued or published, in accordance with applicable laws.

8.06 In-Person Solicitation (RBT)

Behavior analysts do not engage, directly or through agents, in uninvited in-person solicitation of business from actual or potential users of services who, because of their particular circumstances, are vulnerable to undue influence. Organizational behavior management or performance management services may be marketed to corporate entities regardless of their projected financial position.

9.0 BEHAVIOR ANALYSTS AND RESEARCH

Behavior analysts design, conduct, and report research in accordance with recognized standards of scientific competence and ethical research.

9.01 Conforming with Laws and Regulations (RBT)

Behavior analysts plan and conduct research in a manner consistent with all applicable laws and regulations, as well as professional standards governing the conduct of research. Behavior analysts also comply with other applicable laws and regulations relating to mandated-reporting requirements.

9.02 Characteristics of Responsible Research

(a) Behavior analysts conduct research only after approval by an independent, formal research review board.

(b) Behavior analysts conducting applied research conjointly with provision of clinical or human services must comply with requirements for both intervention and research involvement by client-participants. When research and clinical needs conflict, behavior analysts prioritize the welfare of the client.

(c) Behavior analysts conduct research competently and with due concern for the dignity and welfare of the participants.

(d) Behavior analysts plan their research so as to minimize the possibility that results will be misleading.

(e) Researchers and assistants are permitted to perform only those tasks for which they are appropriately trained and prepared. Behavior analysts are responsible for the ethical conduct of research conducted by assistants or by others under their supervision or oversight.

(f) If an ethical issue is unclear, behavior analysts seek to resolve the issue through consultation with independent, formal research review boards, peer consultations, or other proper mechanisms.

(g) Behavior analysts only conduct research independently after they have successfully conducted research under a supervisor in a defined relationship (e.g., thesis, dissertation, specific research project).

(h) Behavior analysts conducting research take necessary steps to maximize benefit and minimize risk to their clients, supervisees, research participants, students, and others with whom they work.

(i) Behavior analysts minimize the effect of personal, financial, social, organizational, or political factors that might lead to misuse of their research.

(j) If behavior analysts learn of misuse or misrepresentation of their individual work products, they take appropriate steps to correct the misuse or misrepresentation.

(k) Behavior analysts avoid conflicts of interest when conducting research.

(l) Behavior analysts minimize interference with the participants or environment in which research is conducted.

9.03 Informed Consent

Behavior analysts inform participants or their guardian or surrogate in understandable language about the nature of the research; that they are free to participate, to decline to participate, or to withdraw from the research at any time without penalty; about significant factors that may influence their willingness to participate; and answer any other questions participants may have about the research.

9.04 Using Confidential Information for Didactic or Instructive Purposes

(a) Behavior analysts do not disclose personally identifiable information concerning their individual or organizational clients, research participants, or other recipients of their services that they obtained during the course of their work, unless the person or organization has consented in writing or unless there is other legal authorization for doing so.

(b) Behavior analysts disguise confidential information concerning participants, whenever possible, so that they are not individually identifiable to others and so that discussions do not cause harm to identifiable participants.

9.05 Debriefing

Behavior analysts inform the participant that debriefing will occur at the conclusion of the participant's involvement in the research.

9.06 Grant and Journal Reviews

Behavior analysts who serve on grant review panels or as manuscript reviewers avoid conducting any research described in grant proposals or manuscripts that they reviewed, except as replications fully crediting the prior researchers.

9.07 Plagiarism

(a) Behavior analysts fully cite the work of others where appropriate.
(b) Behavior analysts do not present portions or elements of another's work or data as their own.

9.08 Acknowledging Contributions

Behavior analysts acknowledge the contributions of others to research by including them as co-authors or footnoting their contributions. Principal authorship and other publication credits accurately reflect the relative scientific or professional contributions of the individuals involved, regardless of their relative status. Minor contributions to the research or to the writing for publications are appropriately acknowledged, such as, in a footnote or introductory statement.

9.09 Accuracy and Use of Data (RBT)

(a) Behavior analysts do not fabricate data or falsify results in their publications. If behavior analysts discover errors in their published data, they take steps to correct such errors in a correction, retraction, erratum, or other appropriate publication means.

(b) Behavior analysts do not omit findings that might alter interpretations of their work.

(c) Behavior analysts do not publish, as original data, data that have been previously published. This does not preclude republishing data when they are accompanied by proper acknowledgment.

(d) After research results are published, behavior analysts do not withhold the data on which their conclusions are based from other competent professionals who seek to verify the substantive claims through reanalysis and who intend to use such data only for that purpose, provided that the confidentiality of the participants can be protected and unless legal rights concerning proprietary data preclude their release.

10.0 BEHAVIOR ANALYSTS' ETHICAL RESPONSIBILITY TO THE BACB

Behavior analysts must adhere to this Code and all rules and standards of the BACB.

10.01 Truthful and Accurate Information Provided to the BACB (RBT)

(a) Behavior analysts only provide truthful and accurate information in applications and documentation submitted to the BACB.

(b) Behavior analysts ensure that inaccurate information submitted to the BACB is immediately corrected.

10.02 Timely Responding, Reporting, and Updating of Information Provided to the BACB (RBT)

Behavior analysts must comply with all BACB deadlines including, but not limited to, ensuring that the BACB is notified within thirty (30) days of the date of any of the following grounds for sanctioning status:

(a) A violation of this Code, or disciplinary investigation, action or sanction, filing of charges, conviction or plea of guilty or nolo contendere by a governmental agency, health care organization, third-party payer or educational institution. Procedural note: Behavior analysts convicted of a felony directly related to behavior analysis practice and/or public health and safety shall be ineligible to apply for BACB registration, certification, or recertification for a period of three (3) years from the exhaustion of appeals, completion of parole or probation, or final release from confinement (if any), whichever is later; (See also, 1.04d Integrity)

(b) Any public health- and safety-related fines or tickets where the behavior analyst is named on the ticket;

(c) A physical or mental condition that would impair the behavior analysts' ability to competently practice; and

(d) A change of name, address or email contact.

10.03 Confidentiality and BACB Intellectual Property (RBT)

Behavior analysts do not infringe on the BACB's intellectual property rights, including, but not limited to the BACB's rights to the following:

(a) BACB logo, ACS logo, ACE logo, certificates, credentials and designations, including, but not limited to, trademarks, service marks, registration marks and certification marks owned and claimed by the BACB (this includes confusingly similar marks intended to convey BACB affiliation, certification or registration, or misrepresentation of an educational ABA certificate status as constituting national certification);

(b) BACB copyrights to original and derivative works, including, but not limited to, BACB copyrights to standards, procedures, guidelines, codes, job task analysis, Workgroup reports, surveys; and

(c) BACB copyrights to all BACB-developed examination questions, item banks, examination specifications, examination forms and examination scoring sheets, which are secure trade secrets of the BACB. Behavior analysts are expressly prohibited from disclosing the content of any BACB examination materials, regardless of how that content became known to them. Behavior analysts report suspected or known infringements and/or unauthorized access to examination content and/or any other violation of BACB intellectual property rights immediately to the BACB. Efforts for informal resolution (identified in Section 7.02 c) are waived due to the immediate reporting requirement of this Section.

10.04 *Examination Honesty and Irregularities (RBT)*

Behavior analysts adhere to all rules of the BACB, including the rules and procedures required by BACB approved testing centers and examination administrators and proctors. Behavior analysts must immediately report suspected cheaters and any other irregularities relating to the BACB examination administrations to the BACB. Examination irregularities include, but are not limited to, unauthorized access to BACB examinations or answer sheets, copying answers, permitting another to copy answers, disrupting the conduct of an examination, falsifying information, education or credentials, and providing and/or receiving unauthorized or illegal advice about or access to BACB examination content before, during, or following the examination. This prohibition includes, but is not limited to, use of or participation in any "exam dump" preparation site or blog that provides unauthorized access to BACB examination questions. If, at any time, it is discovered that an applicant or certificant has participated in or utilized an exam dump organization, immediate action may be taken to withdraw eligibility, cancel examination scores, or otherwise revoke certification gained through use of inappropriately obtained examination content.

10.05 Compliance with BACB Supervision and Coursework Standards (RBT)

Behavior analysts ensure that coursework (including continuing education events), supervised experience, RBT training and assessment, and BCaBA supervision are conducted in accordance with the BACB's standards if these activities are intended to comply with BACB standards (See also, 5.0 Behavior Analysts as Supervisors).

10.06 Being Familiar with This Code

Behavior analysts have an obligation to be familiar with this Code, other applicable ethics codes, including, but not limited to, licensure requirements for ethical conduct, and their application to behavior analysts' work. Lack of awareness or misunderstanding of a conduct standard is not itself a defense to a charge of unethical conduct.

10.07 Discouraging Misrepresentation by Non-Certified Individuals (RBT)

Behavior analysts report non-certified (and, if applicable, non-registered) practitioners to the appropriate state licensing board and to the BACB if the practitioners are misrepresenting BACB certification or registration status.

Appendix B: Glossary

Provided by the BACB

BEHAVIOR ANALYST

Behavior analyst refers to an individual who holds the BCBA or BCaBA credential, an individual authorized by the BACB to provide supervision, or a coordinator of a BACB Approved Course Sequence. Where Code elements are deemed relevant to the practice of an RBT, the term "behavior analyst" includes the behavior technician.

BEHAVIOR-ANALYTIC SERVICES

Behavior-analytic services are those that are explicitly based on principles and procedures of behavior analysis (i.e., the science of behavior) and are designed to change behavior in socially important ways. These services include, but are not limited to, treatment, assessment, training, consultation, managing and supervising others, teaching, and delivering continuing education.

BEHAVIOR-CHANGE PROGRAM

The behavior-change program is a formal, written document that describes in technological detail every assessment and treatment task necessary to achieve stated goals.

CLIENT

The term client refers to any recipient or beneficiary of the professional services provided by a behavior analyst. The term includes, but is not limited to:
   (a) The direct recipient of services;
   (b) The parent, relative, legal representative or legal guardian of the recipient of services;
   (c) The employer, agency representative, institutional representative, or third-party contractor for services of the behavior analyst; and/or
   (d) Any other individual or entity that is a known beneficiary of services or who would normally be construed as a "client" or "client-surrogate" in a health-care context.

For purposes of this definition, the term client does not include third-party insurers or payers, unless the behavior analyst is hired directly under contract with the third-party insurer or payer.

FUNCTIONAL ASSESSMENT

Functional assessment, also known as functional behavior assessment, refers to a category of procedures used to formally assess the possible environmental causes of problem behavior. These procedures include informant assessments (e.g., interviews, rating scales), direct observation in the natural environment (e.g., ABC assessment), and experimental functional analysis.

MULTIPLE RELATIONSHIPS

A multiple relationship is one in which a behavior analyst is in both a behavior-analytic role and a non-behavior-analytic role simultaneously with a client or someone closely associated with or related to the client.

PUBLIC STATEMENTS

Public statements include, but are not limited to, paid or unpaid advertising, brochures, printed matter, directory listings, personal resumes or curriculum vitae, interviews or comments for use in media, statements in legal proceedings, lectures and public presentations, social media, and published materials.

RESEARCH

Any data-based activity designed to generate generalizable knowledge for the discipline, often through professional presentations or publications. The use of an experimental design does not by itself constitute research. Professional presentation or publication of already collected data are exempt from elements in section 9.0 (Behavior Analysts and Research) that pertain to prospective research activities (e.g., 9.02a). However, all remaining relevant elements from section 9.0 apply (e.g., 9.01 Conforming with Laws and Regulations; 9.03 Informed Consent, relating to use of client data).

RESEARCH REVIEW BOARD

A group of professionals whose stated purpose is to review research proposals to ensure the ethical treatment of human research participants. This board might be an official entity of a government or university (e.g., Institutional Review Board, Human Research Committee), a standing committee within a service agency, or an independent organization created for this purpose.

RIGHTS AND PREROGATIVES OF CLIENTS

Rights and prerogatives of clients refers to human rights, legal rights, rights codified within behavior analysis, and organizational and administrative rules and regulations designed to benefit the client.

RISK-BENEFIT ANALYSIS

A risk-benefit analysis is a deliberate evaluation of the potential risks (e.g., limitations, side effects, costs) and benefits (e.g., treatment outcomes, efficiency, savings) associated with a given intervention. A risk-benefit analysis should conclude with a course of action associated with greater benefits than risks.

SERVICE RECORD

A client's service record includes, but is not limited to, written behavior-change plans, assessments, graphs, raw data, electronic recordings, progress summaries, and written reports.

STUDENT

A student is an individual who is matriculated at a college/ university. This Code applies to the student during formal behavior-analytic instruction.

SUPERVISEE

A supervisee is any individual whose behavior-analytic services are overseen by a behavior analyst within the context of a defined, agreed-upon relationship.

SUPERVISOR

A supervisor is any behavior analyst who oversees behavior-analytic services performed by a supervisee within the context of a defined, agreed-upon relationship.

Appendix C: Fifty Ethics Scenarios for Behavior Analysts (With Hints)

INSTRUCTIONS

Read each scenario carefully. Each is based on an actual situation encountered by behavior analysts working in the field. We suggest that you first use a highlighter to mark key words or phrases in the scenario. Next, referring to your index for Behavior Analyst Certification Board (BACB) Guidelines, write in the code number for each key issue highlighted, and under "Principle" indicate in your own words what ethical principle is involved. Note that for each scenario there may be three to four such principles. Finally, after reviewing all the ethical principles involved, indicate what steps you should take to follow the guidelines. There may be several code numbers and principles for an individual scenario. For each scenario, answer the following:

Ethics Code number
Principle
What should you do?

PRACTICE SCENARIOS

1. I am an Applied Behavior Analysis (ABA) program supervisor. I have a preschooler who really needs lots of intervention. The family insists on mixing and matching approaches [e.g., floor time, gluten free and other diets, sensory integration]. This cuts down on the available ABA time to 10 hours. I don't feel that this is enough time but have been unsuccessful so far in convincing the parents. Should I drop this child from our ABA program or give what I believe is a treatment that is insufficient?
   Hint: What *can* you do with the 10 hours?

2. Is it always unethical to use testimonial information? What if a parent shares this information with a prospective client without your knowledge or permission?
   Hint: Think First Amendment.

3. When confronting another behavior analyst that you believe is doing something unethical, what should you do if the other analyst either disagrees with what you are saying or denies that it is occurring?
   Hint: Don't "confront" another professional. Take a look at element 7.02 and the description of Compliance Code Committees at the end of 10.0.

4. Kevin continues to bang his head when attempting to seek attention from his parents and teachers. The following approaches have been implemented: sensory integration recommended by the occupational therapist, deep pressure, joint compression, and jumping on a trampoline.

Kevin continues to bang his head. Sign language was recommended by the speech therapist: Kevin is unable to discriminate between the signs; therefore he continues to bang his head. The use of a helmet was recommended by the physical therapist. Kevin continues to bang his head with the helmet, and he has now begun to bite his fingers. The behavior specialist has now recommended shock therapy, after reviewing all the interventions, or medication. Is it ethical to use an aversive strategy at this point? How long should interventions continue to be in place before medication or shock therapy is considered?

Hint: How do you know attention is a reinforcer? And remember to say, "Show me the data!"

5. Are we always obligated to use the best practices that are scientifically proven effective treatments with no exceptions? What happens if we are a member of a team [e.g., a school Individual Education Plan (IEP) team] and the team chooses to use and agrees on, despite your advice, an approach that is not supported by research?

Hint: Take a look at 7.01 and 7.02(c).

6. An ABA consultant has been working with a child with autism and his or her family. As the child approaches the age of 3, a transition meeting is held between the early intervention program teacher and the school district. This meeting begins pleasantly, with sharing of information from both sides. However, a point comes when the ABA consultant and the family actually become hostile and verbally attack school district personnel out of nowhere, and it becomes obvious during the meeting that the consultant has painted the school district as the enemy who has little to no concern for the best interest of the child. I would say that because this is the first time the district has encountered ABA, their impression of ABA, from the very beginning, is not a positive one. Does this not damage the school's perception of ABA, along with the parents'

perception of a school district (which they will likely be working with for the next 20 years), and in fact distract from what is in the best interest of the child? Is this typical procedure in dealing with school districts?

Hint: If you are in that meeting and this happens, what do you do right then?

7. As professionals in the field of education, we sometimes tend to forget that the children we work with have the right to privacy and their reports are deemed confidential. How can you politely tell another professional that to discuss a child's record without the family consent is not appropriate?

Hint: See Chapter 17.

8. What do you do when you have one member of the family who constantly "sabotages" the positive impact the behavior intervention and your input has on his or her child? In particular, one parent refuses to keep data or to give you honest feedback and offers no encouragement or support to the other parent, who is willing to at least attempt what is asked. The uncooperative parent feels that there is nothing wrong with his or her child and that this intervention is a waste of time. How far, ethically, can you become involved in this family dispute to convince the combative parent to become supportive of what you and the cooperative parent are trying to accomplish on behalf of their child? Is termination of the case a viable option?

Hint: See Chapter 18. Using a Declaration on the front end should prevent this. Also check Code 4.07 and 4.07.

9. Working in a home-based setting stirs up many ethical and boundary issues for therapists that do not occur in school or office settings. When working in a home, the family takes you into its "personal space." Additionally, when you work with someone's children, parents develop strong attachments to their children's therapist, whom they are entrusting with their child's well-being. I have observed

several of my colleagues develop "friendships" with the mothers of the children with whom they work. These relationships start out innocently enough. Usually it is a car ride to the grocery store, or perhaps the therapist and the parent may talk about shopping, and within a matter of a few sessions the two people have planned lunch and a day at the mall. These plans at times have included or excluded the child. Home-based therapy is very tricky, and without the proper supervision and without properly trained staff, there are many opportunities to develop inappropriate relationships that can both jeopardize the child's treatment and engage the parent in an inappropriate manner. My question is actually a request for clarification of the boundary between therapist and the parent in a home-based situation. I am wondering if there are somewhat relaxed criteria for the dual relationship rules in working with children and in working in a home environment.

Hint: To the last question the answer is, "No." Read 1.06 and Chapters 17 and 18 carefully.

10. Many of the requests for my services as a behavior consultant come when agencies or schools are struggling with families and are at odds with what to do to help a child with his or her behavior difficulties. The agency or school provides the funding to pay for my services and is the one who initiates my involvement with the student. At times, my review of the case and the analysis of the data I have gathered lead me to believe that previous interventions were not well thought out and were primarily of a reactive nature. Indeed, they may have actually caused the situation to become worse. Several times, families have asked me point-blank as to the cause of the student's behavior and my opinion of these previous interventions. How do I respond ethically, knowing that if I share my beliefs, I risk alienating the agency or school and possibly giving

the families more reasons not to trust the people involved with their child?

Hint: See Code item 1.04 and take the high road.

11. The client is a 19-year-old girl in high school (diagnosed with mild mental retardation). She has a history of sexual abuse and was a "crack baby" at birth. Last month there was an incident in which it was discovered that she was not riding the school bus and was instead walking to school. The problem is that she would meet with a man and have sexual intercourse in his front yard. At that point, they had an adult female talk to her about safe sex. My supervisor suggests she be provided condoms and given the money to go to a motel instead. The home group manager said she would allow her to have sex in her bedroom; however, there are foster kids present, and that may bring up other issues. I don't agree with directing her to a motel as a replacement behavior. I don't think she should be encouraged to have sex with strangers. She has in the past invited male strangers into the home. I am having a difficult time coming up with a replacement behavior to suit her. She has excellent communication skills and gets great grades in school.

Hint: Think safety for the client, and repercussions if anything bad happens to her.

12. A Board Certified Behavior Analyst (BCBA) has been supervising an ABA educational program for a 3-year-old boy with autism for six months. The child's parents have recently gone through a long, bitter divorce. The BCBA has been subpoenaed to testify as to the child's custody and continued treatment. The BCBA has worked with the mother only during the home visits and knows of the home situation only from the mother's perspective. Despite ongoing parent training, the mother does not have good skills when it comes to managing the child. The

father and his new girlfriend want custody of the child, and they have indicated they want no ABA program or therapist in the home. The BCBA deems the ABA program crucial but does not feel comfortable commenting on or recommending custody since she has met the father only once. The BCBA has been told she will be asked which parent would provide the better home for the child.

Hint: Read and reread 1.04. You can be asked "Which parent . . .?" but if you speak only from what you know, do not show any bias, and answer the questions truthfully, you will be fine.

13. There is a BCBA in my area who often claims she was "trained" by well-known behavior analysts. I believe that to be "trained" by someone you should have been their student for a length of time or worked closely with them. This woman goes to conferences where she sits in the audience and then says she was "trained" by well-recognized behavior analysts. She once received some advice from a leader in the field via email on a research project, and she now claims this person was her "mentor." I am really disgusted by this, and I feel she is misrepresenting herself to families and other professionals. Would it be unethical of me to email some of these well-known people, tell them what she is saying, and ask them about the "training" they have given her? If you don't like this approach, how would you handle it?

Hint: Read 1.04 and send a needlepoint version to her as a gift (this is a joke, no gifting, even for pretenders).

14. In our district, there is a BCBA who charges the school district and other agencies a lot of money for providing services to children with autism—and I mean a lot of money. He tells people who are more than just a BCBA that he is one of the very few behavior analysts in the country nationally certified as a "Behavior Analyst for Verbal

Behavior." What should I do about this? I am not inclined to approach him and would rather deal with someone else.

Hint: Read 7.02 and 8.02. Behavior analysts have to have the courage to step up in situations like this.

15. A BCBA works with a mother who homeschools her child. The child is a 6-year-old boy with autism. The BCBA has done a functional assessment and has identified the controlling variables for the child's target behavior. In the opinion of the BCBA, the best data collection system for gathering baseline data would require daily entries by the mother. A data-collection system has been designed that is easy to understand and score; however, the mother does not take the data despite the BCBA's best attempts to prompt and reinforce her. This child really needs help, but with no data it will be hard to provide treatment. Should the BCBA terminate services?

    Hint: Did you start your service to this mother by reviewing your Declaration of Professional Practice (Chapter 18) with her? And, read 4.05–4.07.

16. What are the ethics related to ending behavioral services because you have not been paid in several months? This happens frequently in my district. I started working with one client in October. It is now March, and I have never received a check. I have called the support coordinator, and she just says sometimes the system is slow. Everyone in our district thinks we have an ethical obligation to provide services, so we can't terminate clients over lack of payment. Somewhere, on someone's desk, I am guessing our behavior analysis invoices are just piling up. Our clients have a "right to treatment." Do we have a "right to be paid"?

    Hint: Read 2.12. And think, "Payment due in 60 days . . ." with contingencies.

17. I am a BCBA working with a 30-year-old adult male client who moved from a large institution to a smaller

64-bed residential facility. This client becomes danger-
ously aggressive to get access to his cigarettes. As a part
of his behavior program, I set up a smoking schedule that
spreads his allotted number of cigarettes out across his day
in even, short intervals. Staff members went to the facility
administrator and said they did not have time to manage
the client's cigarettes throughout the day. The administrator listened to the staff and directed them to give the client all of his cigarettes in the morning along with a small
chart showing him when he can smoke them. This has led
to an increase of aggression because the client ignores the
chart and smokes all of the cigarettes as soon as he gets
them. He then tantrums throughout the day and demands
more cigarettes. I would like to keep on working here, but
I am ready to tell the administrator that I don't come in his
office and work on his budget, so he should not be tam-
pering with behavioral programs. What should I say to the
administrator to let him know that his conduct is unethical and that it resulted in an increase in severe behavior
problems?

Hint: Most facilities are now nonsmoking, so this problem
  has likely been solved.

18. One of the schools for which I provide BCBA services sent
  me a request to provide services for a 10-year-old girl who
  has been having multiple behavior problems in the classroom. She has been noncompliant (refusing to do what
  the teacher asks), frequently off-task and out of her seat,
  swearing at the other students on the playground, and not
  completing work in class. The parents are taking the child
  to a clinical psychologist. The psychologist has never seen
  the child in the classroom, but she created a "point sheet"
  for the teacher to use. I was told after I agreed to provide
  services that I should design a behavior plan around the
  point sheet designed by Dr. X. because she spends a lot of
  time with the child, the parents trust her and want her to

be at the center of the therapy, and she is very well known in the community. The fact is, the point sheet is not effective, and the child's behavior is getting worse. I am a new BCBA and don't want to present myself as a know-it-all, but I think I should be able to develop my own behavioral plan. Any advice?

Hint: This is what we call a "No win" situation for you; consider all your options.

19. My guess is that most of the people who ask ethics questions are BCBAs and Board Certified assistant Behavior Analysts (BCaBAs). My situation is somewhat different, as I am a professional who is responsible for approving behavioral services for clients. From time to time, I get a request for a significant amount of behavioral services. The consultant is requesting "prior service authorization," meaning I am being asked to pay for a certain number of hours before the work is actually done. This is a standard practice. In the most recent case, I was familiar with the client. The client was an adult male with a history of behavior problems. According to other professionals who work with the client, the behavior problems are under control at this time. I requested more information from the behavior analyst who requested that I approve consulting hours. All I got was a one-page document with suggestions for guidelines to follow when the behavior occurs. There were no data. The behavior analyst attached a note to his "guidelines" saying that, since the client was moving to the community after many years in an institution, there would probably be problems related to the transition and behavioral services should be in place.

Hint: Read 2.13.

20. The Medicaid waiver agency where I am providing behavioral services billed for behavioral services that were not provided to the client. I am sorry to say this was probably not just an error because this is not the first time it

has done this. My ethical conflict is that the agency did provide another service the family desperately needed, so the family has not reported the agency. The family did not want to lose the best personal care attendant it has ever had. Does this balance out? The family and child really did need the personal care attendant. Can I get in trouble for not reporting this? And I don't even know to whom or how I would report this.

Hint: Read 2.12 and focus on (d).

21. Sometimes it is very clear when you are about to set yourself up to fail. I don't like to do that, but I want to do the right thing. I have been asked to take a case of a severely autistic child who has no language at all. She has never received services. The child is 6 years old. She wets her pants and has tantrums. She will throw food if she does not like it. She screams and cries at night when her parents try to put her to bed. The insurance company is willing to pay for only two hours of behavioral services each week. I feel like this isn't going to make any kind of difference. The parents are at a point where they are literally crying and saying they are desperate for any level of service. The service coordinator who has recently taken the case agrees with the parents. She says, "Something is better than nothing."

    Hint: This motto is wrong more often than not. Read Chapter 4 and think Legal Aid as a resource for the parents to gain some leverage with the insurance company.

22. Where I live, many BCBAs working in the area of autism promote interventions that are ineffective or not based on research. Examples are casein-free diet, essential fatty acids, facilitated communication, auditory integration training, sensory integration therapy, secretin, megavitamins A, B6, and C, and chelation therapy. These BCBAs say, "I just don't want to argue with the parents; they want to try these things and are willing to pay for both them

and behavioral services. As long as it is not hurting anything and my programs are working, I don't see this as an
ethical issue."

Hint: Read 4.01.

23. A group of local behavior analysts gets together quarterly for a continuing education presentation followed by
a group social and informal dinner. One of the members
of our group is the owner of a large consulting firm. At a
recent dinner, he mentioned that on Saturday morning he
was having some parents of clients come to the office to
have their photos taken for his new Web page. "We'll have
a statement from each one about the great things we did
for their child," he said. Someone at the table told him that
behavior analysts were not supposed to solicit testimonials. His response was that doctors, dentists, and other professionals did this and that there was no problem as long as
the parents could choose to not participate. Was he wrong
about this? Is there any situation under which testimonials
would be acceptable? He said what he was doing was not
what the Code referred to in the section on testimonials.

Hint: Have him read Chapter 13 and focus on 8.06.

24. A child in one of the schools where I am the new BCBA
has multiple behavioral issues. I believe that he may need
to be on medication for behavior control. I was called in to
assess the child. I talked to the principal and told her we
would be recommending a medical work-up to start with
and a functional analysis. The principal said, "We just need
to get him out of here. I need you to write a report that
says this child can't be managed in a school setting like
ours and that he needs to move to a special program." I am
afraid that the principal's mind is made up and that if I tell
her what I really think of her approach, I won't be working
at this school much longer.

Hint: You are in a "No win" situation. Read Chapter 4.

25. In our district, a 12-year-old boy with severe developmental disabilities is in a foster placement. The client is ambulatory, and he roams at night. He will go in the kitchen and try to get knives to make a snack, and a few times he went outside and started walking down the road at night. The neighbor of the foster mother called one night at 3 a.m. to alert the foster mother that the boy was walking down the street in his underwear. The neighbor woke up when dogs started barking and looked out of her window to see what was happening. So, for now, to keep him safe, his "treatment" is a "cage" for sleeping. It looks like an old institution crib with a top that locks so he can't get out. A BCBA was involved in this intervention. Is something like this okay if it is used to keep the client safe?

    Hint: Review 4.0, considering in particular the limiting conditions of ABA treatment.

26. I know the new ethics Code says I should not accept gifts or socialize with clients and that I should not be giving them gifts (e.g., meals). I understand this on a big scale—it could lead to a bad situation. But sometimes, there are some fine lines where I think it might be okay to do this. Is the Code really still just a set of "guidelines" and not rules? Specifically, for one of my cases, I work in the home with a preschooler. The family is poor, and the mother is in a wheelchair. Sometimes, when I go to the home around dinnertime, I will take some burgers, pizza, or sandwiches so the mother doesn't have to cook dinner. I feel this helps me bond with this mom. Plus, if she doesn't have to cook and start getting dinner ready, she has more time to be with the child and me in our therapy sessions. Someone told me I should not be doing this. I believe that you should look at the results, and if the food or gifts are not expensive and no one is getting beholden to the other person, that this would be acceptable. If the mother started saying,

"Can you bring some steaks the next time?" I would know I've gone too far.

Hint: The ethics Code is serious about this, these are no longer *guidelines*. Review 1.06.

27. In my consulting job as a behavior analyst, I have been working with a consumer who is a recipient of Medicaid waiver services. Recently, there was a breakdown in the service authority approval process, meaning that my upcoming hours were not approved in writing. Should I still provide behavior analysis and oversight even if I do not have a written authorization? I know it sounds like an obvious yes, but legally the rules say that if my hours are not approved in advance, the agency does not have to pay me.

Hint: Read 1.05(a).

28. Third-party payers for services are starting to employ behavior analysts to review behavior programs provided by other behavior analysts. While this is better than having psychologists or bean counters reviewing behavior plans, are the behavior analysts who are employed to review the plans unethical because they are making decisions about services without observing the client, reviewing data, and so forth?

Hint: Review 2.09(b) and 3.01(a).

29. I work with clients who are developmentally disabled both in their homes and at school. There is a behavioral consultant in our area who will frequently recommend that a punishment procedure be implemented with a client without having seen the client himself. This professional basically hears from school staff of Board Certified assistant Behavior Analysts that the client has behavior problems, but he has never worked with or observed the child himself. I am fairly sure this is unethical, but I am not his supervisor, he doesn't work in the same consulting firm I do, and I am only a BCaBA. Should I do anything about this?

Hint: Review 3.01 and 4.08. In order to report someone to the BACB, you must have firsthand knowledge. If others tell you they have seen the behavior, you should encourage them to make the report.

30. A BCBA is in business with a person from another field who was the lead author on a study that has been shown to have serious methodological flaws. The other authors have retracted its findings. The lead author was found to have a serious conflict of interest that was not disclosed when the study was published and is being investigated for scientific misconduct. Nevertheless, the BCBA continues to promote the person's unsubstantiated theory about the etiology of autism and treatments that have not been tested scientifically.
   Hint: Read 1.0 and 6.01(a).

31. I am a BCBA working for a state-funded program. The problem concerns a BCaBA coworker and her relationship with a client who is a dependent caregiver. The relationship is not romantic; the two have become best friends. The BCaBA sees the client in her home on a weekly basis. My colleague asked if it would be appropriate to maintain a personal relationship with this client after she leaves her job with our program. I suggested that at the point that she ceases employment, she cut the relationship and not try to treat her former client as a friend. I want to make sure that the client does not feel pressured into a relationship with my coworker. Should I follow up with the client to see if this was done, or is it okay for these two women to be friends once there is no longer a professional connection?
   Hint: Review 1.05(f) and 1.06 as well as 1.07.

32. We have an 8-year-old client with a diagnosis of attention deficit disorder. According to her parents, the little girl has a history of "lying." We have not seen this behavior at our treatment center. Yesterday, she told two of our staff members that, some time back, she was roughhousing with her

dad and that he squeezed her so hard that she fainted; she said that later she was sent to bed without dinner. This client also reported that her dad squeezed her wrists "really hard" on past occasions, although we have not seen any sign of bruising. I documented all of this in her clinical file. Do I need to report this incident to the Florida Abuse Hotline, or should I just talk with the parents first and get their side of the story? I don't want to bother the hotline if this is just a case of a girl who fabricated a story.

Hint: Review the *Definitions for Reporting Abuse under the MyFLFamilies.com.*

33. When I was an undergraduate, I was given the opportunity to have a practicum in a classroom for children with autism. Basically, I was a volunteer who helped the teacher, but I was not responsible for any aspect of behavior programs. I was also permitted to observe treatment team meetings. The whole experience inspired me to go on to earn my master's degree in applied behavior analysis. One student who was very hyperactive was not doing very well on his goals. A therapist from another discipline came to a treatment team meeting and made the recommendation that the student be put in a weighted vest. She said it would help his "concentration, ability to learn tasks, reduce his behavior problems, and result in faster learning." This therapist was fast-talking and funny, and everyone liked her. I think she could sell snowballs to Eskimos, and that day she sold this concept to the whole team. I did not agree with this approach at all. I told my faculty supervisor later, and he told me, "You need to keep your mouth shut." I didn't say a word in any of these meetings, and the weighted vest was implemented a little later as the "treatment." Ever since then, I have felt guilty for not having the courage to speak up on behalf of effective treatment for this child. After my supervisor warned me, was there anything else I could have done?

Hint: Review 5.0 regarding supervisor responsibilities and recall that this Code only applies to those who are board certified.

34. One part of my new job is to write up client progress notes. I use these notes and my data to keep track of where I am with my clients. My supervisor also uses my notes to determine if I am handling cases efficiently and effectively. If a client meets a goal, I record it in my notes. I became aware recently that my notes are also being used to document the need for continuing funding for clients. While I am excited that I have helped someone, the administration is upset that because I have written "Goal met" or "Case closed," the funding stream for this client will dry up. A recent conversation with my supervisor was quite disturbing—it was suggested to me in a somewhat roundabout way that rather than saying that the client had reached his goal, I should indicate that there were other goals for him to work on and that further training was indicated. I thought about it and went back the next day for a clarification, just to make sure I understood; the answer was, "Yes, that's right." I have been following these directions now for a couple of months, but it doesn't feel right to me. If a client has met his goal, it seems to me that this should be a cause for celebration and an opportunity to take in a new client who needs our help. Am I missing something here? Am I harming the facility because it gets less funding when I terminate a client?

    Hint: Read 4.11, and remember that in the same way that accepting clients (2.01) is a group decision, so is discontinuing services.

35. I am the supervisor for a team of behavior analysts who provide behavioral services in the homes of children. I have an unusual ethics question. One of my newly certified BCBAs was recently assigned to work in the home of a preschooler; the child lives in a rough neighborhood.

After the second visit, the consultant came to my office and said she believes there is drug use in the home. The child's mother is single, and reportedly her boyfriend and his friends come to the house often. The consultant said that she has seen evidence of drug activity (including use of drugs and dealing) in the home and that she feels uncomfortable going there. I am not sure what I should do. I have studied the Code very carefully. What I get from my common sense and my reading of the Code does not match. For example, the Code say a client has the right to effective treatment and that behavior analysts do not terminate services and leave a client with nothing. What would you advise me to do?

Hint: While it is not in the Code, "do no harm" is the watchword of all human services. This sounds like a classic 9.01 issue.

36. As a Board Certified Behavior Analyst, I am a member of a local peer review committee (LRC). The LRC looks at behavior plans for the clients in my area. I get along well with everyone on the committee. Here is my problem. The chair of the committee is also our regional behavior analysis director. I have to review her programs, make comments, and present my review on the committee date scheduled. I am not sure if she is just overloaded or what, but this person's programs are very weak. The protocols she suggests are not behaviorally sound. She should stick to being an administrator, because she is organized. I am in an awkward situation, because this is the person who gives me cases and basically controls how much money I can make each month. My boyfriend is in law school. He told me to send a strongly worded letter about the quality of the programs to this woman. Other people on the committee have dropped subtle hints that the programs need to be improved, but she ignores the suggestions. One would think the chair would have the best programs of all

of us, but she was trained in the early 1980s and is out of touch. Any ideas for an ethical and diplomatic solution?

Hint: Review all of Code 7.0 and see if something comes to mind; often a group of people can be more effective than one alone.

37. I am a student in a behavior analysis program. I am not yet Board Certified at any level, but I would like to become a BCBA. I have gone to some conferences, and I know about the Code although I am not an expert on it. To get experience with children, I have been working at a private daycare center that has private clients as well as a few children with disabilities. We have one little boy who is very hyperactive. He does not speak well, and you can't understand him. He will spit on you, try to bite you, and kick you if he does not get his way. Sometimes, even when staff members are being nice to him, he just "goes off." There is a program that involves the teacher giving him treats when he is good, putting stars on a chart, and using time-out. Here is my concern: I have seen one teacher's aide smack this child if he spits on her or tries to bite her. When she does this, he starts acting right and behaves himself. I know behavior analysts are not allowed to hit children; however, this is a private daycare, and parents will say, "Spank him if you need to." I have not reported this aide, because one time when the child spit on me I grabbed him by the ear to take him to time-out. The aide gave me a little smile, and she did not report me. I am starting to feel nervous about all of this.

    Hint: Code 9.01 applies here.

38. I am an assistant behavior analyst. I am in graduate school in psychology and work part time at a facility for people with developmental disabilities. I am lucky because several of us who are in school together also work for the same consulting firm and work at some of the same schools and facilities. One of our friends is more advanced than us in

her graduate studies. She is working on a research project that has been all she has talked about for months. Our professor said if the study was done right and the data looked good, this was the kind of study that could be easily published. Our friend talked us into being observers for her. At the end of the study, when we were all out eating pizza and drinking beer, our friend proudly announced that our professor was going to help her submit her work for publication. She said the professor was impressed that the treatment she developed resulted in all of the clients in the study having dramatic improvements in their behavior. "What about Participant #3?" I said. We all knew this participant's behavior got worse over the course of the study, and so did another one. Our friend got a desperate look on her face and admitted to us that she had thrown away the data for two clients who did not perform well. "This is probably done all the time in research; I *really* want to have a publication—you guys have got to stand by me on this. I need to graduate."

Hint: Review 9.02.

39. I am the behavior analyst who works with Jason, an 8-year-old boy who is in a third-grade class for special needs children at an elementary school. This is the first year Jason has attended our school; his family moved here from another state. Jason's school records from first and second grades indicate that he has been "hyperactive," although there has been no formal attention deficit hyperactivity disorder (ADHD) diagnosis. In the past six months, teachers have noted that Jason has frequently appeared tired and irritable. Although he has lost some weight, Jason seems to be very motivated by food, often pushing and shoving other children out of the way to get to the head of the lunch line. The school requires a medical check-up at the beginning of the year. We have asked Jason's mother if we can see

the results of his physical or have permission to talk to his doctors, and she says no. She will not share his medical information, and she says there is no need for a physical; he is just misbehaving. Is it ethical to proceed even though I have a strong hunch that Jason has a medical condition that is related to his hyperactivity? Can I tell the mother, "I have to have the records or he will get no services at all?" Or should I just drop the case altogether since I don't think Jason has a "behavior" problem?

Hint: This is above your pay grade; find a higher authority.

40. I am a graduate student working part time in a facility for adults with developmental disabilities. For severe behavior problems, clients have BCBA services and behavioral programs. But for all the clients who don't have behavioral services, the caregivers in the facility often make up their own behavioral interventions. They act as though the clients are their children and they are the parents. For example, they will say, "You can't go to (a scheduled special event) because you did (whatever the unwanted behavior was)." Often, the punishment is too severe for whatever the misbehavior was. I know if I file a complaint, I run the risk of being ignored by staff. Or worse, they would dislike me, and it would be impossible to work with them. I am already a little different and seen as an outsider because they have all been there 20 years or more. Once, when I tried to get them to do something a different way, a staff person told someone about me, "That little girl has never had any kids; she doesn't have to manage these clients five days a week, and she will be gone as soon as she graduates."

Hint: Review the requirements in 7.02.

41. From a behaviorally trained Special Education Itinerant Teacher[1] (SEIT): A father had to go to the bank, which closed by the time my session ended. He wanted me to stay

356 • Appendix C: Fifty Ethics Scenarios for Behavior Analysts (With Hints)

home with the child while he went. I told him "No, this is not allowed." He begged and said, "Just trust me, I'll be right back," and started to leave. I again said, "No—this is against the law; if you have to go, we will end the session early." He said fine; I grabbed my stuff and left. The next day we discussed the situation, and he apologized for putting me in an uncomfortable position.

Hint: Good work.

42. From a speech therapist: I have had many parents suggest paying me for extra sessions over holidays and school breaks. I have also had parents who suggest that I bill and hold sessions to use on a holiday or school break.

    Hint: Use Nancy Reagan's frequent refrain: Just say "No."

43. Jane, a SEIT teacher, is providing in-home behavioral services to a 3-year-old girl, Mary P. The IEP goals include increasing Mary's appropriate interactions with other children. Mrs. P., knowing that Jane has a 3-year-old child, has repeatedly asked Jane to bring her child to play with Mary. Jane told Mrs. P. that this was not professional. However, Mrs. P. stated that Mary does not really know any other children and that she needs to work on her social skills. When Jane suggested putting Mary into a preschool, Mrs. P. stated that the family could not afford this financially. Jane has felt increasingly uncomfortable with the family's request for a play date. Last week, Jane called Mrs. P. to cancel a session, saying that her babysitting fell through at the last minute. Mrs. P. insisted that Jane bring her own child to the session rather than cancel. Jane did not know what to do.

    Hint: See #42.

44. One colleague said that she gets pressure from families to do make-ups on Saturdays.

    Hint: See #42.

45. Another one of our team's therapists, a speech therapist, has a reputation as a "Chatty Cathy." It is her personality

and her way of connecting, but she chats up a storm about her own personal life with her clients. Here's the dilemma: she is very funny, and the clients actually love the wild stories about her zany life. Should we intervene?

Hint: Natural consequences will eventually fix this one.

46. A parent is transitioning her child from Early Intervention to Committee on Preschool Special Education[2] (CPSE) funding and wants to get different services upon transition than she thinks the committee will approve. The child has a diagnosis of autism and is receiving extensive hours of applied behavior analysis as well as related services at home. The parent has exercised considerable control over the employment of providers in the home under early intervention. She and a lead member of the home-based team communicate to the speech/language therapist that she needs to write a progress report emphasizing the child's weaknesses and not emphasizing the progress that the child is making. They want this report faxed to the committee chairperson right before the next meeting. The committee has not requested a progress report from this provider. The therapist feels uncomfortable with the parent's somewhat manipulative request. The therapist senses, however, based on past events, that if she does not please the parent and the lead member of the home-based team, she will be removed from the case.

Hint: Read Code 1.04 closely; therein lies the answer.

47. A child with a diagnosis of autism has been recommended by the Committee on Preschool Special Education for placement in a full-day center-based program designed to service children with autism. The parent has visited the program and accepted placement. The CPSE is planning to reconvene prior to transition, as was stipulated at the initial meeting, to ensure that the recommendations that were made earlier are still appropriate. The parent is now feeling that her child should not attend the

center-based program but rather that the child should continue with extensive home-based ABA services under CPSE and also with a teacher accompanying the child to typical nursery school. The parent asks the lead teacher of the home-based team to contact the staff members of the center-based program to let them know that the parent does not really want their program. The home-based teacher knows that this may result in the center-based program not sending a representative to the Committee on Preschool Special Education meeting, which may make it easier to drive a change in the recommendation. There is a conflict between what we think the child needs and what the parent wants.

Hint: Ordinarily, parents get what they want, but occasionally an ethical professional will say, "Yes, but not from me."

48. A behaviorally trained teacher providing services in the home is aware that the family is struggling financially and that it will not be able to provide even a simple birthday party for the child. The teacher would like to pay for a modest party because she feels sorry for the child. She knows that the family will accept this gift from her.

Hint: Take a look at Code 1.06(d).

49. Guidance is needed for these three situations: (1) Currently, we have therapists and some teachers attending children's birthday parties or attending family parties. (2) They may also accept monetary gifts or gifts of high value (in our district, occasional gifts with a token value of less than $50 are permitted). To skirt this rule, some parents try to give frequent gifts with a value of $50 or less, and the total of these gifts well exceeds $50. (3) Occasionally, to make a little extra money, therapists and teachers offer to babysit and get paid directly by the family.

Hint: Take a look at Code 1.06(d).

50. Our consulting firm wants to make an ad for television. A few of our clients' parents have told others our services changed their lives. Since they are very vocal with no prompting from us, can we ask them to appear for a short sound bite in our TV and print ads?
    Hint: Review 8.06.

Notes

1 These are special education teachers who have been trained in the use of behavioral interventions.
2 This is a special funding source in New York State.

Appendix D: Suggested Further Reading

Bersoff, D. N. (2003). *Ethical Conflicts in Psychology.* Washington, DC: American Psychological Association.

This third edition of Bersoff's text includes material on ethics codes, applying ethics, confidentiality, multiple relationships, assessment, computerized testing, therapy, and research. Additionally, he covers supervision, guidelines for animal research, ethics in forensic settings, ethical practice within the boundaries of managed care, the American Psychological Association (APA) 2002 2Ethics Code, and the revisions to the rules and procedures for adjudicating complaints of unethical conduct against APA members adopted by the APA's Ethics Committee in August 2002.

Canter, M. B., Bennett, B. E., Jones, S. E., & Nagy, T. F. (1999). *Ethics for Psychologists: A Commentary on the APA Ethics Code.* Washington, DC: American Psychological Association.

The three main sections of this volume are Foundations, Interpreting the Ethics Code, and Conclusions. The bulk of the book is the section on "Interpreting the Ethics Code," in which each ethical standard is analyzed and commentary is provided.

Danforth, S., & Boyle, J. R. (2000). *Cases in Behavior Management.* Upper Saddle River, NJ: Prentice Hall.

This book begins by presenting social systems theory; models of treatment including the behavioral, psychodynamic, environmental, and constructivist models; and information on analyzing cases. The second half of the book features 38 cases that illustrate behavior management issues faced by teachers, parents, and caregivers. A number of the vignettes are related to school settings (preschool through high school). Cases are very detailed, with most being three to four pages in length.

Fisher, C. B. (2003). *Decoding the Ethics Code: A Practical Guide for Psychologists.* Thousand Oaks, CA: Sage.

The 2002 American Psychological Association's Ethical Principles of Psychologists and Code of Conduct is presented in this volume. After an introduction describing how the code came to be developed, the foundation and application of each ethical standard is discussed along with enforcement of the code. Other topics presented include professional liability issues, ethical decision making, and the relation between ethics and law.

Foxx, R. M., & Mulick, J. A. (2016). *Controversial Therapies for Autism and Intellectual Disabilities: Fad, Fashion and Science in Professional Practice.* New York: Routledge, Inc.

A decade has passed since the first edition of this book was published. While much has changed in the world, the field of autism and intellectual disabilities continues to be fraught with fads, controversial, unsupported, disproven, invalidated and politically correct treatments that either were present in 2005 or have appeared since then. All are covered in this book, as is teaching ethics for behavior analysts by Bailey and Burch and why ABA is not a fad.

Hayes, L. J., Hayes, G. J., Moore, S. C., & Ghezzi, P. M. (1994). *Ethical Issues in Developmental Disabilities.* Reno, NV: Context Press.

This volume is a collection of theoretical articles by a variety of authors. Some of the topics include choice and value, moral development, morality, ethical issues concerning people with DD, competence, right to treatment, ethics and adult services, and the pharmacological treatment of behavior problems.

Jacob, S., & Hartshorne, T. S. (2003). *Ethics and the Law for School Psychologists.* Wiley, New York.

This text provides information on professional standards and legal requirements relevant to the delivery of school psychological services. Topics covered include students' and parents' rights to privacy and informed consent, confidentiality, assessment, ethical issues related to Individuals with Disabilities Education Act (IDEA) and Americans with Disabilities Act, educating children with special needs, consultation with teachers, school discipline, school violence prevention, and ethical issues in supervision. *Ethics and the Law for School Psychologists* addresses the changes in the 2002 revision of the American Psychological Association's Ethical Principles and Code of Conduct.

Jacobson, J. W., Foxx, R. M., & Mulick, J. A. (Eds.). (2005). *Controversial Therapies for Developmental Disabilities: Fad, Fashion, and Science in Professional Practice.* Mahwah, NJ: Lawrence Erlbaum Associates.

John Jacobson, Richard Foxx, and James Mulick have done our field a great service in compiling this encyclopedia of fads, fallacies, "faux fixes," and delusions in the treatment of developmental disabilities. This must-have reference should be required reading for all behavior analysts. A few sample titles from the 28 chapters will give you some idea of the approach taken by nearly 30 experts—"Sifting Sound Practice From Snake Oil," "The Delusion of Full Inclusion" and "Facilitated Communication: The Ultimate Fad Treatment."

Koocher, G. P., & Keith-Spiegel, P. C. (1990). *Children, Ethics, and the Law: Professional Issues and Cases.* Lincoln: University of Nebraska Press.

Children, Ethics, and the Law outlines ethical and legal issues encountered by mental health workers in their work with children, adolescents, and their families. This volume addresses issues pertinent to psychotherapy with children, assessment, confidentiality and record keeping, consent to treatment and research, and legal issues. Case vignettes are provided to illustrate the ethical and legal dilemmas under discussion.

Lattal, A. D., & Clark, R. W. (2005). *Ethics at Work.* Atlanta: Aubrey Daniels International, Inc.

For behavior analysts who work in business settings, this is the book you want to use as your standard. Lattal and Clark discuss all the important issues, including building moral integrity, achieving ethical sales, behaving ethically, and making ethics a habit. There are plenty of case examples that can be used to stimulate discussion in class.

Nagy, T. F. (2000). *An Illustrative Casebook for Psychologists.* Washington, DC: American Psychological Association.

An Illustrative Casebook for Psychologists was written to accompany the 102 standards of the American Psychological Association's Ethics Committee's Ethical Principles of Psychologists and Code of Conduct. Fictional case vignettes are used throughout the text to illustrate the key areas of the APA Code, which include General

Standards; Evaluation, Assessment, or Intervention; Advertising and Other Public Statements; Therapy; Privacy and Confidentiality; Teaching, Training Supervision, Research, and Publishing; Forensic Activities; and Resolving Ethical Issues.

Offit, P. A. (2008). *Autism's False Prophets: Bad Science, Risky Medicine, and the Search for a Cure*. New York: Columbia University Press.

"Paul Offit, a national expert on vaccines, challenges the modern-day false prophets who have so egregiously misled the public and exposes the opportunism of the lawyers, journalists, celebrities, and politicians who support them. Offit recounts the history of autism research and the exploitation of this tragic condition by advocates and zealots. He considers the manipulation of science in the popular media and the courtroom, and he explores why society is susceptible to the bad science and risky therapies put forward by many antivaccination activists" (from the dust jacket).

Pope, K. S., & Vasquez, M.J.T. (1998). *Ethics in Psychotherapy and Counseling*. San Francisco, CA: Jossey-Bass.

This text addresses areas in which ethical dilemmas occur in the work of mental health practitioners. Issues covered include informed consent, sexual and nonsexual relationships with clients, cultural and individual differences, supervisory relationships, and confidentiality. There are appendixes of codes of conduct and ethical principles for psychologists and guidelines for ethical counseling in managed-care settings.

Stolz, S. B., and Associates. (1978). *Ethical Issues in Behavior Modification*. San Francisco, CA: Jossey-Bass.

In 1974, the American Psychological Association formed a commission to examine issues related to social, legal, and ethical controversies in psychology. The commission also provided recommendations regarding the use and misuse of behavior modification. This historic volume addresses the ethics of behavior modification in settings that include outpatient settings, institutions, schools, prisons, and society. The volume also addresses the ethics of interventions.

Van Houten, R., & Axelrod, S. (Eds.). (1993). *Behavior Analysis and Treatment*. New York: Plenum Press.

Van Houten and Axelrod persuaded over 30 experts in applied behavior analysis to give their assessment of the field and to suggest ways to create optimal environments for treatment and to provide assessments for quality care and state-of-the-art treatment. Chapter 8, "A Decision-Making Model for Selecting the Optimal

Treatment Procedure," served as a foundation for Chapter 16 in this Third Edition.

Welfel, E. R., & Ingersoll, R. E. (2001). *The Mental Health Desk Reference.* New York: Wiley.

Part IX of *The Mental Health Desk Reference* is "Ethical and Legal Issues." This section of the text addresses procedures for filing ethics complaints, clients' rights to privacy, informed consent, responsible documentation, reporting child abuse, recognizing elder abuse, supervision, and responsible interactions with managed-care organizations.

Notes

Chapter 3

1 Submitted cases that are direct quotes from people who work in the behavior analysis field are indicated by quotation marks.
2 Rafting. Retrieved from Wikipedia December 23, 2015, https://en.wikipedia.org/wiki/Rafting
3 RBT=The Code element is relevant to Registered Behavior Technicians.

Chapter 7

1 For a more detailed definition of what "protected population" means, visit the web page of Ball State University's Office of Research Integrity at http://cms.bsu.edu/about/administrativeoffices/researchintegrity/humansubjects/resources/protectedpopulationgroups

Chapter 9

1 Source: The Pennsylvania Code. The provisions of this § 6400.191 amended through January 22, 1982, effective March 1, 1982, 12 Pa.B. 384; amended August 9, 1991, effective November 8, 1991, 21 Pa.B. 3595. Immediately preceding text appears at serial page (131375). Found at: www.pacode.com/secure/data/055/chapter6400/s6400.191.html

2 VB-MAPP Transition Assessment, p. 32.
3 VB-MAPP Milestones Assessment, p. 21.

Chapter 10

1 Corrective feedback is comprised of seven components: Provide a positive/empathetic statement, describe supervisee's correct performance, specify supervisee's incorrect performance, provide a rationale for the desired change in performance, provide instructions and demonstrations of how to improve the ineffective performance from step 3, provide opportunities to practice the desired target performance, and, finally, provide immediate feedback and positive reinforcement (if appropriate). Adapted from Reid, Parsons, and Green (2012) and BACB (2012).

Chapter 11

1 For more information on Reiki, see www.reiki.org/faq/whatisreiki.html

Chapter 12

1 Note that this Code element does not cover any acts that constitute actual illegal behavior. In situations where you are aware of illegal behavior, you would need to contact the proper authorities and let them handle the matter.
2 The company World Evolve, Inc. of Miami, Florida, includes this statement for employees on their webpage, http://www.world-evolve.com
3 (The relevant code is 42 USC § 1320d-5).
4 Information about HIPAA was obtained from http://www.ama-assn.org/ama/pub/physician-resources/solutions-managing-your-practice/coding-billing-insurance/hipaahealth-insurance-portability-accountability-act/hipaa-violations-enforcement.page?

Chapter 13

1 For more information about alternative treatments, see http://www.sciencedaily.com/releases/2015/02/150226154644.htm
2 For additional information about alternative treatments, see http://www.forbes.com/sites/emilywillingham/2013/10/29/the-5-scariest-autism-treatments/

3   Quoted from "Premera hack exposes 11 million financial and medical records," March 18, 2015, Computerweekly.com, retrieved December 12, 2015, http://www.computerweekly.com/news/2240242508/Premera-hack-exposes-11-million-financial-and-medical-records

4   The podcast interview is available at http://www.stitcher.com/podcast/wwwstitchercompodcastspecialparentsconfidential/special-parents-confidential/e/special-parents-confidential-episode-15-applied-behavior-analysis-33753177

5   The Commission tested the communication of advertisements containing testimonials that clearly and prominently disclosed either "Results not typical" or the stronger "These testimonials are based on the experiences of a few people and you are not likely to have similar results." Neither disclosure adequately reduced the communication that the experiences depicted are generally representative. Based upon this research, the Commission believes that similar disclaimers regarding the limited applicability of an endorser's experience to what consumers may generally expect to achieve are unlikely to be effective.

    Nonetheless, the Commission cannot rule out the possibility that a strong disclaimer of typicality could be effective in the context of a particular advertisement. Although the Commission would have the burden of proof in a law enforcement action, the Commission notes that an advertiser possessing reliable empirical testing demonstrating that the net impression of its advertisement with such a disclaimer is nondeceptive will avoid the risk of the initiation of such an action in the first instance.

    Advertisements presenting endorsements by what are represented, directly or by implication, to be "actual consumers" should utilize actual consumers in both the audio and video, or clearly and conspicuously disclose that the persons in such advertisements are not actual consumers of the advertised product.

6   The relevant FTC regulations are: § 255.2 Consumer endorsements.

    (a) An advertisement employing endorsements by one or more consumers about the performance of an advertised product or service will be interpreted as representing that the product or service is effective for the purpose depicted in the advertisement. Therefore, the advertiser must possess and rely upon adequate substantiation, including, when appropriate, competent and reliable scientific evidence, to support such claims made through endorsements in the same manner the advertiser would be required to do if it had made the representation directly, i.e., without using endorsements. Consumer endorsements themselves are not competent and reliable scientific evidence.

(b) An advertisement containing an endorsement relating the experience of one or more consumers on a central or key attribute of the product or service also will likely be interpreted as representing that the endorser's experience is representative of what consumers will generally achieve with the advertised product or service in actual, albeit variable, conditions of use. Therefore, an advertiser should possess and rely upon adequate substantiation for this representation. If the advertiser does not have substantiation that the endorser's experience is representative of what consumers will generally achieve, the advertisement should clearly and conspicuously disclose the generally expected performance in the depicted circumstances, and the advertiser must possess and rely on adequate substantiation for that representation.

7 Permission to use this material was granted by IBS.

Chapter 14

1 See the full language of the act at the Health and Human Services website at http://www.hhs.gov/ohrp/humansubjects/guidance/belmont.html
2 "U.S. Study Finds Fraud in Top Researcher's Work on Mentally Retarded," May 24, 1987, The New York Times, retrieved from http://www.nytimes.com/1987/05/24/us/us-study-finds-fraud-in-top-researcher-s-work-onmentally-retarded.html
3 Read the relevant U.S. Code at http://www.acl.gov/programs/AIDD/DDA_BOR_ACT_2000/p2_tI_subtitleA.aspx
4 Thanks to Dr. Dorothea Lerman, Behavior Analysis Program, University of Houston Clear Lake, for sharing these scenarios.

Chapter 19

1 A correction fluid, or white-out, is an opaque, usually white fluid applied to paper to mask errors in text. Once dried, it can be written over. It is typically packaged in small bottles, and the lid has an attached brush (or a triangular piece of foam) which dips into the

bottle. The brush is used to apply the fluid onto the paper. Information from "Wite-Out," retrieved August 14, 2015, from Wikipedia, https://en.wikipedia.org/wiki/Wite-Out

Chapter 20

1 For an up-to-date version of the organization Code, go to: COEBO. com
2 Originally drafted by Jon S. Bailey, PhD, BCBA-D.
3 If you would like to become involved in the COEBO Movement, contact Adam Ventura at adamvent@gmail.com.

References

Administration on Intellectual and Developmental Disabilities (AIDD).
(2000). *The developmental disabilities assistance and bill of rights act
of 2000*. Washington, DC: Author.

American Psychological Association (APA). (2001). *PsychSCAN: Behavior analysis & therapy*. Washington, DC: Author.

American Psychological Association (APA). (2002). Ethical principles
and code of conduct. *American Psychologist, 57*, 1060–1073.

Axelrod, S., Spreat, S., Berry, B., & Moyer, L. (1993). A decision-making
model for selecting the optimal treatment procedure. In R. Van
Houten and S. Axelrod (Eds.), *Behavior analysis and treatment*
(pp. 183–202). New York: Plenum Press.

Ayllon, T., & Michael, J. (1959). The psychiatric nurse as a behavioral
engineer. *Journal of the Experimental Analysis of Behavior, 2*,
323–334.

Baer, D. M., Wolf, M. M., & Risley, T. R. (1968). Some current dimensions of applied behavior analysis. *Journal of Applied Behavior
Analysis, 1*, 91–97.

Bailey, J. S., & Burch, M. R. (2010). *25 Essential skills and strategies for the
professional behavior analyst: Expert tips for maximizing consulting
effectiveness*. New York: Routledge.

Bailey, J. S., & Burch, M. R. (2011). *Ethics for behavior analysts*. New
York: Routledge.

BBC Radio. (1999, January 26). *Ten least respected professions* [Radio].
Retrieved December 30, 2015, from http://news.bbc.co.uk/2/hi/
uk_news/politics/2013838.stm

Behavior Analyst Certification Board (BACB). (1998–2010). *Disciplinary standards, procedures for appeal.* Retrieved January 2, 2005, from www.bacb.com/redirect_frame.php?page=discipline-app.html

Behavior Analyst Certification Board. (2012). *BACB newsletter, special edition on supervision.* September 2012. Retrieved August 9, 2015, from http://bacb.com/wp-content/uploads/2015/07/BACB_Newsletter_9–12.pdf

Behavior Analyst Certification Board. (2014a). *BACB newsletter, special edition on supervision.* November 2014, p. 10. Retrieved August 9, 2015, from http://bacb.com/wp-content/uploads/2015/07/BACB_Newsletter_11–14.pdf

Behavior Analyst Certification Board. (2014b). *Professional and ethical compliance code for behavior analysts.* Retrieved August 8, 2015, from http://bacb.com/wp-content/uploads/2015/05/BACB_Compliance_Code.pdf

Behavior Analyst Certification Board. (2014c). *BACB newsletter.* September 2014, p. 2. Retrieved August 10, 2015, from http://bacb.com/wp-content/uploads/2015/07/BACB_Newsletter_09-14.pdf

Binder, R.L. (1992). Sexual harassment: Issues for forensic psychiatrists. *Bulletin of the Academy of Psychiatry Law, 20,* 409–418.

Borys, D.S., & Pope, K.S. (1989). Dual relationships between therapist and client: A national study of psychologists, psychiatrists, and social workers. *Professional Psychology: Research and Practice, 20,* 283–293.

Carnegie, D. (1981). *How to win friends and influence people.* New York: Pocket Books/Simon & Schuster, Inc.

Chhokar, J.S., & Wallin, J.A. (1984a). A field study of the effect of feedback frequency on performance. *Journal of Applied Psychology, 69,* 524–530.

Chhokar, J.S., & Wallin, J.A. (1984b). Improving safety through applied behavior analysis. *Journal of Safety Research, 15,* 141–251.

Cooper, J.O., Heron, T.E., & Heward, W.L. (2007). *Applied behavior analysis,* (2nd ed.). Upper Saddle River, NJ: Pearson Education.

Crouhy, M., Galai, D., & Mark, R. (2006). *The essentials of risk management.* New York: McGraw Hill.

Daniels, A., & Bailey, J. (2014). *Performance Management: Changing behavior that drives organizational effectiveness,* (5th ed.). Atlanta: Performance Management Publications.

Eliot, C.W. (1910). *Harvard classics volume 38.* New York: P. F. Collier and Son.

Foxx, R. M., & Mulick, J. A. (2016). *Controversial therapies for autism and intellectual disabilities: Fad, fashion, and science in professional practice.* New York: Routledge, Inc.

Hill, A. (1998). *Speaking truth to power.* New York: Anchor.

Iwata, B. A., Dorsey, M. F., Slifer, K. J., Bauman, K. E., & Richman, G. S. (1982). Toward a functional analysis of self-injury. *Analysis and Intervention in Developmental Disabilities, 2,* 3–20.

Jacobson, J. W., Foxx, R. M., & Mulick, J. A. (2005). *Controversial therapies for developmental disabilities.* Mahwah, NJ: Lawrence Erlbaum Associates, Inc.

Koocher, G. P., & Keith-Spiegel, P. (1998). *Ethics in psychology: Professional standards and cases* (2nd ed.). New York: Oxford University Press.

Krasner, L., & Ullmann, L. P. (Eds.). (1965). *Research in behavior modification.* New York: Holt, Rinehart and Winston, Inc.

Lenard, J. A. (2012). *K.G. vs. Elizabeth Dudek,* Case No. 11–20684 Florida Agency for Health Care Administration, Judge Joan A. Lenard, presiding, March 2012.

Mason, S. A., & Iwata, B. A. (1990). Artifactual effects of sensory-integrative therapy on self-injurious behavior. *Journal of Applied Behavior Analysis, 23*(3), 361–370.

May, J. G., Risley, T. R., Twardosz, S., Friedman, P., Bijou, S. W., Wexler, D., et al. (1976). Guidelines for the use of behavioral procedures in state programs for retarded persons. *M.R. Research, NARC Research & Demonstration Institute, 1*(1), 1–73.

McAllister, J. W. (1972). *Report of resident abuse investigating committee.* Tallahassee, FL: Division of Retardation, Department of Health and Rehabilitative Services.

Miltenberger, R. G. (2015). *Behavior modification: Principles and procedures,* (6th ed.). Farmington Hills, MI: Wadsworth Publishing.

National Association for Retarded Citizens. (1976, November). *Mental retardation news.* Arlington, TX: National Association for Retarded Citizens.

Neuringer, C., & Michael, J. L. (Eds.). (1970). *Behavior modification in clinical psychology.* New York: Apple-Century-Crofts.

Ontario Consultants on Religious Tolerance. (2004). Introduction to the ethic of reciprocity (a.k.a. the Golden Rule). Kingston, ON, Canada. Retrieved November 12, 2010 from http://www.religioustolerance.org/mor_dive3.htm

Reid, D. H., Parsons, M. B., & Green, C. W. (2012). *The supervisor's guidebook: Evidence-based strategies for promoting work quality and enjoyment among human service staff.* Morganton, NC: Habilitative Management Consultants.

Scott, J. (1988, September 20). Researcher admits faking data to get $160,000 in funds. *The Los Angeles Times.* Retrieved from http://articles.latimes.com/1988-09-20/news/mn-2318_1_research-fraud

Shermer, M. (2002). Smart people believe in weird things. *Scientific American,* August 12, 35.

Skinner, B. F. (1938). *Behavior of organisms.* New York: Appleton-Century.

Skinner, B. F. (1953). *Science and human behavior.* New York: Macmillan.

Skinner, B. F. (1957). *Verbal behavior.* New York: Appleton-Century-Crofts.

Sprague. R. (1998). *Telling people what they do not want to hear: Making a career of this activity as a psychologist.* Division 33, American Psychological Association conference, San Francisco, August.

Spreat, S. (1982). *Weighing treatment alternatives: Which is less restrictive?* Woodhaven Center E & R Technical Report 82–11(1). Philadelphia: Temple University.

Sundberg, M. L. (2008). *The verbal behavior milestones assessment and placement program: The VB-MAPP guide.* Concord, CA: AVB Press.

Tufte, E. (1983). *The visual display of quantitative information.* Cheshire, CT: Graphics Press.

Ullmann, L. P., & Krasner, L. (Eds.). (1965). *Case studies in behavior modification.* New York: Holt, Rinehart and Winston, Inc.

U.S. Equal Employment Opportunity Commission (EEOC). (2004). *Sexual harassment charges: EEOC & FEPA s combined: FY 1997–FY 2009,* p. 288. Retrieved November 12, 2010, from http://www.eeoc.gov/eeoc/statistics/enforcement/sexual_harassment.cfm

U.S. Equal Employment Opportunity Commission (EEOC). (2014). *EEOC Releases fiscal year 2014 enforcement and litigation data.* Retrieved July 27, 2015, from http://www1.eeoc.gov/eeoc/newsroom/release/2-4-15.cfm

U.S. Study Finds Fraud in Top Researcher's Work on Mentally Retarded. (1987, May 24). *The New York Times.* Retrieved from http://www.nytimes.com/1987/05/24/us/us-study-finds-fraud-in-top-researchers-work-onmentally-retarded.html

Van Houten, R., Axelrod, S., Bailey, J. S., Favell, J. E., Foxx, R. M., Iwata, B. A., et al. (1988). The right to effective behavioral treatment. *Journal of Applied Behavior Analysis, 21,* 381–384.

Wolf, M., Risley, R., & Mees, H. (1964). Application of operant conditioning procedures to the behaviour problems of an autistic child. *Behaviour Research and Therapy, 1,* 305–312.

Wilson, R., & Crouch, E.A.C. (2001). *Risk–benefit analysis,* (2nd ed.). Cambridge, MA: Harvard University Center for Risk Analysis.

Wyatt v. Stickney. 325 F. Supp 781 (M.D. Ala. 1971).

Index